Coaching for Performance: Realising the Olympic Dream

This book celebrates two important aspects of the London 2012 Olympic and Paralympic Games. (1) For those involved in any aspect of Olympism, and particularly coaches and athletes, London 2012 was about realising dreams, achieving success and participating in competitive sport at the highest level. This book sets out some of these dreams and the part coaches play in this. (2) The book also looks at the notion of 'coaching-for-performance' and does this from an international and multi-sport perspective. From interviews with Olympic coaches, the experiences of those working in the field of high performance and from applied sport researchers, the book uses the metaphor of the 'coach-as-alchemist' in order to capture the dynamics of coach-athlete relationships and performance. Sports such as diving, swimming, gymnastics, skiing are included together with examples from a range of individual and team Olympic sports.

The book is set within the context of elite sport, high performance and coaching. Its contents illuminate two important kinds of reflective practice: (a) Reflection-ON-action (b) Reflection-FOR-action. The style of presentation includes narratives, reflective conversations, ethnographic work, interview analysis and video-clips available on-line.

This book was published as a special issue of *Reflective Practice*.

Sarah Lee is Subject Leader of Applied Sport Science, University West of England, Hartpury, UK and an elite netball coach.

Martin Dixon is a Lecturer in Sport Coaching and Professional Development, Staffordshire University, UK and UEFA-licensed football coach.

Tony Ghaye is a positive psychologist and Director, Reflective Learning-International, Gloucester, UK.

Coaching for Performance: Realising the Olympic Dream

Edited by
Sarah Lee, Martin Dixon and Tony Ghaye

Routledge
Taylor & Francis Group

LONDON AND NEW YORK

First published 2014
by Routledge
2 Park Square, Milton Park, Abingdon, Oxfordshire OX14 4RN

Simultaneously published in the USA and Canada
by Routledge
711 Third Avenue, New York, NY 10017

First issued in paperback 2014

Routledge is an imprint of the Taylor & Francis Group, an informa business

© 2014 Taylor & Francis

This book is a reproduction of *Reflective Practice*, vol. 13, issue 3. The Publisher requests to those authors who may be citing this book to state, also, the bibliographical details of the special issue on which the book was based.

British Library Cataloguing in Publication Data
A catalogue record for this book is available from the British Library

ISBN 13: 978-0-415-82652-5 (hbk)
ISBN 13: 978-1-138-85073-6 (pbk)

Typeset in Times New Roman
By Taylor & Francis Books

Publisher's Note
The publisher would like to make readers aware that the chapters in this book may be referred to as articles as they are identical to the articles published in the special issue. The publisher accepts responsibility for any inconsistencies that may have arisen in the course of preparing this volume for print.

Contents

CONTENTS

Routledge Online Studies on the Olympic and Paralympic Games Series

Routledge Online Studies on the *Olympic* and *Paralympic Games* (ROSO) is a unique learning resource, publishing scholarly and multidisciplinary research on the Games. Aimed at academics, researchers, lecturers, students, authors, educators, athletes, coaches, journalists, Olympic and Paralympic centres, policy-makers, professionals and anyone with an interest in the Games, it aims to stimulate the production of new knowledge and facilitate dialogue and connections across disciplines.

ROSO contains over 1000 journal articles and book chapters, including handbooks and major reference works dating back to the 1960s on themes including: the media, education, gender, politics, governance, management, law, business, ethics, legacies, the environment, disability studies, athletic performance and history. ROSO's Managing Editor, Dr Vassil Girginov of Brunel University, UK, has curated the site thematically to enable users to search their areas of interest effortlessly.

Routledge has also commissioned over 40 new journal special issues across disciplines on Olympic and Paralympic Studies that will be unveiled on this innovative platform and published as books.

http://www.routledgeonlinestudies.com/

Titles in the Series

Rule Britannia: Nationalism, Identity and the Modern Olympic Games
Matthew P. Llewellyn

Olympic Aspirations
Realised and Unrealised
Edited by James A. Mangan and Mark Dyreson

Olympic Reform Ten Years Later
Edited by Heather Dichter

The Triple Asian Olympics
Asia Rising - the Pursuit of National Identity, International Recognition and Global Esteem
Edited by J. A. Mangan, Sandra Collins and Gwang Ok

Encoding the Olympics
The Beijing Olympic Games and the Communication Impact Worldwide
Edited by Luo Qing and Giuseppe Richeri

The Olympic Movement and the Sport of Peacemaking
Edited by Ramón Spaaij and Cindy Burleson

Olympic Ethics and Philosophy
Edited by Mike McNamee and Jim Parry

Bearing Light: Flame Relays and the Struggle for the Olympic Movement
Edited by John J. MacAloon

Coaching for Performance: Realising the Olympic Dream
Edited by Sarah Lee, Martin Dixon and Tony Ghaye

Citation Information

The chapters in this book were originally published in *Reflective Practice*, volume 13, issue 3 (June 2012). When citing this material, please use the original page numbering for each article, as follows:

Chapter 1
Realising the Olympic dream – bring on the alchemists
Sarah Lee, Tony Ghaye, Martin Dixon and with a contribution from Beth Tweddle, MBE
Reflective Practice, volume 13, issue 3 (June 2012) pp. 327-338

Chapter 2
Coaching for performance: an interview with Olympic diving coach, Andy Banks
Martin Dixon, Sarah Lee and Tony Ghaye
Reflective Practice, volume 13, issue 3 (June 2012) pp. 339-354

Chapter 3
Coaching for performance: reflections of Olympic diving coach, Andy Banks
Martin Dixon, Sarah Lee and Tony Ghaye
Reflective Practice, volume 13, issue 3 (June 2012) pp. 355-358

Chapter 4
Reflection and the art of coaching: fostering high-performance in Olympic Ski Cross
Matthew Lyons, Steven B. Rynne and Clifford J. Mallett
Reflective Practice, volume 13, issue 3 (June 2012) pp. 359-372

Chapter 5
'One door closes, a next door opens up somewhere': the learning of one Olympic synchronised swimmer
Natalie Barker-Ruchti, Dean Barker, Steven Rynne and Jessica Lee
Reflective Practice, volume 13, issue 3 (June 2012) pp. 373-386

Chapter 6
Stories of success: Cultural narratives and personal stories of elite and professional athletes
David Carless and Kitrina Douglas
Reflective Practice, volume 13, issue 3 (June 2012) pp. 387-398

Realising the Olympic dream – bring on the alchemists

Sarah Lee[a], Tony Ghaye[b], Martin Dixon[a] and with a contribution from Beth Tweddle, MBE

[a]UWE Hartpury, Gloucester, England; [b]Reflective Learning – International, Gloucester, England

Going to the Games: This paper is in three parts. First we set out some of the dreams of some London 2012 Olympic medal hopefuls. We call it, 'Daring to dream'. Second, we discuss some of the important factors that can help or hinder the realization of Olympic dreams. Finally we focus exclusively on coaches of elite athletes and use the metaphor of the 'coach-as-alchemist' to describe and explain some of the major themes, concepts and ideas we have learned in constructing this Special (Para)Olympic Issue of *Reflective Practice*.

London calling

On 6 July 2005, the International Olympic Committee announced that London would host the 2012 Olympic and Paralympic Games. This has acted as a catalyst for raising the profile of sport in the UK, and amongst the UK's elite athlete population it has cultivated their ambition for the ultimate sporting achievement. The prospect of a 'home' Olympics has fuelled a dreaming process for these athletes, their coaches, their performance directors and their support teams. The dream of personal and team Olympic glory. The dream of finishing fourth in the Olympic medal table and 'moving towards first' in the Paralympic medal table (National Audit Office, 2008).

Olympism represents a set of ideals which encapsulate significant aspects of these dreams. It connects the Games with the values of human endeavour, competition and achievement, the joy derived from effort, and the educational value of 'good example'. For some, these are aspects that constitute the Olympic ideal. An ideal worth financing, hosting and protecting. Dreams worth defending and safeguarding. A 2012 Olympic Games that goes much further than just the athletic competition, but is also aligned with the notion of a 're-generation game' due to its post-event legacy of long-term sustainable community development. London is calling. But what about legacy? It is now a prerequisite for any potential Olympic host. It was London's successful bid for the 2012 Olympics which set the precedent. Rewind to that triumphant day back in July 2005 and speeches from Lord Sebastian Coe and his team were littered with references to the 'L' word. In a nutshell, Coe promised London would not only regenerate a run-down part of East London but use the 2012 Games to increase sporting activity in Britain and around the world, particularly among the young. He pledged to re-engage the world with the Olympic movement. He also promised none of the costly venues would become white elephants.

Whether you believe it to be an over-hyped commercial extravaganza or a gross mass spectacle where, 'corruption and nationalism are more important than high-minded idealism' (Fussey Coaffee, Armstrong, & Hobbs, 2012, p. 16), one thing is for sure, dreams will be both dashed and realized. With this in mind, this paper will focus on these Olympic dreams, and the role that these play in preparing individuals for competition and the process of turning a dream into reality.

Daring to dream

In general, some dreams can be a source of energy and provide a sense of direction. When athletes and coaches lose sight of a positive image of their future performance, passion suffers and energy with it. Dreaming, or for some, in more performance terms, the outcomes of particular visualization or imagery techniques, help to determine what we become (Short, Tenute, & Feltz, 2005; VaezMousavi & Rostami, 2009). A compelling and meaningful vision of a future, like representing your country in your home Olympics, can provide everyone associated with the athlete with the optimism, strength, energy and efficacy needed to move confidently toward realising that dream. By thinking about what might be possible, we experience hope and release a multitude of positive emotions. Jessica Ennis, one of Team GBs 2012 Olympic hopefuls, illustrates this energizing effect of daring to dream big in the following video clip:[Full video available online at http://dx.doi.org/10.1080/14623943.2012.674771]

Here Jess talks about the motivating effect that can come from thinking about and visualizing success and achievement. It is these dreams that provide the impetus for staying focused, concentrated and committed during arduous training sessions, even in the face of setbacks, such as injury. The dream provides athletes with a constant incentive to do all they can to realize their lifetime ambition.

Within competitive sport dreams often need to be transformed into more systematically thought out and planned competitive and mastery goals. It is these goals that provide the much needed focus and direction for athletes, and their support teams, as they prepare for competition. The dream often takes a back seat as goals become the priority. But imagining and dreaming about what could be possible engages the emotions of athletes and can provide an important source of motivation. Arguably, halfway between dreaming and a performance goal are the outcomes of visualization techniques. In the context of a winning mindset, Shinar (2008) stressed how important it is to, 'visualize achieving your goal, visualize how you are going to achieve it practically, step-by-step; visualize coping well with any nerves and pressure; visualize what it will feel like, how it will feel afterwards and what effect it will have' (p. 46). Practical realism, however, tells us that dreams can be transient. They can fade and change. Dreams can get lost if coaches and athletes take their eye off their goals and get consumed, for example, by media and sponsorship commitments.

Tom Daley (GB diver) has these dreams. 'I sometimes dream about diving or podiums, and hear the national anthem in random places. But it's never been at the

Olympics in my dreams – and I've never found out the result. I'm always left in anticipation' (Lewis, 2011).

Jodie Williams (GB sprinter), who some suggest could be a female version of Usain Bolt, is reported to have dreamt that even before she ran, she wanted to be in the Olympics. 'The Olympics is always on my mind now. I'm so excited. I find myself welling up at the London 2012 adverts – it's a bit tragic' (McRae, 2011). In the same article McRae reports that Williams shows just the right amount of relish at the prospect of becoming the fastest in the world. He quotes her saying:

> Sometimes I lie awake and think how cool it would be. If you look at all the people in the world and you think "I'm the best on earth at this age", it can seem weird. Sometimes I sneak a look at someone and think, "I'm faster than you!" Imagine how it would feel to be to the world's fastest woman?

The dreams of Aaron Cook (GB Taekwondo) are a reminder that from dreams dashed (tears in Beijing) his dream for 2012 emerged stronger than ever. In the Beijing Olympics, Aaron Cook, then 17 years old, finished fourth in the 80 kg class His tears were a defining image of the Games. He has since ascended to world number one and won the European championships. McRae (2011) reports Cook's experience thus:

> I had a bit of a mental breakdown after Beijing. … Then seeing Sarah Stevenson get her bronze medal and everyone being so happy, I was feeling really bad inside that it didn't quite happen for me. But I think that has definitely helped me now – when times are hard, I remember that I'm not going to let anyone take it away from me this time. If I get in that situation, I can do something about it, I can knock them out – my destiny is in my own hands. Taekwondo has been my life since I was 10 years old. My parents were always telling me that I had the ability to be an Olympic champion, and then it was announced that London had the Games and I thought: "Oh my God, I can do this at home" – a once-in-a-lifetime opportunity. I will do whatever it takes to win gold, and everything – all the blood, sweat, tears, sacrifice, money, my family moving from Dorchester to Manchester, giving up jobs – will all be worth it. There were always the days when I wanted to go out with friends or play football, but my dad used to sit me down and say: "To be an Olympic champion, you have to do things differently". You have to train, and other people are out there doing the training, so that's what you've got to do. I have no friends outside taekwondo and I've got a girlfriend I see maybe once or twice a week if I'm lucky… My family and my coach all wear a gold bracelet. It says: "Cook. 2012. Gold" and "Impossible is nothing". We've also got London 2012 stuff round the house, and I've got London 2012 bedding on my bed. It's a reminder and a little bit of motivation that if you want something so bad, you'll do everything you can to get it (McRae, 2011).

One of the most astonishing examples of what we are saying here, about daring to dream, is to be found in the personal narrative of Monique van der Vorst, from the Netherlands, now often referred to as the 'miracle rider'. Van der Vorst won two silver medals at the 2008 Beijing Paralympics, was elected Dutch disabled athlete of the year in 2009, was the first hand-cycle athlete to win the 2009 Ironman world championship in Hawaii, and has a dream of riding in the 2016 Rio Olympics. Her experience is remarkable. Monique van der Vorst has miraculously become an able-bodied Olympic hopeful after a crash reversed her paralysis. The story of van der Vorst is of a woman who was good at tennis and hockey in her early teenage years. When 13 years old she suffered nerve damage during a routine ankle operation and was paralyzed from the hip down. Van der Vorst had turned to hand-cycling after losing feeling in her legs as a teen. She got very good at this. That problem was compounded by a car accident in 2008. She was hit by a vehicle while hand-cycling in Amsterdam. Her spine was injured. However, in 2010 while she was on the road, training for the 2012 London Paralympics, van der Vorst was hit again, this time by a speeding bicyclist. While in the hospital after the collision, van der Vorst says she suddenly developed a tingling in her legs and within a year she was walking again. She now has a new dream. It is competing at the Olympics as an able-bodied athlete in Rio in 2016.

Realising the dream

Double gold medallist in the 2004 Olympics, Dame Kelly Holmes wrote in her autobiography: 'I had always thought of my athletics as coming second to my career in the Army. Whatever my other childhood dreams, I hadn't dared believe they might really come true' (Holmes, 2005, p. 109). She went on to say:

> I believe in fate, but I also believe that you must be passionate about your dreams and never give them up … Life is never easy. There are always obstacles to overcome. But fighting for your dreams will make the eventual achievement of them all the more satisfying. (Holmes, 2005, p. 115)

So how might an athlete realize their Olympic dream? There are of course many important factors and influences. Some help and some get in the way of high performance. Some talk about the need for a vision, being supported and challenged (Arthur, Hardy, & Woodman, 2012). Some debate natural aptitude, physical capabilities and mental toughness. Others think about access to good facilities and equipment such as rubber running tracks, lighter racquets, aerodynamic suits and so on. Then there is the use of modern technologies, that aim to provide coaches with relevant, timely and performance enhancing data. Technologies that help us better understand the athlete's physical actions like slow motion video and the body's response to training, such as physiological monitors like heart rate recorders and max. VO2 data. The ultimate aim, of course, is to enable an athlete to perform at his or her optimum at a given time.

But the athlete is not alone. Elite performers have a team of coaches, performance directors, therapists, conditioners and sports psychologists who work alongside them. Coaching, for some at least, has become part of a field called 'coaching science' that endorses a practice-based profession which aims to enhance athletic performance. Walsh (2008) continued to try to discover the skills and qualities that were common to expert coaches. Using data gathered from a coaching accreditation process for experienced coaches, Walsh required coaches to sit a 'coaching viva', which took the form of a semi-structured interview, focused on reflective practice. Viva transcripts were content analyzed to identify key themes. The following key facets of an expert coach emerged:

(1) Coaching agility: the ability to flex to the needs of different athletes or different situations.
(2) Athlete-centred mindset: the ability to close off to the voice in one's head that may be making judgements or giving answers.

(3) Clear coaching identity: understanding one's values, ethics and motivation for being a coach.
(4) High performance approach: the importance of reflective practice and continual development.
(5) Effective knowledge application: making sense of frameworks, models and techniques. Knowing the right times to use the right tools.

Walsh went on to suggest that moving from novice to expert in the area of coaching requires development of the 'mindset' over and above development of their 'skill set'. This begs the question, 'what kind of mindset?' An ethical and moral mindset perhaps? Sir Jackie Stewart, the successful Formula 1 racing driver, has argued that winning (at all costs) is not enough (Stewart, 2009). The manner of winning is also important (Ghaye, Lee, Shaw, & Chesterfield, 2009; Lee, Shaw, & Chesterfield, 2009). Graf (2005) raised a very provocative question in the context of operating within the letter and spirit of the rules in sport: 'is the lack of ethics the new norm?' Arguably this is a question, not only to be reflected upon in Olympic year, but every year in sport, and should be considered in relation to how performance teams set about trying to enable their athletes to realize their dreams.

Despite current participatory perspectives, coaching in Olympic year at least, is something geared to competitive success and towards winning (Coe, 2009). In the year of the London Olympics, successful coaching and athlete performance is not just about personal bests but about medals won! Just as an 'alchemist' strives to turn poor metals into gold. We suggest that the coach-as-alchemist strives to turn their athletes talent into Gold, Silver or Bronze. Coaching, in any sport, is about making someone better than they were before, continuously improving them and helping them to be the best they can. This is alchemy at work!

Despite many measurable and quantifiable performance criteria, coaching-for-performance is, arguably, fundamentally a moral practice. By this we mean that it is about the nature and quality of sustainable human relationships. Hardman & Jones (2011) argue that there are a number of implications for coaches, and coaching, if we think of it as a moral enterprise. The reasons are because coaching effects: (1) values – what we stand for and represent in sport; (2) attitudes – how athletes feel about themselves and their self belief; (3) behaviours – what athletes can actually achieve in competition; and (4) rules about fair play and drug free performance for example. Reflection-on-practice helps coaches develop a better sense of identity and self-efficacy and can help avoid coaches becoming 'spoilsports'. In addition, coaching-for-performance as a moral enterprise does not only embrace technical and tactical proficiency. It is also about coach-athlete relationships that are laced with integrity (Simons, 2008), should be trustworthy, honest and sincere. Because many coaching relationships are also intense, complex and contextual, this moral dimension is crucial. This is especially important as in many coach-athlete relationships power circulates and is exercised in interesting ways.

Coaching well and coaching ethically are both dependent upon the coach's ability to practice additional kinds of reflection. For example, self-reflection is important for at least three reasons. It enables the coach to: (1) develop their own style and coaching strategies; (2) sort out what interests, in the coach-athlete relationship, are being served (or not) through their coaching practices; (3) check on and exercise some kind of 'duty of care'. This is related to the important notions of athlete well-being and more generally, to human flourishing (Seligman, 2011).

Part of the practices of reflection involve the coach looking backwards to determine what has been achieved already (or what have been the failures), to get a sense of how performance is progressing, and what the 'activities-to-do' list looks like. Another part of the process is looking forward and therefore towards achieving future goals. So, taken together, coaching-for-performance can be said to involve both *projection* and *review*. These are well-known and practised. But there are other reflective practices which are particularly significant. One is reflecting and responding in-the-moment. It is what is often called *improvization*. In many aspects of sports coaching, improvization is necessary. Arguably, it is at the heart of the creative coaching process. For the coach (and athlete) this is often called reflecting-in-action. Some call this 'thinking on your feet'. Much of this can be unconscious and dependent upon tacit knowledge. Elite performers and their coaches act intuitively. They (re)act in the heat of the moment. They keep their 'heads-up'. So reflection-in-action is about making on-the-spot adjustments to coaching to enhance its potency, whilst in the midst of the action. To (re)act requires coaches to be 'resonant'. This begins with coach's thinking about the kind of coach they most want to be.

Bring on the alchemists

In this Special Issue of *Reflective Practice* we find many dreams being alluded to, coaches articulating their philosophies and practical actions and many conceptions of the processes of realising personal and collective Olympic dreams. We suggest that the metaphor of the coach-as-alchemist has emerged as a golden thread within and between the different contributions. At least we, the Editors, have perceived it this way and use this metaphor to make sense of, and derive much pleasure from, the contributions of others. This metaphor also acts as a catalyst for asking questions such as, 'who are these coaches of Olympians?', 'how do they become what they are?', 'what sets them going?', 'what keeps them going?' and 'from where do they draw their inspiration and strength?' Many of these questions are touched upon in the paper in this Special Issue where the thoughts and approaches of Andy Banks, the coach of Tom Daley, the GB diver, are disclosed. These questions and others then emerge as each paper unfurls, culminating in a stimulating 'Thought-piece' by Vassil Girginov who returns us to the notion of the London legacy mentioned earlier.

Arguably, the coach-as-alchemist, can be seen to have four attributes: Passion, Positivity, Persistence and Power.

Passion

Nothing motivates us more than our passions in life. Coaches care passionately about their sport and about the athletes they coach. Passion, like drive, dedication, commitment and even obsession, can be motivating. Being passionate can also be seen as a strength. Buckingham (2007, 2011) offers coaches the radical idea that we should challenge conventional wisdom that advocates that we only learn best from our mistakes and failures. As one person at the vanguard of the strengths-based movement (Yeager, Fisher, & Shearon, 2011), he believes that all we learn from studying mistakes and failures are the characteristics of mistakes and about failure. If we want to learn about our successes, we must study success. To learn about high achievement, we must study it and develop positive action plans to attain it. In the context of building high-performance teams he says:

> While there are many good levers for engaging people and driving performance, levers such as selecting for talent, setting clear expectations, praising where praise is due … The master lever is getting each person to play to his strengths. Pull this lever and an engaged and high performing team will be the result. Fail to pull it and no matter what else is done to motivate the team, it'll never fully engage. It will never become a high-performing team (Buckingham, 2007, p. 9).

Ghaye (2011) argues that coaches and others in human service work need to get passionate about identifying and playing to their strengths. He makes the case for new, strengths-based reflective practices, where reflection is not only about fixing what is wrong and about targeting under-performance. It also needs to be about nurturing, extending and amplifying what is best and what athletes are great at doing. For coaches, the challenge is this: how can you take what you currently do and re-shape it around your strengths? In other words, 'how can you make the best of what you do, the most of what you do?'

Positivity

Coaches strive to form positive athlete relationships, need to be realistic optimists and bring out the best in their athletes. This perhaps goes without saying. Sometimes they may need to stay positive when under pressure and when working within tensioned relationships (Fredrickson, 2011). A recent example of this concerns Jodie Williams (GB sprinter). Last year there were tensions between Charles van Commenee, the head of UK Athletics, Richard Williams, Jodie's father, and her coach, Mike McFarlane. Eager to expose her to more senior competition before the London 2012 Olympics, Van Commenee was displeased by her decision to sidestep last summer's world championship in South Korea and compete instead at the European juniors in Estonia. Van Commenee has a bit of a reputation for having a forceful personality and being used to getting his way. However, in this case he had to succumb to Richard Williams' calm intelligence and McFarlane's gut-feel for sprinting. Williams said, 'My dad sorts this out for me'.

> I'm obviously not old enough to negotiate things with Charles. He would push me over quite easily. But we had a few conversations in Paris because Charles wanted to know, from me, why I didn't want to run in the worlds. I told him I don't feel ready. Physically, I'd be OK. But mentally it's too early. I also don't really know any of the seniors yet and it would feel hard. In the juniors I'm going to be under real pressure to win – but that's healthy pressure (McRae, 2011).

In attempts to explore this notion of positivity in athletes further, we had an email conversation with Beth Tweddle MBE, Britain's most successful gymnast. We explored six questions with her, which are summarized in Table 1. They represent one elite performer's views of aspects of positivity in relation to her Olympic dreams and how the coach-athlete relationship can impact and influence the realization of this dream.

These responses illustrate Beth's Olympic dream acting as a positive energy source as she prepares for London 2012. Importantly, she identifies the enormous

Table 1. Expressions of positivity and coach-athlete relationships.

	Our questions to Beth	Beth's responses
1	We read reports that you are determined to do everything you can to realize your dream of winning an Olympic medal. When did you start dreaming of winning an Olympic medal?	I guess before Beijing I realized that an Olympic medal was a realistic dream.
2	You have been with your coach Amanda, since you were 12 years old. You say that without her you would not be where you are today. In what ways has she been influential in helping you achieve your Olympic dreams?	Amanda has been there throughout both the good and the bad times. She has picked me up when I was low and celebrated with me after a great result. She knows me inside out and always designs my training programme to ensure she gets the best out of me whether I am feeling great or struggling.
3	What are the main challenges in an athlete-coach relationship in a run-up to an Olympics?	I wouldn't say there are challenges! I have been with her that long and there is a line of respect. I know if I work hard and keep at it then she can't ask anymore of me.
4	What standout strengths do you feel a successful Olympic coach needs to have?	An Olympic coach has to have patience, be committed, determined and very hard working.
5	What has been a major setback for you, in your career, how did you recover from it and/or turn it into a positive?	There have been a few injuries and poor results. You just have to remember that everything happens for a reason and take the positive from it. Go back in the gym and work harder ready for the next competition if you didn't get the result you wanted or find a training programme that works on the part of your body that isn't injured.
6	We read that your wish is to end your career on a high in London. We also read that you feel you have to, "take risks to try and walk away with a medal". What kinds of risks are you having to manage?	I have to go to the Olympics with routines that are hard enough to get to finals. With difficulty comes a slight edge of risk. I am just working hard day in day out to work on my routines and hopefully they will be ready for the summer.

value of having a strong coach-athlete relationship in order to build positivity that enables her to bounce back from setbacks and keep on improving. These are necessary qualities in the quest to realize Olympic dreams. Beth's positive attitude also serves to build her psychological and emotional resources. We know from Fredrickson's 'broaden and build' theory (2010), that having a positive mindset can increase performance and broaden our thought-action repertoires. This means that when we feel positive we are more open to suggestions (for example, from an athlete's coach) about new and different ways of performing.

Persistence

This often shows itself in the encouragement and practices of coaches around the phrase, 'you should never give up!' No matter what the odds, no matter what the obstacle, no matter how much others might doubt, you (the athlete) need to believe in yourself, know that you can do your best and then be relentless in the pursuit of that objective. Never Give Up! Arguably, ability and talent alone are not enough to inspire greatness in others and in ourselves. Persistence is also needed. World class rowing coach, Carlos Dinares (2012), suggests that successful rowing coaches need to be persistent. He asks: 'Do you know of any successful rowing coach that doesn't spend all his day, energy and passion on making his rowers faster?' 'Do you know of any of these coaches that don't think all day long about how to make his rowers faster?' He argues that these top coaches are normally very persistent and never give up. They want to give the best they have to their athletes to see them succeed. These coaches get things done and make a direct impact on each rower they coach. They are action people. The conclusion he comes to is this. World class rowing coaches (just like rowers) will not become the best without being persistent.

Persistence is also linked with determination. The coach-as-alchemist knows how to ignite this in their athletes. They infect their athletes with the persistence virus. A good example of this is the case of Beth Tweddle, MBE. She is three times World Champion, double European Champion for two years running as well as National Champion. She is a double Olympian and has her eyes firmly set on a medal at the London Olympics 2012. At 26 years of age she is very much a 'senior' in gymnastics performance terms, a good 10 years older than many of those against whom she normally competes. 'I always thought I'd retire in 2006', she admits.

> But I didn't do as well as I wanted to at the Commonwealths that year. I got injured. So that spurred me on to stay for Beijing. After Beijing I really thought that was it. Coming fourth was the hardest. Normally if I don't do as well as I want, I balance out pretty quick. But Beijing was hard to get your head round. First couple of days after flying back, everything was about how well Team GB had done, we had our own flight back, medalists in business class, and I wasn't part of that. So I went to a travel agent and said, sort me a flight tomorrow. I went off with my flat mate, wondering if that was it. But she said to me after about three days it was obvious I wanted to be back in the gym training, working to put it right. Which is what I've done. Disappointment makes you stronger (White, 2011).

In an article by Patel and Whittington (2012) they ask Beth, 'What is the most important thing that sport has taught you?' Beth's response is another expression of persistence.

> It's taught me discipline and determination. Things don't always go right first time, so get back up and have another go and obviously that can be transferred into any part of your life, whether that's with your job or friends. If something goes wrong make sure you get back up and sort it out.

Power

Power manifests itself in sport and coaching in many ways. When thinking about power in the context of this Special Issue, three expressions come to mind. First there is the 'power to' do something. A skill, a routine, a move and so on. Then there is the 'power over' someone. This term reflects what most of us think of when we consider the use of power in human relationships, within teams and in organizations. It means that the person using this power is exercising control over another person, or people, through the use of formal authority and position. Then there is the term 'power with'. This means finding the leverage to meet one's needs and accomplish one's goals in partnership with others, not by dominating them. It is about working with each other, with one's coach, therapists, and so on. Cultivating the discipline to do this does not mean, as so many people fear, a subordination or loss of self, but precisely the opposite. Nor does it mean the sudden disappearance of any conflict or differences. What it does mean is that athlete well-being is the means to an agreed end, namely high performance.

In a recent, real life pre-Olympic scenario, aspects of power were expressed and circulated in a significant way. In the scenario there was a London 2012 pin-up diving boy, (Tom Daley), his coach, his agent and the British Diving's Performance Director, Alexei Evangulov. In February 2012, the young diver in question was accused by the Performance Director, a powerful man, of endangering his Olympic medal chances because of his media commitments. Reportedly, Evangulov is a strict disciplinarian. He is a former Russian diving champion and familiar with Eastern bloc-type training regimes, which hot-house divers in sports schools away from their parents. The former Russia coach claimed Daley's main rivals in China were training three times harder and said Daley's fifth place at last year's World Championships was a true reflection of his standing in the 10m platform. Jamie Cunningham, Daley's agent, responded strongly by saying that diving, family and school were always the priority for Tom and that they constituted 90% of his life, and that this was agreed between Tom, his family and British Diving. Corporate, media work and friends were the other 10%. In situations like this, which are not unusual in sport with high-profile athletes, the coach-as-alchemist becomes crucial. Tom Daley is an ordinary young man. With the support of those around him, and especially his coach Andy Banks, he has, and will, no doubt, go on to do even more extra-ordinary things.

As we now open the way to the first paper in this Special Issue, by Tom Daley's coach Andy Banks, some things have become very clear to us. Coaches-as-alchemists seem much more interested in doing what they believe in and enjoy than starting a dynasty, amassing huge piles of money or acquiring celebrity status. They play to their strengths and are open to new ideas and ways of doing things. This is an important attribute of their success. Arguably it is the possibility of dreams coming true that makes coaching and performance interesting to research and develop. For many athletes, coaches and spectators, chasing and achieving dreams captures the essence of the Olympic and Paralympic Games.

Notes on contributors

Sarah Lee is a subject leader of Applied Sport Science at UWE Hartpury. She has worked in this field since postgraduate study developing her expertise in performance psychology. Her doctoral research focuses on building high-performance environments. She also provides education and consultation to grassroots and elite performers and coaches alike. She is an elite netball player and holds extensive netball coaching roles within the southwest, including an England Netball Talent and Performance Centre role for developing youth elite performers.

Tony Ghaye is the director of Reflective Learning – International. He is a member of BASES, a positive psychologist, and strength-based performance enhancer. He has worked at numerous universities within the UK and overseas, has written 24 academic books and 108 refereed papers on personal performance and organisational improvement through reflective learning. His interest is in developing more strengths-based reflective practices that build and sustain high performance and supportive cultures.

Martin Dixon is currently lecturer in Sports Coaching and Leader in Curriculum Development at UWE Hartpury. Following postgraduate study in Coaching Science, Martin's teaching is centred on the application of reflective practice within sports coaching. He is a UEFA Licenced football coach and previously held coaching roles at a Premier League Academy and several regional Centres of Excellence. Martin has presented innovative research on sports coaching and pedagogy at international conferences, and his interests focus on coaching for performance through teaching.

References

Arthur, C., Hardy, L., & Woodman, T. (2012). Realising the Olympic dream: Vision, support and challenge. *Reflective Practice, 13*(3), this issue.

Buckingam, M. (2007). *GO put your strengths to work: Six powerful steps to achieve outstanding performance*. London: Simon and Schuster.

Buckingam, M. (2011). *Standout*. Nashville, TN: Thomas Nelson.

Coe, S. (2009). *The winning mind: My inside track on great leadership*. London: Headline.

Dinares, C. (2012). *World class rowing*. Retrieved February 16, 2012, from http://www.carlosdinares.com/

Fredrickson, B. (2011). The role of positive emotions in positive psychology: The broaden-and-build theory of positive emotions. *American Psychologist, 56*(3), 218–226.

Fussey, P., Coaffee, J., Armstrong, G., & Hobbs, D. (2012). *Securing and sustaining the Olympic city: Reconfiguring London for 2012 and beyond*. Farnham: Ashgate.

Ghaye, T. (2011). *Teaching and learning through reflective practice. A practical guide for positive action* (2nd ed.). Abingdon: Routledge.

Ghaye, T., Lee, S., Shaw, D.J., & Chesterfield, G. (2009). When winning is not enough: Learning through reflections on the 'best-self". *Reflective Practice, 10*(3), 385–401.

Graf, J. (2005). Ethics. In C. Reynaud (Ed.), *She can coach*. Leeds: Human Kinetics Publishers.

Hardman, R., & Jones, C. (2011). *The ethics of sports coaching*. Abingdon: Routledge.

Holmes, K. (2005). *Kelly black, white & gold Holmes: My autobiography (with Fanny Blake)*. London: Virgin Books.

Lee, S., Shaw, D.J., & Chesterfield, G. (2009). Reflections from a World Champion: an interview with Sir Clive Woodward, Director of Olympic Performance, The British Olympic Association. *Reflective Practice, 10*(3), 295–310.

Lewis, T. (2011, July 24). London 2012: The home straight, *The Observer*.

McRae, D. (2011, April 19). Jodie Williams: 'Even before I ran, I wanted to be in the Olympics', *The Guardian*. Retrieved February 16, 2012 from http://www.guardian.co.uk/sport/2011/apr/19/jodie-williams-olympics

National Audit Office. (2008). *Preparing for sporting success at the London 2012 Olympic and Paralympic Games and beyond*. London: NAO.

Patel, H., & Whittington, J. (2012). Five minutes with Beth Tweddle, Sportsister. Retrieved February 16, 2012, from http://www.sportsister.com/2012/01/31/5-minutes-with-beth-tweddle/

Seligman, M. (2011). *Flourish: A visionary new understanding of happiness and well-being*. New York: Free Press.

Shinar, Y. (2008). *Think like a winner*. London: Vermilion.

Short, S., Tenute, A., & Feltz, D. (2005). Imagery use in sport: Mediational effects for efficacy. *Journal of Sports Sciences, 23*(9), 951–960.

Simons, T. (2008). *The integrity dividend: Leading by the power of your word*. San Francisco: Jossey-Bass.

Stewart, J. (2009). *Winning is not enough: The autobiography*. London: Headline Publishing Group.

VaezMousavi, S., & Rostami, R. (2009). The effects of cognitive and motivational imagery on acquisition, retention and transfer of the basketball free throw. *World Journal of Sport Sciences, 2*(2), 129–135.

Walsh, K. (2008). *The anatomy of an expert coach*. Retrieved February 16, 2012, from http://www.lane4performance.com/The-Anatomy-of-an-Expert-Coach.html?page=1

White, J. (2011). *Beth Tweddle is fired up for home run*. Retrieved February 16, 2012, from http://www.telegraph.co.uk/sport/olympics/8809091/London-2012-Olympics-British-gymnastics-standard-bearer-Beth-Tweddle-is-fired-up-for-home-run.html

Yaeger, J.M., Fisher, S.W., & Shearon, D.N. (2011). *Smartb strengths: Building character, resilience and relationships in youth*. Putnam Valley, New York: Kravis Publishing.

Coaching for performance: an interview with Olympic diving coach, Andy Banks

Martin Dixon[a], Sarah Lee[a] and Tony Ghaye[b]

[a]UWE Hartpury, Gloucester, England; [b]Reflective Learning – International, Gloucester, England

Scholars from the field of sports coaching have widely accepted the practice of coaching as a complex activity due to the necessity to manage performers and the dynamic environments within which they operate (Cassidy, Jones, & Potrac, 2004; Cushion, 2001; Jones, Armour, & Potrac, 2004; Knowles, Tyler, Gilbourne, & Eubank, 2006). It therefore stands to reason that the higher up the performance chain you get, the more complex the process becomes as a result of more multifaceted competitive environments. This has led to a research focus on understanding not only what coaches do, but unravelling how they think and acquire knowledge. Much of the work conducted within this discipline has been based around the underlying fact that the sports coaching industry is results driven. Certainly at elite and Olympic level a key focus when evaluating sports coaching effectiveness is based on competitive performance and attainment, placing significant expectation and responsibility on the coach. However, it remains to be seen if coaches themselves actually use an outcome focus as the key driver when designing and managing their performance programmes, and what they do in terms of process that ensures they are meeting performance targets. The experiences of practicing coaches working with elite and Olympic performers provides invaluable insights into the coaching process at this level, and what it really means to be a coach and develop athletes that have World Class potential. In order to explore these concepts further we interviewed diving coach Andy Banks, known primarily for his role as coach to World Champion and 2012 Olympic hopeful Tom Daley. Here we present a reflexive conversation with him. We hope that reading this will inspire you, the reader, to think about how you can develop the performance potential of those people you work with.

MD: Andy, just to start with, I'd like you to give us a biography about yourself and how you came to this point in your coaching career.
AB: I started diving when I was nine; I was taken to holiday courses by my parents and enjoyed those, then got involved with a club. For a number of years I was in different clubs as my parents moved from the South to North. I got to National level and thought that if you were launched into the abyss and landed the right way

Figure 1.

up or thereabouts, and if it didn't hurt, then that was a good dive. I did wonder why I didn't do brilliantly at Nationals. Then, at the back end of my career I'd left school and gone down to London to work in the Police. I came across a coach there who basically switched the lights on and started talking to me about things like Biomechanics. I thought 'bio who?!' And psychology, physiology…, dry land training for diving. I thought you just swung your arms around a bit then got in. So it really was an eye opener for me that there was a science behind this sport which I had no concept of whatsoever. That helped me a little bit, but it was too late for me then. Whether there was enough talent there anyway I think is arguable. But it was too late. That enthused me. He got me involved in coaching some of his younger groups, seeing if I could go off and actually learn about what this sport was all about, and put that knowledge and experience together eventually to create people who did have talent to actually achieve right up to the end of their talent. I'm a big believer that you do have to have talent to succeed but also if the coaching isn't correct then you're likely to limit the ceiling of what that talent can achieve. So my goal was to find the talent and then help it to achieve its ceiling.

So I left the Police. Having run away from my A-Levels initially, I went back into college and did a degree in Human Movement which I completely biased towards diving. My majors were biomechanics and psychology and physiology. I did strength training for younger age group divers. Everything we did really by way of assignment I tried to bias towards diving and did the research around it and tried to learn as much as I could about what I was going to do. In effect I used the degree course not just to get a degree but to increase the knowledge base that I had. At the same time I set up a programme in Bradford which was just two hours a week for beginner divers. By the end of the three year college course that had two kids on the Junior National team and had grown from two hours for beginners to a fairly extensive programme. I stole, grabbed, pinched and argued for more pool time. I said to them, 'I've finished my degree course, I've done all this over the last three years, I need a job please'. They had a small pool that was shutting, and a swimming teacher who had retired so there was a salary available. I was given that under the education budget for a year's contract. That role became the first full-time diving coach position that there was. So professionalism in diving came about through that. It of course then expanded along with other white elephants as they were, around the country in pools that had been built but hadn't really been used, with people like myself who were keen to get involved in diving professionally and work as a full-time coach.

I wanted to get into 10 metre level. Bradford was only 5 metre level and Plymouth was a 10 metre pool that was relatively new at the time. But they had no money. A few people had tried to get in and they were like 'sorry no room at the inn'. I'd seen a programme set up by a guy called Chris Snode who came back from the '84 games and set up a private company at Crystal Palace doing pre-school gymnastics, trampolining, recreational diving and elite diving and the whole thing developed as a financial base to help an elite programme. So I nicked that idea and went and spoke to the guy who had been diving mentor, and he was also a city accountant. His history was diving at the '60 Olympic Games, he'd gone off and done his professional accountancy course, although he still coached in his spare time. He said 'well, come in with me, I'll be your partner'. I knew nothing about running or setting it up or budgets or accounting or anything about business so that was kind of a godsend. He came as a partner initially in the business we set up down here. We put together a proposal presented to Plymouth Council in 1992, they approved it and we've been here ever since. So it's fundamentally been about growing that base so that there's money to make sure we're still here the following month which obviously is important. So I have had to spend some time running round the floor playing lions with the three year olds, I still do on occasion when absolutely necessary.

Through the funding that came around, particularly following the Olympic medal that we got in Athens, the sport itself has professionalised. The elite coaches from the different programmes were sent around by the performance director at the time to all the competitions all over the place, so we'd do European Cups, World Championships, Commonwealth Games and ultimately the Olympics, which meant that experience was developed, knowledge was developed and those competitions really became normal as opposed to 'wow'. There's a thing called 'kit and trips' where initially all you want is a tracksuit and a ticket to get on a plane. Well I can set up a sports shop with the amount of kit that I've got and I'm sick to death of Heathrow Bloomin' airport! So it's not about that anymore. I think it's really about the performance and the competition and setting up the programme. Fundamentally it's about the right developmental build up if you like into the major event of the year.

We put all of the top kids into one squad and they work together as a unit. Tom (Daley) at that time was the baby, so although we'd already identified the fact that he was pretty damn good, he was put into a squad where he was the worst. Well not the worst but the least experienced. He trained with a whole load of people who were already on the international scene, doing more difficult dives than he was, but he could look up to. And he still has that really in Tonia. Tonia and him have been everywhere together. At the Games he was seventh and she was eighth. He's had his world championship obviously which she hasn't achieved but they have always been there or thereabouts. They have a mutual respect I think and friendship and ability to train together which I think is fundamental. I also think as an aside it's been extremely important for Tom to come through in an environment where he isn't 'top dog'. I don't think, given his personality, that he would ever have developed into an obnoxious little whatsit, but the fact that he's been in that environment I think has really helped to make sure that hasn't been the case. You look at other people who are big fishes in little ponds, it doesn't help. Staying at the right level of the pond on the way through I think is good because it means you are forever aspiring to achieve what the others are doing.

MD: You talked about this academic side and developing your knowledge of biomechanics and psychology, and you've got experience as a performer as well. How would you say these have developed your strengths as a coach?
AB: I think in some ways not being a good performer has helped because I didn't achieve as a performer and therefore achieving as a coach has been a big deal. If I'd been an Olympic medallist five times then maybe I wouldn't be so into pushing the talent to be great, and maybe I wouldn't understand so much when things weren't going right, why you can't do it.

SL: How do you define achievement as a coach?
AB: Well for me it's very much taking whatever kid it is to their ceiling. I mean Tom obviously as an accolade to me is what most people talk about. In terms of actually coaching him it's been relatively easy. Technique and mechanics are very interlinked, so learning how it works mechanically so you have a full understanding of exactly what it is you are trying to achieve I think is massively important. You can then mould what you see. Tom's ability to make change was really good and that's part of his talent, so given that I knew this, it was very easy to mould what I wanted into very good technique which then allowed him to progress quickly through the difficult skills and the more difficult dives.

TG: Is that why you use this notion of the putty?
AB: Absolutely. If you have quality clay then you can make a Ming Vase. If you don't then you might as well just stick with a load of coffee cups. Having said that you still need the skill to be able to mould it; you can't make a Ming Vase if you don't know what you're doing. So the two came together I think. Another one of my analogies is the racing car, in that there's a whole team of people now it's not just coach and diver. It's very much led by the coach I guess but if I want strength and conditioning done, we've got access to strength and conditioning now and I'll sit down with him and say 'this is what I want to achieve' they're the experts, they can get on with it. The nice thing about the degree course is that it does give you a jack of all trades scenario, so I can understand when they start talking in strength and conditioning speak but it is very much down to them to get on with the programme. We'll then monitor that and see if it's achieving what we're trying to achieve and if it's not we'll try and reason out why it's not and how we can tweak that programme in order to change it so that it does achieve it. Similarly with the physios and massage, we have those there and we do a lot of work now with those guys on pre-hab work. So our medics and our physios and our strength and conditioning people are involved in regular screening to identify weak areas that can then be worked on specifically with an individually tailored programme to make sure that those people are strong enough, flexible enough and able to do the workload that I'm asking them to do so injury levels are decreased as much as possible. We still obviously get injuries and it's important then I think to have the physios and medics on hand immediately. So we have a great link with the hospital.

MD: In terms of the resources you have here in Plymouth, how does that help to develop a winning culture? You've had several divers from Plymouth go on to do very well, so how have you established this winning culture within this area of the country?

AB: It's partly a British Diving thing. As an example, in the beginning of 2005 Tom was 10 moving onto 11; that's when I thought there was an outside chance that he maybe could make 2008. 2012 was always the ultimate goal, but to do an Olympics first to give him that experience, I'm really happy we managed to do that. I went to Athens as a voyeur not as an actual part of the team so Beijing was actually my first Games as part of the team as well and it is amazing how much of a culture shock it is. It's massive; the food hall is the size of two football pitches; you're sitting down and Andy Murray or someone comes in and sits next to you for breakfast; there's the games room, there's stuff going on all the time in the village and it's actually quite difficult to keep your eye on the ball. So I think having done that and seen that and having been there and done that if you like, Tom will be much more prepared to go to London and still enjoy the experience but to be able to carve the pathway that he needs to without being 'oh what's going on there' and be much more 'this is what I'm focused on'.

From 2008 we did a plan backwards, saying 'this is where he needs to be, this is where we are now, so what are we going to do now to achieve that, and the British Diving junior programme bought into that very much so. They went off and organised for him to compete in Aachen which was set up for 14 and 15 year olds, normally when the juniors first start competing. We went off to the Australian Youth Games, again before he was old enough to compete but people had heard about him so the deals were done if you like; the politics was dealt with by the management team and they got him on those planes and got him into those competitions. So it's not just a Plymouth culture. One of the nice things that our PD (Performance Director) did is send everybody all around the place. There had been a little bit of 'this is my baby and you lot can all back off' and we've very much changed that culture now into 'this kid is a bit of a wonder boy, what can we do as a unit to make sure this guy is successful for British Diving as a sport'. If we're successful as a sport then funding stays, the jobs stay, everybody wins. So we try to work very much as a team and I've had people helping me with the coaching. I've got people on the end of the phone and I can say 'I've got this problem, what do you think I should do? What could you do?' And the discussions are always there and in many cases it's a good example of 'more heads are better than one'.

TG: Would you say Andy that what you are describing now is also another strength of yours? This notion of knowing how to make the best of a team. Knowing where people's strengths are. Knowing where to put Tom and your other divers at the right place at the right time?

AB: I think it stems from the fact that I believe that the coach is the facilitator and it goes back to a philosophy that I built for myself when I was at college with a book that I'd read from a gymnastics coaching point of view, and that is, particularly when working in kids' sports; you start off as a dictator and the kids down here somewhere because they haven't got a clue about anything so you tell them what to do. Then gradually that should change and you come up to more of a par and ultimately become the advisor. I think that's very true because I'm asking someone like Tom to stand in front of thousands of people in an auditorium on his own and perform to the best of his ability. I just need to be 'right off you go boy', job's done, let's get on with it. So everything I do is about facilitating his ability to be him and the divers that I work with. That's what it's all about. It's not about 'oh this is Andy Banks, its Tom Daley's coach isn't he great?' I'm much more the sort of person who'll sit there, love the performance and then go and have beer with the other coaches. I don't need to be stood on the rostrum with him. Its job done then, and that's cool and the accolade comes from within the peer group.

TG: This dictator to facilitator journey – when you say you do that it looks like a smooth process but I guess there are times when Tom doesn't want you to facilitate, wants you to dictate?
AB: Absolutely. He said that to me once when I'd tried to push that but it's a relationship and therefore there are times when it does and doesn't work. In his first International he'd just split the Chinese as a young kid. Moving into the next round I thought it might be worth a try so I said to him 'what do you want to do for your build up to your final?' He just looked at me and said 'I want you to tell me what to do and I'll go and do it like you always do'! It was fine, that wasn't an issue I just thought I'd see what the score was and he obviously wasn't ready at that point. Whereas now, he's 17 now and he's quite a mature young man and we discuss stuff a lot more. I've been to the school to meet with his deputy head to discuss his A-Levels and what he's gonna do with them, when he's gonna do his exams and how that fits into this year, how that fits into next year and how that fits into 2013 as an addendum. That's all well and good, I can help set that up, I can help make sure the right people are there, but at the end of the day the decision is his; 'if you want to do your a-Levels this year that's what you're gonna do, these are the pros and cons of doing that, this is what might happen if you do that, what do you think?' I think it's very much a case of yes we'll steer and nudge and I know what I would prefer and I'll tell him what I would prefer, but ultimately I'm not telling him what he's doing, he will make that decision himself and if he needs help with it then we'll get other people in, then we'll get the psychologist to come in and talk to him, or his teachers will talk to him. So he's getting as many inputs as possible. It's not just about me and him, it's about the team again to try and make sure he gets absolutely everything that he needs to make the value judgements and decisions that he needs to make, hopefully in the right way.

TG: OK, so if facilitation is a strength that we're hearing here, what about working with somebody like Tom, initially a boy, now a young man and the kind of emotional journey he's been on. What kinds of strengths have you had to call on to enable Tom to keep it together emotionally?
AB: Have you heard the story about what I said when I first saw him? I was asked to go over and see him and I stood there and watched him for about 15 minutes and turned round to everyone there and said 'that boy will not make a diver whilst he's got a hole in his arse'. Now in my defence I didn't actually see him get in the pool. What I saw was a kid who stood at the back of the first board, the 1 metre board, refusing to get on it, crying, and he didn't even dive in. It was just a 'no' and he had basically lost the plot emotionally and was very much in that downward spiral then. When I did see him in the pool it was obvious that there was talent there and the other people were right. But he needed help with that emotional journey because he would very often just lose the plot. As a child I think one thing

that's very obvious is that they don't know about emotion, they don't know why it happens, they just react to emotion as it happens. As an adult the difference is that you understand emotion a bit more and realise that you can, to a certain extent, control it. So with Tom initially, as an example, I use what I call the Peter Pan theory. If he wanted to fly, he had to think happy thoughts. Basically the first stage was realising that there was this knot and the emotional kick-in was starting, the downward spiral was on its way. So the recognition of that was important. Then we'd stop. It was a bit more difficult in competition but in training we'd stop, he'd go for a shower or a swim or whatever, coming back with a happy thought, and then we'd see if we could start to fly again. It didn't just work like magic, often he'd fall out of the air, fairy dust or not. But gradually that started to work.

TG: What did he say to you when you said 'we're going to do a Peter Pan now?' Did he look at you in that strange kind of way, or did he welcome that?
AB: He was nine years old so he kind of realised. I always spoke to him when he wasn't in 'dodgy mode'; I spoke to him in 'happy mode'. I said 'this is what happens when you lose the plot, you realise that that means the session is a waste of time, we don't get anything done in a competition, potentially you give up, there's no point carrying on the competition and you need to change that'. And he had experiences along the way, and one of the things I tried to do with Tom is what I call 'bank experiences'. So the first competition he did with me, he fell off the board on the last dive. He was winning it but he ended up not getting a medal. He screamed and ran out of the fire exit and almost knocked someone in the pool on the way out. Similarly at one of his Internationals, he was gonna get a medal and then didn't because he dropped the last dive. I sat down with him after and said 'right, you were concentrating on everything else that was going on in that competition, not focusing on your process and your dive and staying in your bubble'. So part of the psychology work we have done is about focusing on process and totally ignoring everything else that's going on.

Competition is very much performance related. I don't do outcome goals. With an outcome goal he's gonna under-perform. We only do performance goals and the reason for that is you can only control the performance. Tom is doing six dives for example; each of those with me is its own individual competition. He does it, forgets about it, and we'll analyse it later but we'll move onto the next competition, the next dive. When he won his gold medal, he went into the last round in fourth place, which is where I expected him to end. If he'd have sneaked onto the rostrum it would have been a massive bonus. And then everyone's wheels fell off; they didn't do what he'd done. They did what he'd done in yesteryear, and they were focusing on 'shit I might win this' or 'I've got to dive really well because that little whatsit has just nailed his last dive' and they all went 'miss, miss, miss' and all of a sudden, he's on top. Now the media jumped on that and said 'oh yeah well the others lost it', well maybe they did but at the end of the day, from a whole performance scenario, his performance on that day was better than the others because they messed up at the end. All the way through, the top three doing what they should have done, they had more degree of difficulty than Tom, they were doing it well and they were staying steadily one step ahead of the game. Tom was doing what our goal was which is go in there and nail the crap out of all of your dives and he just kept the pressure on the whole time. I've got another story from 2008; we went there and the media were all over him after the last World Cup because he got a medal with his synchro partner; 'how many medals are you gonna win here?' Outcome, outcome, outcome. So we had three goals going into the Olympics; one was to be happy and be proud of his performance, two was to learn as much as possible, and three was to have fun. I remember coming away from that final and the media clobbered me before they did him and I just said 'job done; those three, done'. Arguably, he dived safely, which is not surprising really in your first Olympic final I don't think. In 2008 he'd also been to the junior worlds, which was his first ever junior competition and he dived brilliantly. Obviously he went there to win it, but that still wasn't the goal. And this little whatsit from China came out of nowhere, who is now the World Champion from this year. They had a real punch-up, they were 70 points ahead of the field and this guy beat Tom by two points. But his performance was fantastic. So I'd reviewed what he'd done there and said OK, let's forget about new dives and hit the 2009 senior circuit with the same aggression and confidence that you did on the junior meet. And that's what he did throughout 2009 and ultimately ended up with that gold medal. But it's an example I think of where good things have come from bad again with Tom.

TG: Just to go back just briefly, you said that when you first spotted him you thought 'yeah, this boy's got talent', when you first saw him in the pool. What was it that kind of stood out for you?
AB: I think it's about his awareness, that kind of sticks out. He manages to find the right way up relatively easily. He also looks aesthetic. Some kids have knobbly knees and look like a twiglet flying through the air. He's got the right body shape. He's fast enough which means that things spin around no problem, and as I say, his ability to make and change technique was obvious. Some kids you talk to in numerous different ways and it's head on the wall time and they just don't make the changes. With Tom you kind of say something and it's changed. You say something else and it's changed and you can visually see the process of him making the changes to get that technique better. I think that's what made him better, plus when he got it right he just looked fantastic. And he's got this ability to rip; he's got massive hands and yes, we taught him the technique but that rip action is pretty natural to be honest, it's not like we spent forever and ever trying to teach him how to do that, he learnt how to do it pretty quick and he disappears and the judges love it.

MD: One of the things I think is quite fascinating about your scenario with your athletes, is that you have these athletes from a young age; with so much one to one contact over a long duration, how do you make sure things don't go stale and stay fresh? I read for example that you have a very good coach athlete relationship with Tom for example but you don't go for a drink with him...
AB: It's very, very rare that I'll do social stuff with them; I do do it because I think it would be a bit too anal not to.

MD: So you always have to manage that distance?
AB: Yeah I think so, it has to be close; there has to be a mutual trust and respect I think. At the end of the day I'm getting those guys to learn dives that they know when I say it's ready, it's ready, I'm not making it up as I go along. So there has to be that trust, and that's developed over time I guess, when you get it right more often than when you get it wrong. Tom's only 17 so that's not really been an issue

yet. I mean it's probably made easier by the fact that I'm not really in their peer group now. You know when I was a 20 year old it was kind of difficult to not be involved in some of the older divers' social lives as we were kind of the same age.

MD: And in terms of keeping them fresh, because you're with them for such a long time.
AB: It's all about having fun for me and if they're not having fun, then they don't want to be there, and they need to want to be there. So yes I want to put together a programme that means they are competitive in the world, but we still play silly games as part of our warm-up. We often play coaches against divers, so the S & C people are on the coaches' side and the divers, whoever's there will be together. We just do games as part of the warm-up and it's a monthly competitive thing. And it's very competitive! But it's a bit of fun. That's what training should be and if it's all just come in and do this and do this and do this, it's not much kop really.

SL: Do you think you're constantly changing what you do with the athletes to keep it fresh like that?
AB: I try and mix it up but ultimately trying to achieve a six dive list that's the same six dives is there's double the learning so in terms of pushing the boat with that it's more difficult. We do awareness stuff which is slightly different and we do try and make competitions within that and they quite enjoy that. Tom particularly loves competition whatever it might be so even if they're just doing entry practices where they're falling off the board, they're trying to see who can rip the best. So it's just things like that that make it a bit more interesting, but yeah they need to want to come training and therefore the environment has to be such that it makes it more interesting and fun.

SL: Well that's your ability to hook into them I guess?
AB: Yeah well we are known as the fun programme, I think, which I don't have a problem with at all. I think that's great. But they are a bunch of nutters, and I guess I foster that because I think that's good. Ultimately, I'm asking them to go up onto the 10 metre and chuck themselves off doing fairly complex skills which are quite scary.

TG: So you want them to have fun and enjoyment and those things you talked about, but just listening to you and just looking as you are just talking to us it sounds like its got to be fun for you the coach too, because you've got this drive and energy.
AB: I wondered how many hours I've sat next to a diving pool, and it's ridiculous. It's not so bad when you're in Fort Lauderdale in the sun but when it's in the Soviet Socialist Republic of Plymouth it's a bit much. I got into diving because the whole concept excited me as I said, for the first time in my life it was like 'this is something that I really enjoy and I can really see myself doing and I really want to be good at and I really want to make a difference at'. So the fact that I kind of had that as an ultimate goal and I'm now doing that, I think is great. I made a living out of something that most people historically did as a hobby. I run it as a business which means that ultimately I've been more successful financially than most of the other people that are involved in diving. I'm hardly Alan Sugar, but then that was never the goal.

TG: And you've won many awards too; are these really important to you?

AB: No, not at all. It's a nice dinner and it's nice to stand up and say thank you to a few people, and they look good in a cabinet, but I don't do it for the awards at all to be honest. That's just a bonus of being lucky enough to have someone like Tom, and being able to do stuff with him I suppose. I still think that for a coaching accolade, a girl that I used to coach many moons ago who was a novice diver, wasn't great; ultimately got one junior international tracksuit and that's it. She'll always have that, and she should never really have got that. She wasn't good enough. But she worked hard. We worked hard and she got that achievement, and that I think is more of an accolade to the coaching not just getting an award because Tom Daly happens to be doing this, that and the other. It's quite funny, the whole celebrity thing because I've not really been entrenched in that before or experienced it before. It's not me obviously, it's him that's the celebrity, I'm just sort of along for the ride. But it's different, I've known Tom as a kid, as a young man, and as Tom. Everyone else looks at him and goes 'oh god it's Tom Daly!' And that's what they do with celebrities.

MD: Andy, we'd like to talk now about your Olympic dreams. You've talked about not being too outcome driven and focusing more on process, so what would be your Olympic dream?

AB: That obviously is how we treat the competitions, in terms of the dream, that's an easy one really. I was at the Commonwealth Games where we had one and two in the boys in Manchester beating a Canadian superstar and the roof came off there. I've been in Rome when Tom won the World Championships and experienced that. I guess you then put the two together; you've got a home Olympics in a pool which is much bigger, it's gonna be massive, it's gonna be really loud, the home support is gonna be fantastic, and if you could couple that with the euphoria of that result, or a similar one to what happened in Rome then that would just be, you know? It would be an amazing moment. So yeah that's the dream if you like. But dreams then become goals, goals then become the important factor behind that and if the dream happens, it happens.

SL: Do you talk about that a lot?

AB: No. No not at all because at the end of the day we know how tough it's gonna be. There's a number of people out there who could hit that rostrum. The Chinese; they've not done well historically on 10 metres, other than this year where they won it, and they want both of their guys on the rostrum so they are going for it. We've got a plan that's similar. We want to go there and do the absolute best that Tom possibly can do at that event. And then you've got guys from Russia, from America, from Mexico; all of whom can potentially get onto that rostrum and, as I said in Rome, there were four who moved away and it could have been about six. I'd say we're almost up to about eight or nine now, who on their day could get onto that rostrum. So it's not gonna be easy. It's gonna be real tough. But it's not only going to be tough for us, it's going to be tough for them too because they're in the same boat. There could be eight or nine that could get on that rostrum. Everyone's in that fight and someone, well three, will come out on top.

The Chinese are a nightmare because they are just so machine like. But they've cheated in a way, if cheat is the right word because they've picked up numerous kids at the age of five, they've channelled them all into a pretty hectic training programme. The ones that break just get left by the wayside, and the other ones that are successful go through so you only ever see the cream of the cream and you don't see the discarded ones that almost made it but didn't. So if you like the word 'cheat' is more of an ethical thing because I think, what we try and do is nurture the individual and not just match up the sport. Ultimately, Tom is going to go out into the world as an ex-diver and I'd like to think that I can sit back in my rocking chair and say 'yeah he was a good lad, and I helped to be part of that production process'. Significant other is a psychological term for it. I'll never take over or be anywhere near what his dad was to him. I can give him bits of advice and I can help to set up that advice to come in to help him make the very best choice in life as well as within the sport I think.

MD: You've got the dream as this moment that could happen. What about let's say, when the Olympics has finished, what's the legacy and dream after the Olympics; for you and for the sport?
AB: Well this Life Centre is just about to open. I will no longer be running diving as a business. There is an agreement that has been made that everything will come under one banner. So I will have role up there looking after aquatics as well as the diving in an overall role really. We have the local school that Tom goes to, who are chomping at the bit to give scholarships; we've got universities that are also interested in developing the whole sport route. I just need to persuade British Diving that having Plymouth as a major hub for diving moving onwards is the way forwards. I also want to spend some time giving back some of the stuff that I've had. I know that sounds a bit cliché but we have been sent all over the world as a group as some of the top coaches and there is a bit of a gap in terms of experience and knowledge to the next level down. And if we all disappear and just sit on our beach without doing anything then it's gonna take a lot of time for that to catch up again. So I want to try and make sure there's work done before I disappear to try and make that knowledge stay so it's not just about a legacy facility, there's a legacy for knowledge and experience. So when I come back and watch the odd competition, the guys coaching at the top end are possibly even the divers now. It doesn't stop here; it'll move on. Sooner or later there will be other people that are doing this so it's an on-going thing isn't it? And I think what's nice about the London Games is that there are a number of new pools just coming up.

If it wasn't for Tom and Tonia and the programme here, there's no way the council would have spent the money on developing a brand new state of the art facility, not just for diving of course, but diving is very prevalent in there. I think that's brilliant. But there aren't that many facilities around the country. What I want to make sure now is that we use what we've got here because everyone's falling over each other to make it great and if we can get the top kids in the country to come to school here and have a seamless academic pathway, so they move from school to university and get the correct academic background alongside working in a brand new state of the art facility with potentially me and other coaches that we can bring in, maybe to have a sporting development career that is also seamless and good then it's a no brainer isn't it really? I've just got to persuade some other people of that, but I'm working on that behind the scenes. That's the next step really but what happens to funding I don't know. But whether we get a medal or not there will still be funding and I think someone like Tom is going to be looked after because he is the pinnacle of the sport at the moment so I know Plymouth will be there still as an elite programme and Tom is not just talking about 2016, he's talking about 2020 and possibly even 2024 so he's got some longevity in the sport still potentially. Whether he wants to do that here with me again is all up for negotiation and discussion but he's not mentioned anything about moving at all. I don't think he'd move anywhere else in this country and abroad it's difficult to know what's good and what isn't. So if we can keep that legacy going I know Plymouth is going to want to keep him here. At the moment it's kind of planned, next year is obviously the focus but there's life after 2012 as well which is also gonna be quite interesting I think.

SL: You've talked about sharing your knowledge with others; what would you say has been the biggest source of your knowledge? You talked about your degree and that being eye opening.
AB: I'll refer to what I call 'head sitting'. I'm a big believer in if you want to become good at something you find someone that's better than you and sit on their head, and hopefully not be too much of a pain in the neck but ask 'why did you do that?' 'What did you do that for?' 'How do you do this?' 'How do you do that?' Until they swear at you and say 'go away'. I'll try to do that across the board but the education system in diving is pretty rubbish to be fair. It was only earlier this year that I got the next level up, which has only just come about, which is level three. Before that I was qualified to level two the same as everyone else, and that's like a somersault on the 1 metre board and I'm coaching 10 metre multiple somersaults and twists. So the education system isn't there so you have to find it from elsewhere. The degree was a fantastic foundation, and then building on that with the opportunity to go to places like China and Russia and see what they do and watch what they do and film what they do and bring that home and utilise it here and discuss it with the other coaches and discuss it with people from other countries as to what they do and how they develop and how much time they spend on things. I think that's essential.

MD: Is that where you would like to see the future of coach education go, for diving?
AB: Well they've got a system in athletics; and they've got a similar set-up to what they've now got in Canada and their former top coach is now employed by Canadian Diving to work with the coaches around Canada. He does some work with the divers as well but it's mainly with the coaches rather than the divers. I think that's a brilliant idea so whether there would be the money for that or who would do it I don't know. But it does seem to me to be fundamentally important that you have that kind of ability to build on the enthusiasm that the young kids have got to further move into coaching and help foster it. But it's got to come from them too. I do think there's a danger of spoon feeding and often I get the feeling that the people who've come through the professional programmes think it should be on a plate. I remember a guy actually shortly after I had started, he came up and I knew him, again when he was about 12 and he came into the diving pool when I wasn't working professionally at this time, I was only 20 I think. He got involved in the programme and eventually dived with us and moved down to the south and dived there and he came and knocked on my door when he was 19 and said 'I want to be a coach can I stay for a bit'? One of the things I said to him was 'go off and listen to everybody' and he said

'why do I need to do that? You've already done that so I'll just listen to you'. I sort of smacked him around the head a few times 'stupid boy! Yes I've done that and yes listen to me but then go away and do it all yourself and then make your mind up about what you are going to do and how you want to do it'. That's ultimately what he's done and he runs the Leeds programme now. That whole concept I think is massively important because the more you can listen to different people, the more information you're gonna get and you're either gonna be already doing it, or you're going to have not thought about it and you should be doing it, or you were doing it and now you're not doing it and you should be, or it's not really relevant so you disregard it. Either way that information is worth assimilating.

What we don't do enough of as a sporting culture is get into each other's bubbles and it was quite nice to go and speak to Athletics and have some time with them, talking about some of the things that they're trying to do and their initiatives that they've put together and we should do it more often really because there are probably things that they are aware of but we're not, and vice-versa. The nice thing about having the S & C people they come from the EIS (English Institute of Sport) is that they have worked in other sports so we do get a bit of an insight as to what other people are doing from the practitioners that are working multi-discipline, which is good but as coaches and athletes we really just do 'pool home, pool home, pool home' and competition. We don't do the 'get out in the big wide world'.

TG: One of the reasons why we're associated with this journal is because it's all about reflecting on your practice, reflecting on your experience. It seems to me, what you've just said there Andy is that this is what the coach does – you know reflecting on what they do and what they know but also reflecting on what other people know and do, and bringing that in. Would that be right?
AB: Absolutely, I mean we still talk and discuss and argue about technique or programming or periodisation or how to develop into competitions or tapering or psychological aspects or whatever it may be. There's still a wealth of knowledge and experience out there and different ways of doing things to look at and to think about. Just because it works for Tom doesn't mean it works for Tonia or for Brooke or any of the others, so it's about finding something that works for individuals and helping them to develop that. They need to try things out themselves to see whether it works, at which point they'll have a process that they'll buy into. You know Tom used to stand there and look around and gaze at people diving in and this and that. Now he's got a planned pre-prepared process for what he's going to do throughout the whole competition and he knows it back to front and it works for him and that's what he does and he's completely in charge of that. I'm just a part of that at some point during the process. Then he comes up and we just talk about a couple of things to think about.

SL: When you went to the Olympics, what was the biggest eye opener for you in Beijing in terms of preparing for 2012?
AB: I think it was just how gobsmackingly overwhelmingly massive the thing was. The fact that you have to programme when you're gonna leave the apartment, how long it takes you to get to the food hall, how long it takes you to then get food, how long it takes to get from the food hall to the transport area, what times the buses are, when you need to get on a bus and how long it's gonna take you to get to the venue, how long it takes you to get through security at the venue and to get into the pool,

and that's before you've started the warm-up or the process. So all of that needs to be looked at and programmed in and planned. What we did the last time which I think was great is we went into the village when it very first opened so it was really quiet and we got to learn all that so we knew where we were, we knew the food hall and the transport. We knew everything. Everything was planned. Then we got out of there and did a training camp elsewhere, and came back in a bit closer to the competition. So it never got stale but we did the learning bit and the training bit and then the back end of the competition build-up. That went really well, but the villages; you've got thousands of athletes and support staff and the coaches and officials etc. It's like a small city in its own right, and of course you're in a bubble there as well, which is good in many ways; what's going on outside is immaterial.

SL: Do you have to change your approach to how you deal with the athletes because of that environment?
AB: No. The Olympics is no different to anything else. The only difference is the five rings on the wall. Inside there might be but externally it's training sessions, it's competition, it's the build-up to a competition, here we go let's get on with it. It's not 'wow it's the Olympic Games, this is really important'. At Athens the synchro final on the 3 metre went completely tits up for want of a better word. The Chinese diver blew it, the Russian boy hit the board and the American coach went into the back room where the divers were chilling out prior to their dives and said 'these guys have all blown it, we can get a medal!' And you could actually see them on the board they were like this [trembling]!' So I think that's a brilliant example of how not to do it. Everything has got to be normal, normal, normal, normal. So whether it's the Western Counties diving competition or the Olympic final, you do what you do and then you just get on with it, and I think that's really important; that the athletes see that you're just normal.

SL: What do you want your legacy to be as a coach? What do you want to be remembered for as a coach?
AB: If people were to come to my funeral and just say 'ah he was alright, he was a good lad' then that would do me to be honest. The fact that I'm pretty sure that I've been a significant other to a number of kids that are now adults, I actually prefer the adult bit. You know kids are fine and all well and good and cute and nice and whatever but it's easier when they're older. You can reason with them more, you can have a laugh with them, you can swear without worrying about it and it's just an easier scenario. But I think the fact that you have known them, often since they were kids coming through, is a nice transitional thing.

TG: Andy, you talked to us beautifully about the past and your Olympic dream. Between now and next summer, what would you say in your mind is perhaps the single biggest challenge to enable you to realise the dream that you described to us?
AB: The fact that the world is moving on, therefore the performances of everyone else are significantly improved. I think the media will be an issue because they will jump on board and they will want to know what's going on. Last time we had a media day here where they had the opportunity to come down and spend all day talking with Tom, and it is Tom that is the issue really. Then they had to back off. The agent isn't so much of an issue now, they're kind of aware of what the score is

26

so he's only doing stuff that is absolutely essential for his sponsors, so that's kind of under control. The programme he's gonna do is pretty much there. There is a very good tenet around what he's doing. The psychologist we've had around with us for a pretty long time now. She's fantastic and it's somebody that isn't his coach and that isn't his mother and isn't part of his direct family that he can talk to about whatever he wants to and I think that's really useful. He's opened up to her about various things that he wouldn't do to me and he wouldn't do to his family, so having that as an extra thing I think is good. But Tom's very good at compartmentalising his life and always has been; I wish I'd taught it to him but I didn't. He has his different lives; he has his diving life, his school life, his media life, his friends life and he gives time to all of it. When he's doing 'X', 'X' is important, then he moves onto 'Y' and that's important. So if he's planned a meal with his friends, and then something comes up then that's frustrating for him and he doesn't like that because it's planned so that's good, it means everyone else has to be planned too!

TG: What about managing expectations?

AB: Well that'll be part and parcel of being with the media I think and we will discuss that and he knows the media will be asking him how many medals he is going to get. He also knows where the rest of the world is, he also knows where he is and he also knows what the plan is to try and put him in a position where he can do the very best job. He's bought into that programme, we think that programme is right and we'll tweak it as necessary but I think the plan that is in place is a good one for him. It's about developing the sort of consistency and confidence that he had off the back of 2008. So what I'm trying to do with him now is to get a little bit more volume across the techniques and skills that he's doing which means that he will have a bit more water under the bridge in terms of that list moving into next year. So that's the plan, to have him moving to next year feeling pretty comfortable with that list and then going out, competing with it and showing the world that he can do it well, putting the pressure on from the word go really. In terms of goals, obviously they won't be the same as 2008 because it's a slightly different scenario but there won't be any outcome goals in there. It will be very much based on 'we're going to go and perform' and the performance is key. Then we see. Ultimately we go and compare that performance to everyone else and the final performance is that. But I can't see any point in saying 'the aim is to come first, or third'. It's certainly not, because obviously everybody wants him to be on the rostrum and so does he. So that's in the back of the mind, that's the dream, that's what we want but that's no good as a goal in its own right because that means nothing, it's just 'what we want', how are we gonna get there is the important bit and focusing on the how and the performance is key and then we'll see...

Chris Mears, diver and muscle-bound epitome of a London 2012 Olympic contender. But in January 2009 he nearly died. Mears had been competing in the Youth Olympic Festival in Sydney when, at breakfast one morning, he collapsed. At first he was diagnosed with sunstroke, then meningitis. Both were wrong. He had contracted the Epstein Barr virus and had ruptured his spleen while performing a dive the previous day. The prognosis from his surgeon at Sydney's Royal Prince Alfred Hospital was not good. Mears had lost five pints of blood and was given less than a 5% chance of survival. Even when his spleen was removed, a series of convulsing fits left his life hanging by a thread.

Three years later, Mears, who lost three stone and most of his muscle mass in hospital, is able to reflect on his experience as not simply the moment his life was saved, but also the turning point in his diving career. 'The experience changed me, and so much for the better', he said. 'Before the Games I was still at school and had other things I was concentrating on, but when this happened I knew what I wanted to do straight away. As soon as I came back to England I said to my coach, "I want you to make me an Olympic diver". And my dream has almost come true" (Hart & Magnay, 2012).

In the paper that follows called Coaching for Performance: Reflections of Olympic Diving Coach Andy Banks, Dixon, Lee and Ghaye (2012) highlight some of the coaching qualities that begin to answer Mears request − 'I want you to make me an Olympic diver'.

Notes on contributors

Martin Dixon is currently lecturer in Sports Coaching and leader in Curriculum Development at UWE Hartpury. Following postgraduate study in Coaching Science, his teaching is centred on the application of reflective practice within sports coaching. He is a UEFA Licenced football coach and previously held coaching roles at a Premier League Academy and several regional Centres of Excellence. He has presented innovative research on sports coaching and pedagogy at international conferences, and his interests focus on coaching for performance through teaching.

Sarah Lee is subject leader of Applied Sport Science at UWE Hartpury. She has worked in this field since postgraduate study developing her expertise in performance psychology. Her doctoral research focuses on building high performance environments. She also provides education and consultation to grassroots and elite performers and coaches alike. She is an elite netball player and holds extensive netball coaching roles within the south-west, including an England Netball Talent and Performance Centre role for developing youth elite performers.

Tony Ghaye is the director of Reflective Learning − International. He is a member of BASES, a positive psychologist and strength-based performance enhancer. He has worked at numerous universities within the UK and overseas. He has written 24 academic books and 108 refereed papers on personal performance and organisational improvement through reflective learning. His interest is in developing more strengths-based reflective practices that build and sustain high performance and supportive cultures.

References

Cassidy, T., Jones, R., & Potrac, P. (2004). *Understanding sports coaching*. Abingdon: Routledge.

Cushion, C.J. (2001). The coaching process in professional youth football: An ethnography of practice. Unpublished doctoral thesis, Brunel University, UK.

Hart, S., & Magnay, J. (2012, March 8). The London 2012 Olympics, *The Telegraph*. Retrieved from http://www.telegraph.co.uk/sport/olympics/diving/9091922/London-2012-Olympics-GB-diving-contender-Chris-Mears-near-death-experience-helped-him-focus-on-his-dream.html

Jones, R.L., Armour, K.M., & Potrac, P.A. (2004). *Sports coaching cultures: From practice to theory*. Abingdon: Routledge.

Knowles, Z., Tyler, G., Gilbourne, D., & Eubank, M. (2006). Reflecting on reflection: Exploring the practice of sports coaching graduates. *Reflective Practice, 7*(2), 163–179.

Coaching for performance: reflections of Olympic diving coach, Andy Banks

Martin Dixon[a], Sarah Lee[a] and Tony Ghaye[b]

[a]UWE Hartpury College, Gloucester, England; [b]Reflective Learning – International, Gloucester, England

This paper presents a summary of the key themes emerging from the reflexive conversation with Olympic diving coach Andy Banks. Exploration of these themes reveals not only how Banks works in such a high performance environment, but also where this Olympic coach came from, and how his deep-rooted philosophies inform his coaching practice. Projections are also made for the legacy of the London 2012 Olympics including the future of coach development. We begin by reflecting on Banks' ultimate aim; to help athletes achieve their potential, or 'reach their ceiling'.

Reaching your ceiling: identifying and cultivating the strengths of others

As presented in the first paper, the coach as alchemist metaphor reflects the range of contributions from practitioners throughout the Special Issue. This notion is embodied by diving coach Andy Banks and is palpable through the interview transcript as he recognises and develops talent, harnessing the strengths and potential of those around him. Although Banks operates very much in the high performance environment, he defines achievement as a coach not in absolute terms such as attainment of a medal or ranking, but by helping an individual reach their 'ceiling'. Indeed, comparable to turning poor metals into gold, Banks uses his own analogy of sculpting a Ming Vase from clay to epitomise his coaching philosophy. The importance of natural talent is never underestimated however; as Banks explains, even an effective coach can only produce 'coffee cups' without access to quality clay.

This conception is particularly evident in Banks' references to teenage Olympian Tom Daley with the diver's innate aesthetics, natural awareness and 'massive hands' which enable him to rip the water when landing. Whilst these elements are attributed to inherent abilities, the reflexive conversation is loaded with examples where Daley's technique, training regime and emotional control have been moulded and cast through the craft of the coach. The development of athletic and human potential being central to the coaching process is illustrated through an example Banks cites as his greatest accolade. Interestingly, this was not the success of Tom Daley or other divers under his tutelage such as Tonia Couch and Brooke Graddon. Nor does he refer to the substantially raised profile of diving in Great Britain or the numerous awards won by the coach himself. Instead, Banks' greatest success was helping a novice diver win a Junior International tracksuit, stressing that she was never talented enough to perform at that level but through the efforts of the coach-athlete team, she reached and maybe even exceeded her ceiling. This is true alchemy at work.

The ability of identify and foster the strengths of others is not just confined to athletes and coaches, but also to the wider support team as part of a multidisciplinary approach to high performance. Here Banks uses another analogy, that of a racing car, to represent the broader team of people who work to ensure this 'machine' is performing at its optimal level. Indeed, whilst the coach leads and monitors the provision of sport science support, Banks recognises the importance of expertise (probably influenced by his own study of sport science) and encourages practitioners to use their initiative and skills as part of a holistic approach. This resonates with the work of Buckingham (2007) as Banks pulls the 'master leaver' by getting each person to play to their strengths to develop and maintain a high-performing team.

Dictator to advisor: the evolving pedagogical relationship

The notion of developing the strengths of others is reflected further through accounts of the coach-athlete relationship. An athlete-centred approach, identified by Walsh (2008) as a key facet of an expert coach, emerged as a strong theme throughout the reflexive conversation and appears central to Banks' coaching process. In a sporting environment whereby coaches and athletes can work together for a relatively long period of time (for example, Banks and Daley's partnership spans eight years), an empowering approach may be especially pertinent. Arguably, when the athlete is young and inexperienced, they need to be given encouragement and understanding to develop their natural abilities. As the athlete develops and the relationship grows, the performer takes more initiative, with discussion becoming a key feature of the partnership. Ultimately, the advanced athlete takes more ownership of the performance and the coach's role often changes to that of a facilitator, advising the athlete to use the right tools at the right time.

The development of this dynamic relationship is dependent on the context however, and knowing when to 'loosen the reins' can be a challenge to even the most expert of coaches. Banks' example of empowering Daley in his first international competition was met with an abrupt negative response and the athlete was clearly not ready to take such responsibility. Nonetheless, it may be necessary for coaches to 'test the water' and assess the stage of the pedagogical relationship by gradually giving more responsibility and gauging the athlete's response. The following video clip illustrates that Daley, in the run-up to London 2012, is now very much in a position where he is able and willing to take a lot more ownership over his training and performance:

http://www.youtube.com/watch?v=KgjRnbA8RU&feature=related

In this footage he comes across as a confident, experienced performer who is very focused on his diving ambitions. As their coach-athlete relationship has developed, Banks has tuned into Daley and recognised when the timing has been right to readdress the balance of power in order to facilitate his achievement. The contextual nature of the coaching relationship also implies a high degree of coaching agility as

Banks demonstrates the capacity to flex to the needs of athletes in different situations. Moreover, an evolving approach to the coaching process could be crucial in maintaining and regenerating a long-term coach-athlete relationship.

Positivity and persistence through process goals

In addition to an evolving pedagogical relationship, the competitive environment is also kept fresh through a positive approach based on enjoyment. Whilst performing at a world-class level, Andy Banks emphasises the need for fun amongst his athletes and staff and actively fosters this positive atmosphere. This serves not only to motivate and inspire athletes, but helps them to focus on their diving technique in a high pressure environment. Indeed, whilst Banks describes his Olympic dream as a moment of ovation in the new state-of-the-art aquatics centre with the whole nation behind his athletes, he recognises that to obsess over what we want is not productive; we need to focus on how we get there. Dreams must become goals which are the important factors in determining whether the dreams come true.

Banks has previously implemented process goals based on 'fun', 'learning' and 'pride' with successful results, but the 2012 Olympics is expected to present a range of new challenges to his dream. The ever-increasing quality of opposing athletes, excessive media attention and issues within the athlete's personal lives were alluded to as the biggest potential threats. However, with positivity and persistence the expert coach can turnaround adverse situations. Banks offers several examples of where Daley's performance has ultimately turned 'good from bad' through emphasising process over performance. Knowing when and how to adjust process goals is also crucial. After an unsuccessful dive at the 10 metre level which left Daley distraught, Banks set goals exclusively at 7 metres for the next six months, ultimately resulting in improved performances. This ability to turn good from bad, being positive under pressure, maintaining a process focus in a results-driven environment reflects not only persistency, but a high degree of coaching expertise. That much is clear, but now we reflect on how this knowledge and coaching skill has been acquired and developed.

Studying success: development and drive of the Olympic coach

It is appropriate to start here by reflecting on how Andy Banks' passion for coaching initiated and grew, so we can gain an understanding of where the coach came from. As a diver himself, Banks did not reach the elite level and claims this has fuelled his ambitions to achieve success as a coach. Moreover, performing at only a modest level has enabled Banks to understand his athlete's struggles, limitations and learning processes, perhaps more so than if he had greater natural diving ability himself. Whilst this ambition served as the driver behind Banks' passion, academic study was also fundamental to his development as a coach. Banks emphasises that studying biomechanics, physiology and psychology provided a scientific underpinning and increased his existing knowledge base, and now enables him to effectively manage a multi-disciplinary sport science team. Whilst such study can provide coaches with the right tools, knowing when to use them is often a more informal process.

The notion of 'head-sitting' was presented as a method of improving practice by absorbing knowledge from someone who is 'better than you'. Indeed, within a sport which Banks says formal coach education has developed too slowly to facilitate its leading coaches, informal mentoring appeared to be central to advance coaching expertise. Another method of studying success in line with a strengths-based approach is observing other high performance organisations. Banks cites his visits to study diving in China and Russia as essential to furthering the skills of GB coaches, and highlights the necessity for greater knowledge exchange between different sports to optimise coach development.

Values, ethics and coaching identity

Whilst several references are made to the competitive threat posed by Chinese divers at the 2012 Olympics and the clear respect for the talent of their athletes, Banks' coaching philosophy could not be more different to that of his Chinese counterparts. The ethics of Chinese athlete development are questioned as young divers are 'channelled' into intense training programmes at a young age with little support for those who do not reach an elite standard. Conversely, Banks stresses the importance of the coach as a significant other and whilst he refers to 'creating people' and the 'production process', this alludes more to his humanistic approach of nurturing people. The notion of the coach as significant other is reflected through the emphasis placed on enjoyment, support for athletes' education and personal lives, and the dream that they will be 'good people' long after they have finished competing.

2012 and beyond: the coaching legacy

The satisfaction gained from helping to nurture young athletes and seeing them develop into adults resonates most powerfully throughout this reflexive conversation and emerges as key facet in maintaining passion for coaching. Banks takes great pride in explaining how he meets up with adult ex-divers whom he has known since they were children, and he hopes to see this continue in the future. His most high-profile athlete is already thinking about the next three Olympic cycles, and diving has received more media attention than ever before. Whilst pressure and expectation on the GB diving team mounts in anticipation of London 2012, Banks is already looking beyond the Games and makes projections not only for himself and his athletes, but also for the sport and next generation of coaches.

New aquatics centres, an increase in funding, raised profile of diving in Great Britain and the expansion of diving provision in Plymouth as a major hub for the sport all surface as part of the London 2012 Olympic and Paralympic legacy. However, Banks focuses on the 'legacy for knowledge and experience' within coaching as vital to the sport after the 2012 Games. With such vast experience incorporating major competitions and observation of foreign coaches and training regimes, in addition to Banks' craft knowledge developed through years of reflecting on his practice, he aims to pass this on to future coaches. Far from enjoying retirement from the sport and 'sitting on his beach', Banks looks forward to mentoring the next generation, possibly the elite divers of today, helping them to reach their ceiling as coaches too.

References

Buckingham, M. (2007). *Go put your strengths to work: Six powerful steps to achieve outstanding performance*. London: Simon & Schuster.

Walsh, K. (2008). The anatomy of an expert coach. Retrieved February 16, 2012, from http://www.lane4performance.com/The-Anatomy-of-an-Expert-Coach.html?page=1.

Reflection and the art of coaching: fostering high-performance in Olympic Ski Cross

Matthew Lyons[a,b], Steven B. Rynne[a] and Clifford J. Mallett[a]

[a]The University of Queensland, School of Human Movement Studies, The University of Queensland, Brisbane, Queensland, 4072, Australia; [b]The Olympic Winter Institute of Australia, Ski Cross, Level 1, 1-3 Cobden St, South Melbourne, 3205, Australia

In preparation for the 2010 Vancouver Winter Olympic Games, the lead author engaged in systematic reflection in an attempt to implement coaching behaviours and create practice environments that promoted athlete development (psycho-social and physical performance). The research was carried out in relation to his work as head Ski Cross coach working with (primarily) three athletes in their quest for Olympic qualification and subsequent performance success in the Olympic Games. This project sought to examine coach-athlete interactions. Of particular interest were coach and athlete responses regarding the implementation of autonomy supportive coaching behaviours in a high context. Autonomy supportive coaching behaviours have previously been strongly associated with positive athlete psycho-social and performance outcomes, however, a paucity of research has examined its implementation in high-performance contexts. Through the use of participant ethnography, it was possible to gain considerable insights regarding athletes' perceptions of choice, implications of perceived athletic hierarchies, as well as cultural and experience-related influences on training and performance expectations.

Introduction

High-performance sports coaching such as that associated with the Olympic Games involves the highest levels of athlete and coach involvement, public performance objectives, intensive commitment to the development and implementation of programmes, highly structured and formalised competitions, typically full-time work, heavy emphasis on decision making and data management, extensive interpersonal contact, and very demanding and restrictive athlete selection criteria (Lyle, 2002; Rynne, Mallett, & Tinning, 2010; Trudel & Gilbert, 2006). Coaches undertake this complex work in an attempt to foster the improved or sustained performance of their athletes towards identified goals such as high quality performance at an Olympic Games. This paper examines the journey leading into the Olympic Games of one high-performance coach pursuing excellence in practice. The high-performance coaching work discussed in this paper relates specifically to the Olympic sport of Ski Cross.

Ski Cross involves head-to-head racing in heats of between four to six competitors, on an undulating, downhill course incorporating rolls, jumps, dips and berms. The discipline requires traditional downhill alpine ski racing technical skills and in addition, combines terrain park and big air-type challenges, mixed in with the unique, direct competition element of racing to a 'first past the post' style finish. The Vancouver 2010 Winter Olympics was the event's Olympic debut.

Because of the somewhat related coaching and athletic requirements, the majority of the current field of Ski Cross competitors and coaches at the Olympic level have come from downhill alpine ski racing. A major issue, however, is that there are several elements of Ski Cross that are unique to the discipline (e.g. group racing, the Ski Cross start gate and a variety of course features). Furthermore, performance on these unique elements impacts upon overall performance (i.e. these elements are crucial for achieving strong outcomes). For this reason, having a background as an alpine coach (or athlete), while useful, may not be sufficient in developing specific coach knowledge and skills. Consequently, coaches that transfer from the alpine disciplines have probably evolved their practice through more informal learning opportunities (Mallett, Trudel, Lyle, & Rynne, 2009).

This serendipitous and pragmatically driven approach to coach development is similar to the broader high-performance coaching context in that, despite agreement regarding the critical role of the coach in supporting and directing elite performance (see e.g. Gilbert, Côté, & Mallett, 2006; Starkes & Ericsson, 2003), in most sports and in most countries there is an absence of clear developmental pathways for high-performance coaches. So how do coaches continue to develop their craft and foster the improved performances of their athletes? Previous research has consistently shown that coaches learn through practical coaching experiences (i.e. learning in and through their coaching work) (Gilbert & Trudel, 2001; Rynne, et al., 2010). Further to this, reflection has been positioned as a key mechanism by which 'learning through experience' might be conceptualised (Cushion, Armour, & Jones, 2003; Gilbert & Trudel, 2005). To this point, no research has considered the rapidly evolving context of Ski Cross coaching.

Ski Cross athletes are required to adapt and perform 'on the run' to be successful in the dynamic environment of each competition. The more capable athletes are of directing and contributing to their own development, the more likely they will be to operate effectively on the field in practice and in successful performance outcomes during competition (Amiot, Gaudreau, & Blanchard, 2004; Beauchamp, Halliwell, Fournier, & Koestner, 1996; Kidman, 2005; Mallett & Hanrahan, 2004). For this reason, a personal orientation toward an organismic view of human development (Self-determination theory; Deci & Ryan, 1985) and the central role of others were central to the conceptualisation of this study.

Self-Determination Theory

Self-Determination Theory is a multidimensional social-cognitive theory of human motivation, behaviour, development and wellness (Deci & Ryan, 2008) that evolved from the belief that humans have innate tendencies to pursue personal growth in the development of a congruent, unified self (Chatzisarantis & Hagger, 2007). This self, moreover, operates largely through autonomous, responsible behaviour. Self-Determination Theory preferences the influence of innate organismic tendencies (Deci & Ryan, 2002) in our interactions with the social world with regard to impacts on personality. The SDT concept does not deny the contextual environment with regard to its impact on an individual's psychological growth and subjective well-being (Blanchard, Amiot, Perrault, Vallerand, & Provencher, 2009). Rather, it incorporates this notion of influence to explain the "broad array of developmental outcomes" that occur (Deci & Ryan, 2002, p. 5).

While the natural, innate and constructive tendencies for inner organisation, holistic self-regulation (autonomy), and integration of oneself with others (homonomy) are key concepts behind the self-determination framework, they are by no means taken for granted as guaranteed outcomes. There are clear social-contextual factors that support or thwart these tendencies. The above factors lead to the conclusion that psychological growth is "a dynamic potential that requires nurturing" (Deci & Ryan, 2002, p. 6).

These innate components of SDT are categorised as three basic and universal human needs: autonomy, competence and relatedness. It is argued that humans will pursue these needs consciously or unconsciously (Deci & Ryan, 1985). The universality of these three basic psychological needs is demonstrated through their existence in all development stages and across cultures. They are said to be "nutriments" to psychological health and well-being (Deci & Ryan, 2002, p. 76). The satisfaction of the three universal psychological needs – autonomy, competence and relatedness – promotes personal growth. Alternatively, if these needs are not satisfied personal growth will be inhibited (Deci & Ryan, 1985). Although conceptually interrelated, each of the basic needs may be considered independently.

Autonomy reflects the need to be the origin of one's own behaviour (deCharms, 1968), to have volition, choice, self-directedness (Deci & Ryan, 1985), and be agentic (McDonough & Crocker, 2007). Behaviour becomes an expression of the self, even if other outside influences have some effect (Deci & Ryan, 2002). Competence can be defined as the need to feel as if one is acting effectively within the environment in order to produce desired outcomes and prevent undesired ones (Blanchard et al., 2009; Deci & Ryan, 1985; Hollembeak & Amorose, 2005; White, 1959). Competence involves not only the attainment of skill or capacity but also "the sense of confidence and effectance in action" (Deci & Ryan, 2002, p. 7). Relatedness is the degree to which we feel connected to those significant others around us (Deci & Ryan, 1985; Hollembeak & Amorose, 2005; Vallerand & Ratelle, 2002). It is a state of mutual caring, authenticity and involvement in the social context in which we find/place ourselves (Hodge, Lonsdale, & Ng, 2008; McDonough & Crocker, 2007). These basic psychological needs provide an essential link between various goals and outcomes and the basis on which we organise our behaviours in order to achieve them; this being motivation.

SDT in sport

In the sport setting, motivation is considered an integral factor regarding initiation, participation, persistence, dropout, burnout, enjoyment, attitude, effort and performance (Weiss & Amorose, 2008). The type of motivation (self-determined versus non-self-determined) one experiences has important consequences for learning and perceptions of experience, and is more likely to effect outcomes and achievements. These last being particularly relevant in a high-performance sporting context (Duda & Treasure, 2001). Several studies have examined the mediating effects of the psychological needs of autonomy and competence on social contextual variables (e.g.

coach behaviours) and, in turn, on different forms of motivation and related outcomes (Hollembeak & Amorose, 2005; Ntoumanis, 2001). In particular, the behaviours of coaches have been examined with regard to the impact on the athletes under their guidance. Coaching behaviours encompass areas of practice, training structures and operations. They also include game structures, how decisions are made and communicated, the quality and quantity of feedback, how relationships are established and maintained, and what techniques are used to motivate and encourage (Harwood, Spray, & Keegan, 2008; Hollembeak & Amorose, 2005; Mageau & Vallerand, 2003, Smoll & Smith, 2002).

Autonomy-supportive coaching behaviours have been found to have particularly beneficial impacts on the participation, enjoyment, persistence and subsequent performance of athletes in a variety of sports settings that include rugby (Ahlberg, Mallett, & Tinning, 2008), golf (Beauchamp et al., 1996), track and field (Mallett, 2005; Mallett & Hanrahan, 2004), and judo (Gillet, Vallerand, Amoura, & Baldes, 2010) amongst others (Amiot et al., 2004; Kidman, 2005). Coaches' (pedagogical) behaviours that foster satisfaction of the three psychological needs are considered to be autonomy-supportive rather than controlling (Mageau & Vallerand, 2003). This focus on autonomy-supportive behaviours and their adaptive influence on athletes have important implications for coaches in the field and suggests some practical areas for future interventions designed to better facilitate optimal functioning of athletes (Gagné, Ryan, & Bargmann, 2003; Reinboth & Duda, 2006; Vansteenkiste et al., 2004). To this point, however, there has been a relative lack of studies examining the use of an autonomy-supportive coaching approach in high-performance sporting environments.

High-performance sport can be generally considered as involving athletes and coaches who are members of a national squad or team, have represented their country at an international level, and/or those who perform at the highest level of their chosen sport (Thelwell, Weston, Greenlees & Hutchins, 2008). High-performance sporting environments' participants form a very small segment of the athletic population. The specific environments many experience are characterised by "extreme training loads, injuries, solitude, competition schedules and travel demands ... [that] make the lifestyle extremely arduous and define the social conditions of the context" (Treasure, Lemyre, Kuczka, & Standage, 2007, p. 154). This means that the impacts and effects these particular contexts have may differ considerably based on the levels of self-determined motivation and perceived needs satisfaction. The combination of motivational orientations and levels of integration and identification may have more relevance in high-performance sport than has been seen in other contexts (Treasure et al., 2007).

Despite some limited research, further investigations in high-performance sports coaching contexts is underscored, especially given the oft-prevailing conditions and culture of high-performance sport and its emphasis on successful performance outcomes and subsequent external rewards (Amiot et al., 2004). Those concepts are seemingly at odds with the overall tenets of SDT and other motivational theories that have been well supported across varied domains. The potential impact of autonomy-supportive coaching behaviours in this highly contested performance environment on the nature of coach-athlete interactions was a key factor considered in this study. Specifically, a coach's personal orientation towards an autonomy-supportive approach to coaching was considered interdependent with athletes' preferences for this approach and subsequent adaptive psycho-social (e.g. improved self-esteem) and performance (e.g. faster times) outcomes.

Participant ethnography

The key purpose of this research was to examine a strategic approach to improving professional practice. A deliberate strategy of 'extended professionalism' (Stenhouse, 1975) was the means chosen to determine the effectiveness and desirability of the autonomy-supportive coaching approach. Extended professionalism has been characterised by: a commitment to a systematic self-study (in coaching); the need to acquire skills adequate to participate in that study process; and the willingness to test ideas of theory in practice through the use of those skills, as a basis for autonomous, professional development (Stenhouse, 1975). Participant ethnography was seen as an appropriate methodological choice in the application of this notion of extended professionalism.

Participant ethnography originated from anthropology and the ethnographic approach to the study of human cultures and the place they occupy in human affairs (Chambers, 2000; Kelley & Gibbons, 2008). Influenced by the work of Malinowski, Radcliffe-Brown, and the Chicago School of Sociology it is a process that combines various methods of research inquiry with characteristics including holism, contextuality, reflexivity, lengthy and sustained engagement, a naturalistic inquiry, and an expression of multiple meanings and perspectives (Barton, 2008; Sands, 2002). Along with more traditional forms of ethnography, participant ethnography has been found to have value in a number of applied settings. In sport, it can provide for an in-depth examination and understanding of the complexities of sport-related behaviour in context (e.g. Jones, 2009).

Participant ethnography was appropriate for the context of this research project, as it applies where the participant and practitioner are one and the same, and where the principal researcher is already an established member of the proposed sample group. Notwithstanding the criticisms that such an 'insider' approach can engender (Chambers, 2000), a key feature of value for this study was the focus on practical change and improvement, rather than description and evocation (Barton, 2008).

Method

Participants

The lead author and his practices and behaviours as a coach for a national sporting institute programme were the focus of this participant ethnographic study. The lead author's past athletic experiences and experiences as a coach in the traditional alpine ski racing environment for 17 years helped develop and inform a personal orientation toward the tenets of SDT. This interest was further strengthened from personal experience attempting to implement a more autonomy-supportive approach to coaching behaviours in previous roles and contexts (from club, through state, and into national/international level sporting environments) over a period of six years.

Integral to the unique coach-athlete environment in this study and a central component of participant data sources, were three athletes of differing ages, genders, sporting experience and performance levels. One athlete was a multiple representative at the international level, including at a previous Olympic Games (albeit in another skiing discipline). Another athlete had been a promising junior level alpine athlete with a number of representative team selections to their name, and the third athlete had been a skilled child-athlete but had moved away from the alpine disciplines and sport in general prior to accepting a position with the Ski Cross national programme. All had experienced varied coaching approaches over the years, however, the majority of the experiences were of coaching that was typically controlling in nature. The three athletes had been involved in a coach-athlete relationship with the lead author, ranging from periods between eight months to eight years.

This participant ethnographic study was based on the premise that a self-reflective approach would guide any increase in awareness and improvement in subsequent practice (Grimmett & Erickson, 1988). The major research questions for this study related to (1) whether an autonomy-supportive approach was being implemented effectively by the head coach; (2) whether the approach was in accordance with what the athletes themselves perceived they needed in order to improve and perform optimally; and (3) whether there were some observable perceived benefits in training and performance outcomes for the athletes.

In addressing these questions, multiple data collection methods were used to inform the reflective practice of the head coach over the course of the lead-in to and eventual competition in, the Olympic Games. A combination of reflective coaching journal entries (27 entries), audio recordings of coach-athlete interactions *in situ* (53 recordings), questionnaires (four), and direct written athlete responses to events and circumstances as they unfolded (e.g. four emails, two letters, six training reflection forms) were collected and collated. These multiple data forms were then used to inform the design and conduct of semi-structured interviews with each of the three high-performance athletes involved.

Semi-structured interviews

The narrative interview is the most common method of qualitative data collection (Gubrium & Holstein, 1995; Sands, 2002). The inclusion of semi-structured interviews in this project was to allow for an exploration of issues that were identified in various forms throughout the course of the examined training and competition period. In addition, the semi-structured interviews provided an opportunity to delve more deeply into the notion of athlete perceptions of coaching behaviours, in relation to individual expectations and perceived needs.

As part of the conduct of these semi-structured interviews, direct audio excerpts from various coach-athlete interactions were replayed during the course of the interview to the athletes. These audio excerpts would likely assist in eliciting a more accurately remembered experience of events and circumstances and was in line with the concept of *stimulated recall*, used extensively and successfully in other research domains (e.g. Bloom, 1954; Lyle, 2003). Prompts to elicit clarification and elaboration were used throughout the semi-structured interviews (Patton, 2002; Wengraf, 2004).

The recordings of the interviews were then transcribed by a professional transcription service. A sound checking review of both transcriptions and the audio recordings was then undertaken to ensure the accuracy of the written format.

Data analysis

Data analyses were conducted through both a 'template approach' whereby categories are applied based on prior research and theory, and an 'editing approach' that was in keeping with the grounded theory concept (DiCicco-Bloom & Crabtree,

2006). These two approaches to analysis were combined for this research project in a form of *content analysis* (Elo & Kyngäs, 2008). This dual method application maintained the balance between the inductivist and deductivist methodologies described by Weber (1990) and allowed for a "units of analysis" format (Wengraf, 2004, p. 214). These units of analysis were consolidated into key findings, largely determined by information elicited from the other data collection methods used in the study, the SDT concepts of Deci and Ryan (2000), and the key research questions that formed the basis for the project from the outset.

In a form of triangular consensus, each of the original interview recordings were provided to outside researchers, not associated with the project, who then detailed their own interpretations and insights. These were then compared and contrasted with the chief investigator's insights. This presented the possibility of uncovering previously un-discovered themes or emphasis that might be present in the responses of participants, while at the same time maintaining focus on the main research questions (Elo & Kyngäs, 2008). Agreement was subsequently reached regarding key findings.

Results and discussion

Five key findings emerged from the content analysis of the data:

(1) The presence of autonomy-supportive (AS) coaching behaviours within and throughout the specific sporting context examined was evident.
(2) There was agreement, between the perceptions of both coach and athletes, as to whether those behaviours occurred and whether they were considered desirable – with some notable exceptions.
(3) The distinction between control and choice in relation to coach-athlete interactions warrants further elaboration.
(4) There were changes in the nature of coach-athlete interactions that can perhaps best be characterised as 'shifts along the continuum' between autonomy-supportive and controlling coaching behaviours.
(5) The relative importance of the psychological need of relatedness within this particular context emerged quite strongly from the data.

For the primary purpose of this paper, only the first two findings will be discussed in detail. The reflective focus of the study warrants particular attention to the first two themes because the presence or otherwise of an autonomy-supportive approach, and the congruence of that approach with the perceived requirements of the athletes involved, were the central questions in the conduct of the work under investigation (the coaching behaviours and practices), and in the formulation of the study itself. The latter findings, while undoubtedly providing valuable nuances to the main questions, are less relevant in this instance.

Before proceeding, it should be noted that in order to take advantage of the 'enhanced' nature of this special issue, excerpts from the data-set are presented below in the form of short video 'links'. These links will redirect the reader to the main article page on the publisher's website, where the videos can be downloaded from the 'Supplementary' tab toward the bottom of the page. The aim of presenting the information in this way is to give 'voice' to the participant(s) in this study.

Evidence of autonomy-supportive (AS) coaching behaviours

There was strong evidence of AS coaching behaviours as perceived by the coach and the Ski Cross athletes. Specifically, the (pedagogical) autonomy-supportive behaviours, which were consistent with those espoused by Mageau and Vallerand (2003) included: (1) the provision of choice in training and other areas of impact; (2) the provision of rationales for decision making to the athletes; (3) acknowledgment of athletes' feelings and perspectives; and (4) there was limited evidence of the coach as sole decision maker, or having a unidirectional dissemination of information. In addition, the value in providing competence-based (as opposed to performance-based), task and mastery feedback (Allen & Hodge, 2006) within the high-performance sporting environment was evident. This was despite the emphasis of that high-performance environment on external goals and outcomes that potentially conflict with the task and mastery approaches to coaching.

Specifically acknowledged by all was the value of the general conversational nature of exchanges and the development and allowance for independence in the learning process: as a means of personal accountability, as a recognition and acknowledgment of experience, and as a required element of personal growth. These were present in relation to the direct, task-oriented, skill development components of coach-athlete exchanges.

Link 1: full video available online at [http://dx.doi.org/10.1080/14623943.2012.670629] *The AS behaviours were also reported to be present in the less motor-skill based, athlete support components (planning, scheduling, resource allocation) of the role*:

Link 2: full video available online at [http://dx.doi.org/10.1080/14623943.2012.670629].

Some of the perceived benefits of this AS approach were also supported in athlete responses. The approach provided for increased understanding:

Link 3: full video available online at [http://dx.doi.org/10.1080/14623943.2012.670629].

For perceived increases in performance:

Link 4: full video available online at [http://dx.doi.org/10.1080/14623943.2012.670629].

For an allowance for personal growth:

Link 5: full video available online at [http://dx.doi.org/10.1080/14623943.2012.670629].

For greater self-efficacy and confidence:

Link 6: full video available online at [http://dx.doi.org/10.1080/14623943.2012.670629].

These perceived benefits of the AS coaching approach aligned with those put forward by Amorose (2007) with regard to areas of learning, persistence, enjoyment, and competence in self-determined activities. In addition, these behaviours also provided opportunities for athletes to perceive themselves as being valued members of the group that, in turn, reflected some of the importance of the psychological need of relatedness (SDT; Deci & Ryan, 1985) being partially satisfied through their Ski Cross participation.

Link 7: full video available online at [http://dl.dropbox.com/u/33001066/Link%207.mov]. The provision and focus on a competence-based, task/mastery approach to coaching was valued in developing athletes' performances, which is consistent with the findings by Allen and Hodge (2006). It was particularly interesting given that the external expectations of the high-performance sporting environment were very much acknowledged as being present by athletes and were largely considered appropriate given the context in which they were operating.

Link 8: full video available online at [http://dx.doi.org/10.1080/14623943.2012. 670629]. This acceptance, in part however, seemed to be less in relation to the outcome measures themselves, or the requirement of them by the sporting context in which they operated, but more to the fact that they saw themselves as striving for similar external goals from a primarily internally motivated perspective. The alignment of these personal aims with the institutional or organisational expectations may have had a good deal of influence over the observed levels of *integrated* and *identified* regulation (Vallerand, 1997). In some respects, the athletes took ownership over those outcome expectations by dismissing the institutional requirements as being largely irrelevant and ensuring that the personal ones held greater significance in their own stories. This source of motivation fits with the self-determined extrinsic motivation of activities outlined by Deci and Ryan (1985), Deci and Ryan (2000) in reflecting the degree of acceptance and internalisation of outside or extrinsic reasons for participation.

Agreement between the presence and desirability of behaviours

The data showed that both the coach and the athletes were primarily oriented towards a self-determined motivational profile and subsequently a preference for an AS approach to coaching.

Link 9: full video available online at [http://dx.doi.org/10.1080/14623943.2012. 670629]. *These personal orientations and preferences for an AS approach are said to be relatively stable over time and have an impact on the type of motivational processes that determine individuals' choices and decision making, which is consistent with the Causality Orientation Theory within Deci and Ryan's (2000) SDT. There was evidence of the development, facilitation, encouragement and preference for self-determined learning and involvement: Link 10*: full video available online at [http://dx.doi.org/10.1080/14623943.2012.670629].

There was also evidence of some influence from variables such as age, relative experience and varying degrees of perceived competence. While differences in these variables is difficult to demonstrate from the semi-structured interview data without violating participant confidentiality, some of the following excerpts contain differences in language and perspective that can be interpreted as being indicative of some of the influence of relative experience, age and perceived competence:

Link 11: full video available online at [http://dx.doi.org/10.1080/14623943.2012. 670629].

All of the above examples from both coach and athletes point to the presence, orientation and general preference for these types of AS behaviours in this specific context. This was important because it provided an element of external confirmation of both the presence of the elements of behaviours that had been deliberately implemented over time and some of the impact and reception these had from those considered to benefit the most from them: the athletes. If, as Lyle (2002) stated, the coaching process is an interpersonal phenomenon that is shaped by the value systems and personal characteristics of those involved in it, then it is important to have a clear understanding of what those values and personal characteristics comprise, in order to tailor approaches to best effect. These best effects impact on athlete well-being, satisfaction and development (Ahlberg et al., 2008; Duda & Treasure, 2001); they also impact on performance.

The data support the possibility, and indeed the desirability, of the implementation of autonomy-supportive coaching behaviours within high-performance sporting environment structures. In general, along with the stated benefits to learning and adaptation, overall athlete preference, and the clear support to personal growth, well-being and enjoyment, the performance results for all of the athletes involved were above expectations (injury status for one being taken into account). There is a strong case that these enhanced outcomes in the performance sporting environment over the qualification period and during the Olympic Games themselves might be attributable, at least in part, to the implementation of an autonomy-supportive coaching approach. At the very least, one could say that performances were not adversely affected by the introduction of such an approach. This was not to say that the implementation of such behaviours was not without its issues.

One example where the concept of AS behaviour and the implications for self-determined motivation became somewhat 'muddied' or problematic revolved around the congruency between coach and athlete perceptions of behaviours and their desirability. The perceptions of the presence of AS behaviours and their desirability did not always quite align and this was evidenced in an initial resistance to a more autonomy-supportive approach in coaching behaviour. The move to a more AS coaching approach placed some consequent demands on the athlete that did not always match the athlete's perceived requirements. In addition, it thwarted attempts by the athlete in their strategy of 'testing' the coach. This testing or challenging approach was used by the athlete in new and unfamiliar coach-athlete working environments and was a strategy used to help determine both the extent of the coach's knowledge and the alignment in communication between athlete expectations and preferences and coach delivery. The thwarting of this ability to stand back, assess and test due to a request for active engagement by the coach, led to some conflict in the desirability of the presence of those types of AS behaviour.

Link 12: full video available online at [http://dx.doi.org/10.1080/14623943.2012. 670629]. There was also some evidence of a broader, more culturally (sport) based resistance to an autonomy-supportive coaching approach. This resistance was evidenced in some of the responses about what the role of a coach entailed and how it fitted with overall past experiences and consequent expectations developed through those lived-experiences; a form of cultural conditioning into the 'traditional' approach in a high-performance sporting environment. *Link 13*: full video available online at [http://dx.doi.org/10.1080/14623943.2012.670629].

Conclusion

The central aim of this research project was to examine the nature of the principal researcher's coach-athlete interactions. Based on the notion of a critical reflection of practice (Jones, 2009; Mallett, 2004; Schön, 1983), these interactions were examined within a high-performance sporting environment, with the focus on autonomy supportive coaching behaviours. A secondary consideration became how an autonomy-supportive coaching style may be problematic in its implementation, when faced with issues surrounding perceived value and worth.

The high-performance sporting environment of an Olympic qualification period and competition at the Games itself is one characterised by elevated levels of personal, organisational and cultural pressure and expectation. Related elements of scarce resource allocations, injury and associated rehabilitation issues, and medal expectations were all important considerations within the specific sporting context examined in this study. The traditional coaching approach to these types of environments and in these types of circumstances is often based around attempts at controlling all possible variables.

It is possible, however, as evidenced by the findings in this study, to implement a more autonomy-supportive coaching approach within the unique context of high-performance sport that can still lead to strong performances. In the specific context described here, there was a general preference and perceived value in the approach from both coach and athletes, and a consensus and recognition of its psycho-social and physical performance benefits.

Despite these benefits, it must be acknowledged that the implementation of autonomy-supportive coaching is by no means a panacea for all performance related issues in high-performance contexts. Organisational and individual expectations and preferences can present their own complications in high-pressured Olympic environments. However, there is growing evidence of the primacy of coach-athlete interactions within the high-performance sporting context and a growing appreciation that these exchanges influence performance and psycho-social growth through the three essential human psychological needs (autonomy, competence, and relatedness).

There were a number of limiting factors regarding this study. The small sample size and the unique nature of the context means it is impossible to generalise across all high-performance sport, in all circumstances. The relatively limited timeframe of the study also presents some issues regarding more general applicability given that a longer exposure and experience with AS coaching behaviours may engender different outcomes, responses and effects. Within those restrictions and limitations, however, it must be emphasised that there is room for recognition of commonality within the uniqueness of specific contexts (Cushion, Armour, & Jones, 2006). Similarly, while there may be some perceived limitations associated with the lead researcher conducting the interviews, these are acknowledged and accepted within the broader research framework. Moreover, we contend that the reflexive processes encouraged in the literature (Jones, 2009; Mallet, 2004) and presented here, are appropriate for use in both research frameworks and in providing a useful tool for the oft-missing link in the professional development and on-going learning processes of coaches operating in high-performance contexts.

Notes on contributors

Matthew Lyons is the Head Coach of the Olympic Winter Institute of Australia's Ski Cross Program and was the inaugural Australian coach of that program at the sport's debut in the Vancouver 2010 Olympic Games. He carries Level III Canadian and Australian coaching certification and has completed his Masters of Applied Science in Sports Coaching. He in nearing completion of his Master of Philosophy with his project examining Autonomy Supportive Coaching Behaviours in elite sport.

Steven Rynne is a Lecturer and Research Fellow at The University of Queensland. Steven has worked and conducted research with the Queensland Academy of Sport, Australian Institute of Sport / Australian Sports Commission and Cricket Australia in the areas of high performance coach learning and Indigenous sport. Steven teaches graduate students, is a registered HPE teacher and coaches track cyclists.

Cliff Mallett teaches undergraduate and graduate students at The University of Queensland and actively researches in the area of elite sport. He is a registered psychologist and has coached extensively at the elite level coaching track athletes at Olympic Games and other major international competitions.

References

Ahlberg, M., Mallett, C., & Tinning, R. (2008). Developing autonomy supportive coaching behaviours: An action research approach to coach development. *International Journal of Coaching Science, 2*(2), 3–22.

Allen, J., & Hodge, K. (2006). Fostering a learning environment: Coaches and the motivational climate. *International Journal of Sports Science & Coaching, 1*, 261–277.

Amiot, C.E., Gaudreau, P., & Blanchard, C.M. (2004). Self-determination, coping, and goal attainment in sport. *Journal of Sport & Exercise Psychology, 26*, 396–411.

Amorose, A.J. (2007). Coaching effectiveness: Exploring the relationship between coaching behaviour and self-determined motivation. In M.S. Hagger & N.L.D. Chatzisarantis (Eds.), *Intrinsic motivation and self-determination in exercise and sport* (pp. 209–227). Champaign, IL: Human Kinetics.

Barton, T.D. (2008). Understanding practitioner ethnography. *Nurse Researcher, 15*(2), 7–18.

Beauchamp, P.H., Halliwell, W.R., Fournier, J.F., & Koestner, R. (1996). Effects of cognitive-behavioral psychological skills training on the motivation, preparation, and putting performance of novice golfers. *The Sport Psychologist, 10*, 157–170.

Blanchard, C.E., Amiot, C.E., Perrault, S., Vallerand, R.J., & Provencher, P. (2009). Cohesiveness, coach's interpersonal style and psychological needs: Their effects on self-determination and athletes' subjective well-being. *Psychology of Sport and Exercise, 10*, 545–551.

Bloom, B. (1954). The thought processes of students in discussion. In S.J. French (Ed.), *Accent on teaching: Experiments in general education* (pp. 23–46). New York: Harper.

Chambers, E. (2000). Applied ethnography. In N.K. Denzin & Y.S. Lincoln (Eds.), *Handbook of qualitative research* (pp. 851–869). Thousand Oaks, CA: Sage.

Chatzisarantis, N.L.D., & Hagger, M.S. (2007). Intrinsic motivation and self-determination in exercise and sport: Reflecting on the past and sketching the future. In M.S. Hagger & N.L.D. Chatzisarantis (Eds.), *Intrinsic motivation and self-determination in exercise and sport*. Champaign, IL: Human Kinetics.

Cushion, C.J., Armour, K.M., & Jones, R.L. (2003). Coach education and continuing professional development: Experience and learning to coach. *QUEST, 55*, 215–230.

Cushion, C., Armour, K., & Jones, R. (2006). Locating the coaching process in practice. Models 'for' and 'of' coaching. *Physical Education & Sport Pedagogy, 11*(1), 83–99.

DeCharms, R. (1968). *Personal causation: The internal affective determinants of behaviour*. New York: Academic Press.

Deci, E., & Ryan, R. (1985). *Intrinsic motivation and self-determination in human behaviour*. New York: Springer.

Deci, E., & Ryan, R. (2000). The 'what' and 'how' of goal pursuits: Human needs and the self-determination of behaviour. *Psychological Inquiry, 11*, 227–268.

Deci, E., & Ryan, R. (2002). Self-determination research: Reflections and future directions. In E. Deci & R. Ryan (Eds.), *Handbook of self-determination research*. Rochester, NY: The University of Rochester Press.

Deci, E., & Ryan, R. (2008). Facilitating optimal motivation and psychological well-being across life's domains. *Canadian Psychology, 49*(1), 14–23.

DiCicco-Bloom, B., & Crabtree, B.F. (2006). The qualitative research interview. *Medical Education, 40*, 314–321.

Duda, J.L., & Treasure, D.C. (2001). Toward optimal motivation in sport: Fostering athletes' competence and sense of control. In J. Williams (Ed.), *Applied sport psychology* (4th ed., pp. 43–62). Mountain View, CA: Mayfield Press.

Elo, S., & Kyngäs, H. (2008). The qualitative content analysis process. *Journal of Advanced Nursing, 62*(1), 107–115.

Gagné, M., Ryan, R.M., & Bargmann, K. (2003). Autonomy support and need satisfaction in the motivation and well-being of gymnasts. *Journal of Applied Sport Psychology, 15* (4), 372–390.

Gilbert, W., & Trudel, P. (2001). Learning to coach through experience. Reflection in model youth sport coaches. *Journal of Teaching in Physical Education, 21*, 16–34.

Gilbert, W., & Trudel, P. (2005). Learning to coach through experience. Conditions that influence reflection. *Physical Educator, 62*(1), 32–43.

Gilbert, W., Côté, J., & Mallett, C. (2006). The talented coach: Developmental paths and activities of successful sport coaches. *International Journal of Sport Science and Coaching, 1*(1), 69–76.

Gillet, N., Vallerand, R.J., Amoura, S., & Baldes, B. (2010). Influence of coaches' autonomy support on athletes' motivation and sport performance. A test of the hierarchical model of intrinsic and extrinsic motivation. *Psychology of Sport and Exercise, 11*, 155–161.

Grimmett, P.P., & Erickson, G.L. (1988). *Reflection in teacher education.* New York: Teachers College Press.

Gubrium, J.F., & Holstein, J.A. (1995). *The new language of qualitative method.* London: Oxford University Press.

Harwood, C., Spray, C.M., & Keegan, R. (2008). Achievement goal theories in sport. In T. S. Horn (Ed.), *Advances in sport psychology.* Champaign, IL: Human Kinetics.

Hodge, K., Lonsdale, C., & Ng, J.Y.Y. (2008). Burnout in elite rugby: Relationships with basic psychological needs fulfilment. *Journal of Sports Sciences, 26*(8), 835–844.

Hollembeak, J., & Amorose, A.J. (2005). Perceived coaching behaviours and college athletes' intrinsic motivation: A test of self-determination theory. *Journal of Applied Sport Psychology, 17*(1), 20–36.

Jones, R.L. (2009). Coaching as caring (the smiling gallery): Accessing hidden knowledge. *Physical Education & Sport Pedagogy, 14*, 377–390.

Kelley, D., & Gibbons, M. (2008). Ethnography: The good, the bad and the ugly. *Journal of Medical Marketing, 8*(4), 279–285.

Kidman, L. (2005). *Athlete-centred coaching: Developing inspired and inspiring people.* Christchurch, NZ: Innovative Print Communications.

Lyle, J. (2002). *Sports coaching concepts: A framework for coaches' behaviour.* London: Routledge.

Lyle, J. (2003). Stimulated recall: A report on its use in naturalistic research. *British Educational Research Journal, 29*, 861–878.

Mageau, G.A., & Vallerand, R.J. (2003). The coach-athlete relationship: A motivational model. *Journal of Sports Sciences, 21*(11), 883–904.

Mallett, C.J. (2004). Reflective practices in teaching and coaching: Using reflective journals to enhance performance. In J. Wright, D. Macdonald, & L. Burrows (Eds.), *Critical inquiry and problem solving in physical education* (pp. 147–158). London: Routledge.

Mallett, C.J. (2005). Self-determination theory: A case-study of evidence-based coaching. *The Sport Psychologist, 19*, 417–429.

Mallett, C.J., & Hanrahan, S. (2004). Elite athletes: why does the 'fire' burn so brightly? *Psychology of Sport & Exercise, 5*, 183–200.

Mallett, C.J., Trudel, P., Lyle, J., & Rynne, S. (2009). Formal versus informal coach education. *International Journal of Sport Science & Coaching, 4*, 325–334.

McDonough, M.H., & Crocker, P.R.E. (2007). Testing self-determined motivation as a mediator of the relationship between psychological needs and affective and behavioural outcomes. *Journal of Sport & Exercise Psychology, 29*, 645–663.

Ntoumanis, N. (2001). A self-determination approach to the understanding of motivation in physical education. *British Journal of Educational Psychology, 71*, 225–242.

Patton, M.Q. (2002). Enhancing the quality and credibility of qualitative research. *Health Services Research, 34*(5), 1189–1208.

Reinboth, M., & Duda, J.L. (2006). Perceived motivational climate, need satisfaction and indices of well-being in team sports: A longitudinal perspective. *Psychology of Sport and Exercise, 7*, 269–286.

Rynne, S.B., Mallett, C.J., & Tinning, R. (2010). Workplace learning of high performance sports coaches. *Sport, Education and Society, 15*, 315–330.

Sands, R.R. (2002). *Sport ethnography.* Champaign, IL: Human Kinetics.

Schön, D.A. (1983). *The reflective practitioner: How professionals think in action.* New York: Basic Books.

Smoll, F.L., & Smith, R.E. (2002). Coaching behaviour research and intervention in youth sport. In F.L. Smoll & R.E. Smith (Eds.), *Children and youth in sport.* Duduque, IA: Kendall/Hunt.

Starkes, J.L., & Ericsson, K.A. (2003). *Expert performance in sports: Advances in research on sport expertise* (pp. 49–81). Champaign, IL: Human Kinetics.

Stenhouse, L. (1975). *An introduction to curriculum research and development.* London: Heinemann.

Thelwell, R.C., Weston, N.J.V., Greenlees, I.A., & Hutchings, N.V. (2008). Stressors in elite sport: A coach perspective. *Journal of Sport Sciences, 26*, 905–918.

Treasure, D.C., Lemyre, P.-N., Kuczka, K.K., & Standage, M. (2007). Motivation in elite-level sport: A self-determination perspective. In M.S. Hagger & N.L.D. Chatzisarantis (Eds.), *Intrinsic motivation and self-determination in exercise and sport.* Champaign, IL: Human Kinetics.

Trudel, P., & Gilbert, W. (2006). Coaching and coach education. In D. Kirk, D. Macdonald, & M. O'Sullivan (Eds.), *The handbook of physical education* (pp. 516–539). London: Sage.

Vallerand, R.J. (1997). Toward a hierarchical model of intrinsic and extrinsic motivation. In M.P. Zanna (Ed.), *Advances in experimental social psychology* (pp. 271–360). New York: Academic Press.

Vallerand, R.J., & Ratelle, C.F. (2002). Intrinsic and extrinsic motivation: A hierarchical model. In R.M. Ryan & E.D. Deci (Eds.), *Handbook of self-determination theory.* Rochester, NY: The University of Rochester Press.

Vansteenkiste, M., Simons, J., Lens, W., Soenens, B., Matos, L., & Lacante, M. (2004). Less is sometimes more: Goal-content matters. *Journal of Educational Psychology, 96*, 755–764.

Weber, R.P. (1990). *Basic content analysis* (2nd ed.). Newbury Park, CA: Sage.

Weiss, M.R., & Amorose, A.J. (2008). Motivational orientations and sport behaviour. In T.S. Horn (Ed.), *Advances in sport psychology* (pp. 115–156). Champaign, IL: Human Kinetics.

Wengraf, T. (2004). *Qualitative research interviewing.* Thousand Oaks, CA: Sage.

White, R.W. (1959). Motivation reconsidered: The concept of competence. *Psychological Review, 66*, 297–333.

'One door closes, a next door opens up somewhere': the learning of one Olympic synchronised swimmer

Natalie Barker-Ruchti[a], Dean Barker[a], Steven Rynne[b] and Jessica Lee[c]

[a]Department of Food and Nutrition, and Sport Science, University of Gothenburg, Gothenburg, Sweden; [b]School of Human Movement Studies, The University of Queensland, Brisbane, Australia; [c]School of Public Health, Griffith University, Brisbane, Australia

Although training in sport is necessary to reach Olympic status, a conditioned body is not the only outcome. Athletes also learn how to be Olympians. This learning involves taking on certain ways of acting, thinking and valuing. Such learning has implications beyond competition, as athletes eventually retire from elite sport and devote their time to other activities. This paper examines processes of learning and transition using the case of Amelia, a former Olympic synchronised swimmer. Through two in-depth interviews, empirical material was generated which focused on the learning that took place during this athlete's career and after, during her transition to paid employment. A cultural view of learning was used as the theoretical frame to understand the athlete's experiences. Our reading suggests that the athlete learned in various ways to be productive. Some of these ways of being were useful after retirement; others were less compatible. In fact, Amelia used a two-year period after retirement to reconstruct herself. Key to her eventual successful transition was to distance herself from the sport and to critically reflect upon her sporting experiences. We thus recommend that those involved with high-performance athletes foster a more balanced perspective that acknowledges and promotes ways of being beyond athletic involvement.

Introduction

The training of Olympic athletes advances physical performance. Usually beginning in childhood, participants condition their bodies to excel in their chosen sports. In artistic sports such as gymnastics, figure skating and synchronised swimming, training begins at a particularly young age and often peaks during adolescence. These athletes' childhoods are spent in gymnasiums, ice rinks or swimming pools, where they often train over 30 hours per week. During such years of training, athletes' conditioning goes beyond physical training and includes the informal learning of social skills.

Research examining informal learning has predominantly emerged from psychology. Within this perspective, scholars have focused on the learning of specific skills such as stress management (see for instance Gould, Eklund, & Jackson, 1993), teamwork (see for instance Bloom & Stevens, 2004; Bloom, Stevens, & Wickwire, 2003) and motivation (see for instance Naber, 2006). This view of learning has been criticised, mainly by scholars who adopt broader constructivist frames of understanding learning, arguing that the cognitive notion of learning is too narrow.

In sport science, the constructivist view of learning has found resonance, particularly research on school physical education (for useful examples see Kirk & Kinchin, 2003; Kirk & Macdonald, 1998; Kirk & MacPhail, 2002). Learning in non-school sport settings, however, has received much less attention. Constructivist learning theories have the potential to be highly generative, but until now have been under-utilised in analyses of athletes' participation in sport. Three exceptions which involve a process of learning that is inseparable from the development of identity are recent research by Barker et al. (in press), which explores and relates learning during Olympic sporting careers to Olympism, Krogh Christensen's, Nørgaard Laursen's and Kahr Sørensen's (2011) study on learning processes in elite sport talent development and Light's (2006, 2010) research, which has demonstrated how long-term participation in practices of sports clubs (surf lifesaving and swimming in Australia, rugby in Japan) influences identity.

In terms of transfer of learning from sport, both cognitive and constructivist camps have debated this issue. With regard to the former, a number of scholars have discussed the transferability of skills learnt in sport (see for instance Gould & Carson, 2008; Holt, Tamminen, Tink, & Black, 2009). From within the constructivist camp, the idea of transfer has been rejected and replaced with notions such as embodied learning, transition and reconstruction (Hager, 2004; Hager & Hodkinson, 2009). However, very little research on how athletes' learning relates to non-sport areas of life has actually emerged from this perspective. Fleuriel's and Vincent's (2009) study of one French rugby player's career-change difficulties, Carless' and Douglas' (2009) research on career transition in professional golf, as well as Brown's and Potrac's (2009) and Sparkes' (2000) research into identity disruption following premature retirement due to de-selection and illness, are attempts in explaining retirement experiences. These studies do not, however, examine processes of learning related to identity (re-)construction.

This paper sets out to address learning, career transition and identity reconstruction in sport from a cultural perspective of learning. It does this by exploring the *becoming* of one former Olympic synchronised swimmer and to relate her experiences to life after competitive sport. The specific research questions are: (1) How did Olympic sport shape the athlete during her athletic career? (2) How did the athlete experience her move away from high-performance sport? and (3) How did the athlete adjust to life outside of sport? In the following, we present the cultural perspective we have adopted to make sense of learning. We then describe the methods we employed to generate data and interpretations. Finally, we present the athlete's sporting career, and discuss her learning during and after her time in sport.

Theoretical perspective

We adopt an embodied view of learning, which a group of English scholars has recently put forward (Hodkinson, 2005; Hodkinson, Biesta, & James, 2007, 2008; James & Biesta, 2007). Basic to their understanding is that learning involves the construction of embodied subjectivities. That is, who one becomes is a process of incorporation that involves the absorption of skills, knowledge and values. As

Hager and Hodkinson (2009) stated: 'People *become* through learning and learn through *becoming* whether they wish to do so or not, and whether they are aware of the process or not' (p. 633, emphasis ours).

Seeing learning as embodied reflects a cultural view. On the one hand, the frame proposes that learning is about the participation of people in what Lave and Wenger (1991) called, 'communities of practice' (CoP). These communities are defined by agreement on what comprises the group's 'work' and the ways members should go about this work. Lave and Wenger (1991) explored the notion of apprenticeship to explain how communal characteristics and practices emerge. Several scholars have adopted this idea to explain learning in various workplaces (see for instance Billett, 2001; Hodkinson & Hodkinson, 2004). On the other hand, learning as a cultural phenomenon points to how the features of a CoP do not exist in a vacuum, but rather reflect social context. Relations of power shape these communities and affect what individuals learn (Hodkinson et al., 2008). That is, relations of power and processes of normalisation shape what practices, knowledge or values emerge and are perceived valuable and normal. Learning thus not only involves practices (as in practical activity and intelligent action), through which, for instance, an athlete learns to become proficient or adopt particular ways of being that are expected within her sporting community, but also about social structures that provide frames of legitimation. That is, the knowledge and values existing within sporting communities offer its members ways to make sense of the practices, relationships and expectations common-place within them. The proficient athlete, who has adopted her CoP's expected ways, can draw on the underlying values of her community and the practices within it to understand her experiences.

What happens when the athlete retires and enters a new CoP? Hager's and Hodkinson's (2009) 'becoming within a transitional process of boundary crossing', as well as their metaphors 'transition', 'transformation' and 'reconstruction', offer explanations on how the learnt can be moved from one area of life to another. The concept of embodied subjectivity is key, as it explains how a transition is about learning (or change in an individual), rather than a transfer of knowledge. As our athlete from above retires from sport and enters a new CoP, her embodied subjectivity includes the experiences she made in and the ways of being she adopted through sport. Her opinions, beliefs and values will become part of the new situation, and influence how she experiences it. Learning will continue in the new location, as what the now former athlete has brought with her may need to be adjusted or even changed in order to achieve efficient and successful participation.

In this paper, we present the becoming of a two-time Olympian. We explore how the CoP shaped her and how this relates to her life after sport. Before we do this, we describe the research methods and analytics we employed to generate data and interpretations.

Methods

Thinking about learning as situated and embodied has implications for how the topic of learning and career transition should be approached empirically. In the case of our study, it necessitated a detailed understanding of the characteristics of the athlete's CoP, the practices the athlete experienced, the ways she acted in her social world, what was important to her and how others treated her. We felt that extended conversations would fit this purpose.

Amelia,[1] the synchronised swimmer presented in this paper, was recruited as part of a larger case study of eight former Olympic athletes. Amelia was a synchronised swimmer for 16 years (9–25 years of age). During this career, she trained at a high-performance level for approximately 10 years and attended major international competitions (Junior and Senior European and World Championships, World Cups), as well as two Olympic Games. We chose to present the case of this athlete because her accounts provide particular insight into career transition and the reconstruction within the professional sphere she entered after retirement. Furthermore, the career transition of female artistic athletes, although little explored, offers particularly informative insight as their athletic training is intense and at a time when impressionability is considered high (Kerr & Dacyshyn, 2000).

As with all participants in the broader study, two semi-structured interviews (Rapley, 2004) were held with the former synchronised swimmer. The first interview covered topics relating to her athletic career progression, learning and social relationships. The schedule included questions such as: 'How did your sporting participation change over time?' and 'Who was important to you in your sporting context?' After the verbatim transcription of the interview, and in line with Alvesson's and Skolberg's (2000) notion of reflexive methodology, key areas of learning and being were identified. These guided the second interview, within which the interviewee was asked to consider how particular aspects of her sporting experiences played out in her life after high-performance sport. The second interview thus took a more individualised form, in that the questions reflected the comments she had made in the first interview. Both transcripts, as well as the paper that emerged from the data, were sent to the participant for comment.

The transcripts were read repeatedly in order to extract aspects and processes of learning. A table, within which aspects of learning, as well as actors involved in the learning, was coded and sub-coded, and aided the analytic process. This table included columns, detailing the ways the athlete reconstructed herself after retirement, and/or how new aspects and processes of learning emerged. After this process of data collation, a collective element of analysis followed. Dialogue took place between the four researchers, leading to alternative and more sophisticated ways of understanding. Importantly, collaboration was not used as a triangulation-type strategy to ensure convergent interpretations (Cresswell, 2003), but as a way to explore divergent and competing explanations.

In what follows, we briefly describe Amelia's sporting career and transition away from Olympic sport and then delve into key characteristics and practices, through which she learnt to be an Olympic synchronised swimmer. We will then relate these ways of being to her life after elite sport.

Amelia's Olympic career

Amelia began synchronised swimming at the age of nine. She recounted how she had grown bored with ballet and track and field and said that she wanted to do a more intense activity. She chose synchronised swimming and began training once per week for between two and three hours. From the age of 10, she trained three to four times per week. Amelia described how at first, her father struggled to accept her 'commitment', but eventually understood that she enjoyed this relatively intense participation. Her dad stipulated, Amelia remembered, that she could participate as long as she made her own way to training (a train ride to the next village) and maintained her school performance.

As a teenager, Amelia achieved various national titles and quickly moved from national development to junior and senior teams. She competed at a number of international competitions, including European and World Championships, and Olympic Games. Nationally, Amelia frequently held the top ranking and internationally, she consistently placed within the top 10. During her account, Amelia stressed that she received little financial support and paid her own costs.

A number of individuals comprised Amelia's immediate community during her athletic career. From the age of 16, she lived away from home so that she could train with two national coaches. Amelia described these coaches, both from the former Soviet Union, as extremely tough and authoritarian. Other influential members were Amelia's team partners. During the preparation for her second Olympic Games, she lived together with her team partner. She recounted how they used to laugh about their closeness, describing it as more intimate than a romantic relationship.

Amelia retired after the second Olympic Games she participated in. She described how she was glad that her career was finished. A two-year phase, during which Amelia had to adjust to life after sport, followed. Today, she regards herself as happy, having found permanent employment and generally living a 'normal' life.

Becoming Olympic: discipline, self-control and submission

Amelia brought ambition and focus to her training of synchronised swimming. Even as a novice synchronised swimmer, she had the goal of becoming good: 'I wanted to train a lot and I was disciplined, I don't think I could ever have strayed off the path'. She recounted that she did not need somebody to push her; on the contrary, the drive to achieve seemingly came from within. Nevertheless, Amelia described her coach of her early years in the sport as influential in teaching her the basic attitude to high-performance sport. She viewed this coach as being central to a community which she wanted to be a part of; an elite community of synchronised swimmers. This coach adopted particular coaching methods to teach her athletes *discipline*:

> She also made me mentally strong. At the age of 12 we had to, I still remember it was pure horror. Sometimes we really were scared to go to training. We would come to training and then: "Shit, help, I don't want to" and "Oh, how can I do this?" But, [the coach] led you through that, she also gave you the strength that you can achieve a lot if the attitude is right. We had to, for example, swim 50 metres under water two times, we were only 12. Physically, we could do it, we were ready to do it. But mentally, we hadn't had to do it ever before and she just said: "Two times 50 metres under water and a one minute break in between". We already started hyperventilating before we even started and then she said: "If one of the team doesn't manage it, the whole team has to do it again". And then we did it every training until we made it. And we were thinking: "Shit, if I'm the one who comes up too early then the whole team will have to do it again because of me". You already went down thinking that and you had barely swum four metres when you thought: "I've got to go up, I don't have any air left". And we really had, we walked out of training weeping and crying because we didn't know how to carry on, but she always got us back and showed us that you can go through something like that. It has to work in your head. So that was more of a fight with myself.

The coach shaped Amelia to realise that pushing her limits beyond what she thought she could endure, was possible. Indeed, it was made clear to Amelia that if she was to become an Olympic standard athlete, she must push beyond what she felt she was capable of. Amelia referred to this process of emotional dismissal as 'tricking' herself, because she understood that she had 'to get through this, there was no other possibility'.

The form of discipline Amelia learnt was a method for her to control her reactions to the physical and emotional demands placed on her. Amelia provided an example to illustrate her *self-control*:

> The water was 23 degrees, which isn't very warm if you're in there for seven hours. And I lost eight kilos in five weeks. I couldn't keep my weight. I was already very slim when I got there. I froze for seven hours and I was really close to being anorexic. That was psychologically one of the most difficult moments in my life, because I had to get through it. Because I wasn't allowed out [of the water] and I ate as much as I could. But I also totally lost my motivation. I went into hell and that was so crappy. And I wish someone would've just said: "Come out, you don't have to do it". But I was in a team and I had a commitment and I didn't want to go. But that was absolutely horror, it really was.

The discipline to push physical and emotional limits was necessary, on the one hand, to improve athletically, but on the other, to overcome the desire to stop training. Amelia referred to this purpose in training:

> I think the main goal of our trainer, or actually the goal of any trainer, is to bring you to a point emotionally in training, so that you can manage competitions no matter what happens. Or just say if you've got a migraine or if you puke before the free exercise, if you have to puke during the free exercise or if you puke after it. So that you know you can swim the free exercise, maybe not perfectly, but optimally.

In this sense, Amelia developed into a 'training machine', one that continued practising even when she would have preferred leaving sport. Amelia further needed to be disciplined and self-controlled in order to handle her coaches' criticism. She learnt this early on:

> When I was 9 years old [the coach] dealt out blows to the swimmers. One of them was a bit plump. And you have to tread water to stay up, right? And then, she said: "Why are you so low?" and she said: "I don't know". The coach responded: "I always thought fat swims on top". We were nine or 10 years old at the time and when you hear comments like that, that probably influences you. And just to accept it and say nothing at all.

Again, Amelia said that she needed 'to be able to accept criticism … and to make it positive', a practice her coaches used to get their athletes to 'function'. This self-control, Amelia thought, was even more important than physical pre-requisites: 'We saw a lot of people, who had a great body, but they were mentally just weaker and at some point they just didn't make it'. Amelia described how her body suited synchronised swimming, however, she pointed to the mental control she needed to develop in order to succeed in this sport. These practices highlight how Amelia learnt to continuously push her limits, a characteristic that she termed 'sport thinking'. Amelia's description further highlights the utility in adopting a situated view of learning in which learning processes are indivisible from the performance being learnt (Culver & Trudel, 2008). To Amelia, 'sport thinking' was necessary to handle the demands of her sport. In turn, Amelia felt that the mental strength she developed was necessary to achieve. She saw it as the foundation of high-performance sport, a framework that explained and justified her focus and efforts. On the level of the community of synchronised swimming, 'sport thinking' legitimated its characteristics and practices. Although Amelia occasionally questioned the assumptions and conduct, and even left one coach for another because she could not identify with her training philosophy, on many other occasions, she remained in the sport even though she would have preferred to retire. Regardless, other ways of being, such as for instance learning social skills for life after sport, were excluded as they were not seen as useful for the improvement of performance. This is similar to learning in other contexts where the influence of central community members and the prevailing culture mean that certain ways of working and performing are privileged at the expense of other (often more appropriate) ways (Billett, 1994).

The disciplined and self-controlled athlete Amelia developed into involved a further characteristic, namely *submission* to others. To Amelia, the acceptance of her coaches' authority involved respect and responsibility:

> Not for yourself but for others, also your coaches and also towards your fellow swimmers in the team … because it really was a working together, it sometimes was a subordination, but also very consciously so, I always respected it in that sense, because I just knew, it's the only way we'll be successful. You're in a team, so there's a boss who has the say.

The power relations inherent in coach-athlete interactions have led some to suggest that it is more appropriate to conceptualise separate coach CoPs and athlete CoPs (see for example Galipeau & Trudel, 2006). In Amelia's case, the community formed by her teammates was highly influential on her learning and practice. For example, submission was necessary as Amelia was part of a team. At a training camp prior to the qualification phase for her second Olympic Games, Amelia was forced to continue training, despite having fallen seriously ill and being unable to eat. After a blow-out with her coach, Amelia's boyfriend convinced her to continue training. It was at this moment that she swore to herself: 'I'll do it for the others. I'm not doing it for myself, because I don't need all this anymore'. Despite the physical strain and mental demands, Amelia complied so that her duet partner (and her coach) could have a chance at qualifying for the Olympic Games. A fear of regret influenced her decision to continue training. Not surprisingly, all Amelia could feel after her performance at the Games was relief that she 'had gone through with it' and that her duet partner had been able to compete at the Olympics. It was not 'about feelings of happiness' as Amelia described, but rather that 'it was all over' and that she could go home and start planning her new life.

Transition away from sport: perspective, independence and ingenuity

In the first year after retirement, Amelia worked in various jobs to pay off debt and 'finding something [she] would really like doing'. It was a time that she needed for 'peace and quiet' and to 'just do the job and be and live'. This time was spent with her family and friends. The way she described it was as if she had spent over 10 years overseas and had now returned home. Suddenly, she had a lot of spare time to spend with a multitude of people. This included her resuming contact with friends. The community with whom she was associating, and the practice in which she was engaging, had changed dramatically.

Physical adjustments included a change in her perceived need to exercise, which in the beginning included 'training' (e.g. cycling, running, fitness, weight training, swimming) for up to three hours per day. Over time, she exercised less and today, Amelia is happy to be active regularly, but moderately. In contrast, the emotional adjustments appeared more complex and long lasting. Her integration into permanent employment played a key role in this process of change and self-(re) construction. On the one hand, Amelia felt insecure about her professional capabilities. She had been an expert in the synchronised swimming community; in the employment setting, however, she had very little expertise and was a fairly peripheral member. During the application process for permanent employment, she felt that she needed to prove her value as an employee, but also to herself, because this is what she was used to from sport:

> In the company, at the beginning, I had to prove that I could do it. But then I realised, I don't have to prove anything to anybody, all the more to myself. That gives me serenity. Often you can see things from a bird's eye and realise, ok, it's actually not so important, there are other things.

In keeping with workplace studies using situated learning approaches (see for instance Billett, 1996), Amelia's time in employment afforded opportunities to engage in different contexts and with different 'others', enabling her to (re)set her expectations about herself and those around her. But while Amelia's time in employment assured her that she is a capable worker, her Olympic past cannot be ignored. While aspects of her synchronised swimming self could be adjusted and developed in life outside of sport, others need(ed) releasing and involved a process of transformation and renovation. As Hager and Hodkinson (2009) suggested, Amelia had to transform her identity and learn new ways of being. Yet, her embodied sporting self cannot be ignored, as it formed the basis from which Amelia had to reconstruct her identity.

An important feature that Amelia identified as being 'new' after retirement from sport, was that of being able to show weakness and emotions:

> Yes, now I'm actually allowed to show them. I find that's the hardest part. To let it happen, to be able to show weaknesses. I was never allowed to. That was out of the question for us. If you cried, you had to put on your goggles, because the coach didn't want to see you crying. And that's really difficult, on the one hand because, well, I like people, who are strong. I don't want to end up appearing like a greyhound or something weak. But sometimes, it's also good to show weaknesses and also to accept it and to say: "Today, it's just not going to work out and yes, maybe you should just leave me alone". I'm still only learning that to be honest. I'm still in the process of letting that happen.

The practice of being mentally strong had taught Amelia to ignore emotional reactions. As her site of learning had changed, this custom was no longer relevant and Amelia had realised that she did not need to embody mental strength. In a similar way, Amelia was learning to let go of her submissive self:

What I definitely took with me that is something I still think of today: "You have to stop subordinating yourself". And that's difficult to really achieve. I still carry that in me. And it takes a while until I get rid of it or just realise: "You don't have to do it, why are you doing this?" you know. So now I question things. But [in synchronised swimming], to question things wasn't good.

While Amelia has to reconstruct aspects of her being, she is also able to expand ways of being from sport to her non-sport life. First, her experiences of having to continuously push her emotional and physical limits, has given her *perspective*. Her employment, for instance, appears easy to Amelia compared with her former training demands:

Going through the training wasn't always nice. From time to time, someone had to rescue me, because you stayed under water. And to push yourself to this limit requires a lot of overcoming. And it wasn't nice in fact, such a long time. Sometimes I had enough of holding my breath.

With this perspective, Amelia does not look for fulfilment through work. Instead, she carries her sporting achievements with her and does not see herself depending on succeeding professionally in order to feel good about herself.

Another aspect that Amelia identified that she learnt through sport is *independence*. Various situations led to this confidence, one being that she became independent early on in her career:

When I went [overseas] I was 15. It was also interesting that my parents just said: "Yes, you are going [overseas]". I still remember when I was standing on the [train] platform when I went away in September, I said to my mother: "Is it actually ok, if I already move out?" And my mother just stood there and probably thought: "What sort of a question is that? Did that only occur to you now?" Then she said: "No, you know, we have faith in you and we think it's a great opportunity and we just want you to be happy!" And that was somehow really wonderful to take that with me on my way. And I knew I wouldn't take advantage of their trust in me.

A further way of 'being' Amelia is able to draw from is knowing what she is capable of. This includes the physical limits she had to push and the kinaesthetic level she reached, but also the belief that problems can always be solved. Amelia's continuous financial struggles often caused more stress than the physical and emotional demands the sport posed and forced her to develop *ingenuity*:

Because I learnt how to cope with difficult situations. If you have to ring up an insurance [company] to say: "I'm sorry, but I can't pay the bills because I don't have any money" and you're 17 or 18, that's not that funny. But there's always a way and that applied to every other area as well ... Falling over and standing up again. I think that hopefully I will be able to keep that for the rest of my life and that I have basic confidence in life and can keep that confidence. If one door closes a next door opens up somewhere. I think I will be able to go through life easily, I hope I can keep that attitude.

We consider this attitude significant and an aspect of Amelia's self that she has embodied and was able to develop within and take with her from Olympic synchronised swimming. In a similar way, Amelia felt that her early move away from home to train with renowned coaches, as well as her ways of handling financial strains, taught her independence and ingenuity. She developed an 'I can do any-thing' disposition, an attitude she still embodies today. We suggest that this outlook was highly valued by her elite sport community, as well as the new communities she subsequently entered, and this ultimately helped Amelia reconstruct herself after retirement. Moreover, Amelia described how knowing her physical and emotional limits gave her perspective, which she interpreted as a trust in herself and life in general. Despite the perhaps counter-productive learning Amelia made in terms of discipline, self-control and submission, the perspective, independence and ingenuity she adopted through sport gave her confidence and a trust in life that served her after she retired from sport.

Outlook

In this paper, we have demonstrated the learning of one Olympic athlete and have pointed out how the person she became through sport related to her life after retirement. We have adopted learning as cultural and embodied to make sense of Amelia's experiences. In so doing, we have shown how she developed to suit the demands and expectations of her sport and how she was able to use some of those ways of being outside of sport, while others need(ed) transformation and reconstruction.

Amelia's case demonstrates how her Olympic past influences her current experi-ences, as well as her learning since retirement. With regard to the former, she is still looking for a professional and recreational passion. Synchronised swimming had filled her life and although she is giving herself time to decide what she would like to do, she is looking to find a new passion. In a similar way, Amelia said that 'sport thinking' is still part of her today, even though it causes conflict as her work col-leagues, for instance, do not share this attitude. Yet, she remains goal-oriented and highly motivated to work hard, as well as to channel her energy into a professional future. With regard to the latter, her Olympic learning influences her reconstruction after retirement, namely that she is learning to be less submissive and to accept mis-takes and weaknesses. Time in a largely non-sporting community has fostered learn-ing that has de-emphasised the degree of discipline and self-control that was expected in her synchronised swimming community.

The reconstruction Amelia has undergone since retirement included her reflecting on what appeared a key value in Olympic sport: 'sport thinking'. We argue that sev-eral dispositions she developed in sport (perspective, independence and ingenuity) appeared to foster the gaining of distance from this value. However, and importantly, Amelia had described a two-year phase during which this realisation occurred. While she did not seem upset or remorseful for having to undergo such learning, we sug-gest that athletes' transitions from elite sport to a life without sport could be facili-tated through their gaining critical distance *during* their careers. Two points are worth mentioning in this regard. First, gaining critical distance may be particularly necessary and beneficial for high-performance and/or Olympic athletes. Such athletes are involved in high-performance sport at the most intense level and for a significant period of their mostly still young lives. We thus argue, and this has been suggested by other researchers (see for instance Barker-Ruchti, 2011; Shogan, 1999), that the more intense sport participation is, the more the athletes have to adapt to the com-mon values and practices of a sporting community. As Amelia's case has demon-strated, her long-term and intense involvement in synchronised swimming shaped her into a particular person, one that had learned what successful functioning in her sport required. Had she remained training at the club level, we can assume that she would not have become the person she became through elite sport.

Second, gaining critical distance from high-performance sport may not mean that athletes put less effort or focus into their career or training, but rather, that athletes understand that 'there is more to life' than high-performance or Olympic sport. We suggest that Amelia provides an example that illustrates how her distance from sport allowed her to experience communities that accept and embody other forms of being. We speculate that had Amelia been able to develop such a perspective during sport, she would have been able to construct a non-sporting self during her career. Her transition away from sport may have been facilitated. We thus recommend that those forming communities involving (future) Olympic athletes provide athletes with learning experiences that include gaining a more balanced perspective that sport is but one sphere and phase of life and that others will follow after retirement. Research that *listens* to how athletes learn is necessary, however, to further inform the high-performance community on how this balance can be achieved.

Acknowledgments

The authors wish to thank the IOC Postgraduate Research Grant 2011 for financing this project.

Note
1. 'Amelia' is a pseudonym.

Notes on contributors
Natalie Barker-Ruchti is a senior lecturer at the University of Gothenburg. She teaches in the field of sport coaching and researches sport coaches' practices, the coach-athlete relationship and the learning of high-performance athletes.

Dean Barker is a senior lecturer at the University of Gothenburg. He teaches in the field of sport pedagogy and researches issues related to school physical education, in particular in relation to experiences youths with immigration backgrounds make.

Steven Rynne is a research fellow and lecturer at the University of Queensland. He researches and teaches in the field of sport coaching. He is particularly interested in how coaches learn.

Jessica Lee is a lecturer at Griffith University. She researches and teaches in the field of physical activity and health. She is particularly interested in how young people make meaning of health.

References

Alvesson, M., & Skoldberg, K. (2000). *Reflexive methodology*. London: Sage.
Barker, D., Barker-Ruchti, N., Rynne, S., & Lee, J. (in press). Searching for Olympism on Olympus: A pedagogically-oriented investigation of elite sporting communities. *Educational Review*.
Barker-Ruchti, N. (2011). *Women's artistic gymnastics: An (Auto-)ethnographic journey*. Basel: gesowip.

Billett, S. (1994). Situated learning – a workplace experience. *Australian Journal of Adult and Community Education, 34*(2), 112–130.

Billett, S. (1996). Towards a model of workplace learning: The learning curriculum. *Studies in Continuing Education, 18*(1), 43–58.

Billett, S. (2001). *Learning at the workplace: Strategies for effective practice.* Sydney: Allen & Unwin.

Bloom, G.A., & Stevens, D.E. (2004). Case study: A team-building mental skills training program with an intercollegiate equestrian team. *Online Journal of Sport Psychology,* 4 (1). http://www.athleticinsight.com/Vol4Iss1/EquestrianPDF.pdf

Bloom, G.A., Stevens, D.E., & Wickwire, T.L. (2003). Expert coaches perceptions of team building. *Journal of Applied Sport Psychology, 15*, 129–143.

Brown, G., & Potrac, P. (2009). 'You've not made the grade, son': De-selection and identity disruption in elite level youth football. *Soccer & Society, 10*(2), 143–159.

Carless, D., & Douglas, K. (2009). 'We haven't got a seat on the bus for you' or 'all the seats are mine': Narratives and career transitions in professional golf. *Qualitative Research in Sport and Exercise, 1*(1), 51–66.

Cresswell, J.W. (2003). *Research design: Qualitative quantitative and mixed methods approaches.* Thousand Oaks, CA: Sage.

Culver, D.M., & Trudel, P. (2008). Clarifying the communities of practice concept in sport. *International Journal of Sports Science and Coaching, 3*(1), 1–10.

Fleuriel, S., & Vincent, J. (2009). The quest for a successful career among elite athletes in France: A case study of a French rugby player. *Leisure Studies, 28*(2), 173–188.

Galipeau, J., & Trudel, P. (2006). Athlete learning in a community of practice: Is there a role for the coach? In R.L. Jones (Ed.), *The sports coach as educator: Reconceptualising sports coaching* (pp. 77–94). London: Routledge.

Gould, D., & Carson, S. (2008). Life skills development through sport: Current status and future directions. *International review of Sport and Exercise Psychology, 1*(1), 58.

Gould, D., Eklund, R., & Jackson, S. (1993). Coping strategies used by U. S. Olympic wrestlers. *Research Quarterly for Exercise and Sport, 64*(1), 83–93.

Hager, P. (2004). The inescapability of metaphors for thinking about learning. In G. Jover & P. Villamor (Eds.), *Voices of philosophy of educationproceedings of the 9th Biennial Conference of the International Network of Philosophers of Education* (pp. 143–151). Madrid: Complutense University.

Hager, P., & Hodkinson, P. (2009). Moving beyond the metaphor of transfer of learning. *British Educational Research Journal, 35*(4), 619–638.

Hodkinson, H., & Hodkinson, P. (2004). Rethinking the concept of community of practice in relation to schoolteachers' workplace learning. *International Journal of Training and Development, 8*(1), 21–31.

Hodkinson, P. (2005). Learning as cultural and relational: Moving past some troubling dualisms. *Cambridge Journal of Education, 35*(1), 107–119.

Hodkinson, P., Biesta, G., & James, D. (2007). Understanding learning cultures. *Educational Review, 59*(4), 415–427.

Hodkinson, P., Biesta, G., & James, D. (2008). Understanding learning culturally: Overcoming the dualism between social and individual views of learning. *Vocations and Learning, 1*, 27–47.

Holt, N.L., Tamminen, K., Tink, L., & Black, D. (2009). An interpretive analysis of life skills associated with sport participation. *Qualitative Research in Sport and Exercise, 1* (2), 160.

James, D., & Biesta, G. (2007). *Improving learning cultures in further education.* London: RoutledgeFalmer.

Kerr, G., & Dacyshyn, A. (2000). The retirement experiences of elite, female gymnasts. *Journal of Applied Sport Psychology, 12*, 115–133.

Kirk, D., & Kinchin, G. (2003). Situated learning as a theoretical framework for sport education. *European Physical Education Review, 9*(3), 221–235.

Kirk, D., & Macdonald, D. (1998). Situated learning in physical education. *Journal of Teaching in Physical Education, 17*, 376–387.

Kirk, D., & MacPhail, A. (2002). Teaching games for understanding and situated learning: Rethinking the Bunker and Thorpe model. *Journal of Teaching in Physical Education, 21*, 177–192.

Krogh Christensen, M., Nørgaard Laursen, D., & Kahr Sørensen, J. (2011). Situated learning in youth elite football: A Danish case study among talended male under-18 football players. *Physical Education and Sport Pedagogy, 16*(2), 163–178.

Lave, J., & Wengner, E. (1991). *Situated learning: Legitimate peripheral participation.* Cambridge: University Press.

Light, R. (2006). Situated learning in an Australian surf club. *Sport, Education & Society, 11* (2), 155–172.

Light, R. (2010). Children's social and personal development through sport: A case study of an Australian swimming club. *Journal of Sport and Social Issues, 34*(4), 379–395.

Naber, J. (2006). From high school to the Olympic games: Learning from a variety of swimming coaches. *International Journal of Sport Science and Coaching, 1*(2), 125–126.

Rapley, T. (2004). Interviews. In G.C. Seale, B.J. Gobo, & D. Silverman (Eds.), *Qualitative research practice* (pp. 15–33). London: sage.

Shogan, D. (1999). *The making of high-performance athletes: Discipline, diversity, and ethics.* University of Toronto Press.

Sparkes, A. (2000). Illness, premature career-termination, and the loss of self: A biographical study of an elite athlete. In R.L. Jones & K.M. Armour (Eds.), *Sociology of sport: Theory and practice* (pp. 13–32). Harlow: Longman.

Stories of success: Cultural narratives and personal stories of elite and professional athletes

David Carless[a] and Kitrina Douglas[b]

[a]Leeds Metropolitan University, Fairfax Hall, Headingley Campus, Leeds, LS6 3QS, UK; [b]University of Bristol, Bristol, UK

Using a narrative methodology to explore the stories Olympic and elite athletes tell about success, we identified three alternatives to the dominant conception of success as the achievement of performance outcomes. In these alternatives, success is storied as: (1) 'I did the best that I could' – a controllable and sustainable story of effort and application; (2) 'It's the closest thing you can get to flying' – a story where success relates to embodied experience and discovery; (3) 'People I made the journey with' – which prioritises relationships and connection between people. We reflect on three key insights: (1) success is a multi-dimensional concept, broader than the singular conception encapsulated within the dominant performance narrative; (2) through various narrative strategies, experienced athletes resist cultural pressures towards a singular conception of success; (3) for long-term performance and well-being, it is necessary to work towards multiple forms of success over time and across contexts.

Introduction

Success and how it can be achieved generates a great deal of interest and discussion in sporting circles. However, a question that is less commonly asked is: *What is success?* For some, the answer is winning. This orientation towards success – that it is about beating individual/s or teams – is ubiquitous within sport culture and in the media. Increasingly, it seems to be the most stridently voiced perspective among coaches, managers, governing bodies, sport psychologists, athletes, fans, as well as in policy documents. For example, in *Playing to Win: A New Era for Sport* (Department for Culture, Media and Sport, 2008), the UK Secretary of State for Culture, Media and Sport says: 'When you play sport, you play to win. That is my philosophy. It is also at the heart of this plan that, over time, seeks to change the culture of sport in England'. This perspective is not unique to the UK, but holds a good deal of international currency. The following remarks made by the Director of the Australian Institute of Sport (AIS) during a BBC *Horizon Special* television interview in 2006 provide a further clear example:

> The main drive of the AIS is we are here to win. Getting a personal best and trying your hardest is fantastic and you would never knock an athlete for doing that, but you

are here to win. Getting on the Olympic team is fantastic and getting a green and gold tracksuit is fantastic, but you're here to win. No athlete comes in here without fully understanding and being absolutely committed to winning, winning, and winning. That's what it's all about.

Parallel perspectives have been found in recent sport research (Douglas & Carless, 2006a, 2009, 2011) which identified a dominant type of story – termed a *performance narrative* – among elite athletes. This narrative type revolves around performance outcomes (i.e. winning or being the best) which forms the backbone of the story plot. In performance stories, the purpose of sport is competition and the outcome of achieving a win is the point of playing sport. Performance outcomes, therefore, are considered the ultimate (or only) criteria for success. The words of a successful professional golfer provide an illustration:

> I just like competition – I suppose to see how good you can actually be, so you can stretch yourself. I need to stretch myself to see how capable I am. I need competition – that's what it is, that's what you chose to go into. At the end of the day there is a trophy and there is a cheque and another notch in how many wins you've had. (Douglas & Carless, 2006a, p. 19)

In the performance narrative there is also an assumption or belief that prioritising performance outcomes above all else is the *only* way to be successful. This is illustrated by the following statement:

> I couldn't be successful without it being the most important thing in my life. My golf is more important than anything. If I was in a relationship I would have to say to whoever that was, this is huge – it is not a job. It's much more than that. It is not just a career. I think that all of us, it becomes our whole life. Because I don't think that you can possibly be successful without it being the most important thing. (Douglas & Carless, 2006a, p. 20)

As this excerpt suggests, performance stories are totalitarian in the sense that they implicitly exclude or reject alternative stories which prioritise other values, plots or ways of being. They also exclude other ways of conceptualising success. Tellers of performance stories present their own (personal) story as a universal story shared by *all* elite athletes. Within this story, success depends on winning. But is this the case? Is success solely about winning? Or can success be storied as something else? Further, *should* success be storied as more than winning? It is these questions we now consider.

Stories and narratives matter

Insights from the fields of counselling and psychotherapy suggest that problems are likely when particular narratives become dominant because, in Neimeyer, Herrero and Botella's (2006, p. 132) terms, dominant narratives, '"colonize" an individual's sense of self, constricting identity options to those that are problem saturated'. By 'transmitting' cultural meanings and perspectives, dominant narratives shape personal stories. This is because, as McLeod (1997, p. 94) puts it, 'Even when a teller is recounting a unique set of individual, personal events, he or she can only do so by drawing upon story structures and genres drawn from the narrative resources of a culture'. Thus, an individual's story is constructed on the basis of both personal experience *and* the narrative forms that are available within their particular culture (Carless, 2010).

For narrative scholars, personal stories are important not least because identity and sense of self are created and sustained through narrative means (McAdams, 1993). More specifically, as Spence (1982) describes, telling stories of our experiences over time allows the development of a 'narrative thread' which constitutes the core of identity and sense of self. Thus, cultural narratives come to shape each individual's identity and sense of self which, in turn, serves to open or close particular lifestyle possibilities and horizons. The upshot of all this is that, in Somers' (1994, p. 614) terms, 'people are guided to act in certain ways, and not others, on the basis of the projections, expectations, and memories derived from a multiplicity but ultimately limited repertoire of available social, public, and cultural narratives'. Thus, stories and narratives matter.

Narrative research in sport

The ways stories and narratives matter in sport have been charted and explored in recent research which shows the dominant performance narrative has very real consequences for long-term mental health and identity development. In-depth longitudinal research with professional golfers reveals how significant problems (in terms of mental health and sense of self) can result when an individual rigidly follows the contours of the dominant performance narrative, excluding other ways of storying (and living) life (see Carless & Douglas, 2009; Douglas & Carless, 2009, 2011). Other narrative types – termed *discovery* and *relational* – have however been identified which legitimise alternative ways of living and negotiating life in elite sport (Douglas & Carless, 2006a; Douglas, 2009). While documented during interviews with professional athletes, these story types tend to be marginalised, trivialised and/or silenced in sport culture and, therefore, rarely reach the public domain.

The purpose of this study is to explore success stories among elite and Olympic athletes, to establish whether alternative ways of conceptualising success are possible for high-achieving elite sportspeople. On the basis of studies cited above, in addition to personal experience of elite sport (Douglas, 2009), we suspect that diverse conceptions of success are possible but that these stories are silenced within an elite sport culture which prioritises performance outcomes. Our focus is therefore on athletes' stories of their own experiences of success – that is, accounts that elite and professional athletes have offered which shed light on what they consider success to be. At times, this is expressed as what it is they aim for in their sport, at other times through descriptions of what happens when things go well. By considering individual stories of success experiences in this way, we hope to generate a more complex and multidimensional conception of what success *is* and *might be* for elite and Olympic sportspeople.

Methods

Participants

This study draws on data collected for a research project funded by the UK Sport Council (Douglas & Carless, 2006b), which was granted ethical approval by a local ethics committee at Kitrina's (the second author) institution. The participants comprised 21 elite and professional athletes (11 female, 10 male) between 18 and 44 years of age and registered on the UK Sport Council's athlete support programme. Participants were drawn from the following sports: track and field athletics, rowing, rugby union, swimming, cricket, judo, canoeing, hockey and netball.

Procedures

It is widely recognised that researching 'elites' raises several distinct challenges particularly in terms of access and recruitment (Hertze & Imber, 1995; Pensgaard & Duda, 2002). It was therefore necessary that we were flexible and adaptable in terms of, for example, how and when we collected data to fit in with individuals' often busy schedules and geographical location. To balance this with the aims of our research, we employed two methods of data collection: focus groups and one-to-one interviews. Initially, a series of five focus groups were arranged and conducted for those individuals who were able to make pre-arranged times and locations. Subsequently, five one-to-one interviews were conducted at a time and place which suited individuals who were unable to attend a focus group.

While there are sometimes differences in the conduct and purposes of interviews and focus groups, we utilised a similar approach within both which sought – in line with narrative life story approaches (see Crossley, 2000; Lieblich, Tuval-Mashiach, & Zilber, 1998; Plummer, 2001) – biographical, historical and cultural context for each athlete's current life situation and experiences. Kitrina conducted in-depth interviews and led focus groups. As a professional sportsperson, Kitrina is an 'insider' to the population of study and this, we felt, increased the depth of conversations, helping participants feel sufficiently secure to be candid in the stories they shared. During the focus groups, David (first author) noted key issues which emerged, engaging in the conversation when clarifying or contrast questions where needed. Having no personal experience of professional sport, David is an 'outsider' to the population, which helped bring a further critical perspective to the focus groups and subsequent analysis and interpretation.

Analysis and interpretation

Both researchers collaborated in a two-stage processes of analysis and interpretation, incorporating different narrative analytical approaches suited to the purpose of this study. After immersing ourselves in the data, the first stage was conducting a *thematic analysis* (see Riessman, 2008) to identify themes, typologies or instances of paradigmatic categories. This cross-case analysis allowed us to compare and contrast themes and issues evident in the accounts of different participants. During this stage, we identified those stories which, in some way, referred directly to the *experience of success*. The second stage of analysis comprised what Sparkes (2005, p. 195) terms a *narrative analysis of structure and form* in recognition that 'the formal aspects of structure, as much as the content, express the identity, perceptions, and values of the storyteller'. This within-case approach allowed us to focus on one story at a time, reflecting on the underlying theme/s, organisation and plot and considering how broader cultural narratives informed the story's construction. It is the outcomes of this analysis that we present here, in the form of three ways participants storied success which differ from the dominant conception of success as winning.

'I did the best that I could'

A first alternative story of success – subtly different in emphasis to performance stories – is captured by one participant's phrase: 'I did the best that I could'. Whereas performance stories generally include accounts of 'hard work' and 'dedication', these are typically portrayed as essential steps for talented individuals in their ultimate journey towards winning. In contrast, stories which prioritise effort or application portray the *process* of 'being effortful' as a defining characteristic of the teller's sense of self, and a valuable outcome in its own right which (at times) is more important than winning. This sense of evident in the words of Martina, a recently retired rower:

> I've just been to the world dragon boat championships, yeah, and we got a silver and two bronzes but I did 10 minutes training a week. Now I know that medal is sitting on my drawer at home but it has no comparison to a medal that I would get rowing in the rowing World Championship because of the amount of training commitment which has gone with it … Its about being able to put a value on it, saying it was worth me doing that, there's so much I learnt from it and I can look back on it and say you know I did absolutely everything I could, I did the best that I could and it's something I can be completely at peace about.

This story is notably different from the performance narrative in two key ways. First, the application of effort is largely *controllable* and *sustainable*, whereas performance outcomes, generally, are not. A significant problem for tellers of performance tales – over time – is the eventual and inevitable loss of perceived control that occurs when they are simply unable to win. At these times – whether due to opponent quality, injury, ageing, illness, de-selection or career cessation – athletes can find themselves disempowered, feeling impotent or ineffectual. Effort stories, in contrast, are sustainable over time – through injury, poor form and even career transition. The sustainability of this narrative has long-term implications for identity and well-being because, as Spence (1982, p. 458) notes, 'the core of our identity is really a narrative thread that gives meaning to life provided – and this is the big if – that it is never broken'. Being able to maintain a story which revolves around a controllable behaviour is therefore desirable.

Second, as this excerpt illustrates, the teller demonstrates a personalised sense of value and meaning. To achieve this, we suggest, it was necessary that Martina *resisted* the plot of the dominant performance narrative (which would story winning the medals as 'the whole point' of sport) to create a personal story that more closely fitted her own experiences and values. In telling this story, she not only reinforces her own story, values and identity, but simultaneously shares with others an alternative conception of success which allows for value and worth regardless of performance outcome.

We describe this narrative type as *subtly* different to the performance type because effort and performance stories may share some similar features and, therefore, are likely to co-exist more comfortably than other narrative types. Whereas discovery and relational stories tend to be excluded or silenced because they challenge and contravene the core foundations of the performance narrative (see Douglas & Carless, 2008), it may be that effort/application stories are less threatening. For example, Carrie a judo player, put it this way:

> It's weird, the more that I did the more I felt that had one up on people. I don't know, you've probably done the thing when you go out for a run and you see a lamp post

and that lamp post is someone else and once you'd made it you'd beaten them. I still do it now. Like I'd go training on Christmas day, I still do it, so I know that no one else in the country or in the world could have done any more than me. I always wanted to make it feel that there were no minutes in the day that I hadn't been used that someone could have done more than what I'd done.

For us, this excerpt demonstrates the subtle (yet potentially important) difference between the two story types. While Carrie's story shares certain language with the performance narrative (a description of 'beating others'), the underlying plot seems to prioritise the application of effort evidenced here by training on Christmas day. Within the effort/application stories we heard, individuals often portrayed talent and ability as secondary to effort and application. This point also marks a departure from the performance narrative which often stories success as being largely down to 'natural' ability (see Douglas & Carless, 2006a). Carrie had this to say:

My mentality was that if I was training or trying hard enough I could be as good as those people with natural ability anyway. And then people seemed to be confused thinking that I was actually good at the sport and it was like I'd convinced them that was the case. It was a big game I think now looking at it!

Once again, this shift in emphasis reveals a way in which individuals might be able to build and articulate a life story in which a greater degree of control and sustainability is possible.

'It's the closest thing you can get to flying'

A strong narrative thread within some athletes' stories was of success being the actual *embodied experience* of sport, or aspects of it. For some, this was conveyed through stories which focus on the intrinsic pleasure of physical movement. Sam, a Paralympics swimmer, offered this account:

For me, it's the closest thing you can get to actually flying because on land you can only move in two dimensions – unless you jump and then you're momentarily in three dimensions, not truly in three dimensions. But when you're swimming you really can move within this cuboidal space … When I get a good training session it still feels brilliant. I think what it is, it's the ability to get hold of something that you can't get hold of. The water's got this sort of incredibly kind of illusive nature and if you fill up a sink of water and put your hand into it you can't get it but when you swim through it it's solid like a wall. And you know the harder you hit it the harder it will hit you back and it's got this permanent dynamism – it's never the same twice. And I think that's what I really like about it – all its strange kind of vortices and things.

Evident in this excerpt is a sense of flow (Csikszentmihalyi, 1990), comparable to that described by Sparkes and Partington (2003) in their research with members of a university canoe club. Also strongly evident is the sense of taking pleasure or enjoyment through *embodied* movement. There is no reference here to competition, opponents, talent or performance outcomes. In this sense, these stories are distinct from the performance narrative because success is conceived of here not as winning, but as *doing* the movement which relates directly to the individual athlete's sport.

For some participants, success as experience stories revolved around learning or discovering through their sport. Brandon, a rugby union player, shared this account:

[The coach] said: "Right, I'm just going to take you and we'll do a bit of coaching". And I blinked. And he said, "Come on", ... and he took me to one side and just coached with me for an hour. He said, "What are you like with balls along the ground, rolling balls?" And I said I think I'm alright and he said, "Well, we shall see". So he just stood there, he'd chuck balls over my head and I'd turn round and go, you know, and jump down on it and stand up and kick it to touch. I was useless! ... But it didn't matter because here was someone – the coach – actually helping me to be a better player. And I came home absolutely ecstatic, you know, having gone there sort of full of woe and lack of sleep, I came back absolutely buzzing, buzzing and saying, "Look! They took an interest in me! They've accepted that I'm not the be all and end all international player", which I knew I wasn't. But rather than saying, "You're the international – you sort it out", they've said, "You're the international that's why you've got to learn even more".

Once again, absent from this story is a performance outcome achieved through competition with others. Instead, success is realised through solitary practice. Whereas athletes who tell performance tales draw pleasure from their strengths, from doing something better than others, Brandon describes feeling 'absolutely ecstatic' as a result of identifying (and responding to) a *weakness*. Inherent in stories like Brandon's is a sense that despite already having reached the elite or professional level, the teller prioritises personal improvement, learning, and/or discovery. Success for him, therefore, is through experiencing personal development. While, at times, this might be measured or documented in terms of self-referenced performance outcomes (a faster time or a clean execution of a skill, for example), it does not depend upon beating others.

Common, then, to all these type of stories is a tendency towards self-reference rather than other-reference for assessing whether or not one is successful. While experiencing sometimes includes others (in the form of a shared experience), it in no way depends on the demonstration of superiority over those others. These stories have much in common with the discovery narrative described in detail by Douglas and Carless (2006a) and Carless and Douglas (2009) where life is oriented towards exploration and new experiences rather than externally set performance or achievement. Tellers of discovery stories, Douglas and Carless (2006a, p. 22) suggest, see:

self-worth in terms that are not related to achievement in [sport], that bad [sport] scores need not reflect negatively on self-esteem, and that a need for discovery can take precedence over a need to perform in [sport] regardless of the expectations of close relatives, the media, the [sporting] world, and popular western culture.

It is on the basis of these defining characteristics that tellers of discovery stories, while sometimes experiencing tensions within elite sport culture (through *not* subscribing to the dominant performance narrative), are likely to experience a greater sense of alignment and continuity in their lives outside and after elite sport. It seems likely to us that storying success as 'experiencing' – as in the examples above – might be a useful way to move towards the long-term advantages of the dialogical discovery narrative (see Carless & Douglas, 2009).

'People I made the journey with'

Across much of our narrative research with different populations, we have found that many individuals who take part in sport and exercise initially did so through a desire to develop or maintain a relationship, affiliation or connection (see, for example, Douglas & Carless, 2006a; Douglas, 2009; Sparkes & Douglas, 2007). For some, this connection was to significant others (such as friends or family member/s), for others, the connection was to a club or group of some kind. We found similar stories among the participants in this research, when they talked about their early involvement in sport. Shauna, a track and field athlete, offered this story of her early involvement in elite junior athletics:

> We used to have district sports and things like, it was a fun way 'cause we used to meet up with other schools so I used to meet up with cousins and family and friends. On one particular occasion I won and there was a coach for my club at the sideline who gave me a leaflet to join the club and at that age I think I was, "Ooh!" – wowed by the fact that somebody wanted me to join. So I just used to go along. I went down, started off like twice a week, and from the age of 11 until about 13, 14. I was winning everything in the county ... I think I used to see the athletes strutting around in their GB tracksuits and I wanted to be one who had a GB tracksuit – I wanted to be a part of that group.

Often, being a part of a group or team was a central component of participants' stories of their youth sport experiences. Carrie, for example, told of her netball experience while at school:

> You'd see the team lists come up like netball team lists come up and because netball really wasn't my sport, and I'd have said it wasn't my sport, but I'd make sure I was on the list and that in itself would be my winning for that week.

Absent, once again, from these examples are the assumptions and expectations of the performance narrative that winning, competition and talent are the cornerstones of involvement. Instead, these stories have more in common with the plot of a relational narrative (see Douglas & Carless, 2006a, 2009; Douglas, 2009). The relational narrative is a story of complex interdependent connection between two people in which sport performance is essentially a byproduct and where *being with* other/s is storied as more important than achievement in terms of wins or trophies (Douglas & Carless, 2011).

Douglas (2009) has explored the ways that cultural pressures within sport culture can lead to young sportspeople, as they move towards elite level, to either revise or silence the relational stories that characterised their initial sport involvement. As a result of pressure to conform to the terms of the performance narrative as the behaviours it prescribes are widely assumed to be essential to success, some individuals consciously silence their own story in order to tell a performance tale, which satisfies the media, coaches, selectors, sponsors, family members, and/or fans (Carless & Douglas, 2009). A damaging outcome of this is a severing of the 'narrative thread' that, in Spence's (1982) terms, constitutes the core of a person's identity.

Among the participants in this research, however, there were some who continued to hold to the values of a relational story. Martina, for example, reflecting on her sport career, identified relational factors to do with respect as central to her satisfaction and achievements:

> People always ask me: "What was it? Why did you want to win? Was it the accolades?" Because there's no money involved and, you know, I'd chosen a sport with a particularly low media profile. I wanted, I wanted to be able to walk down the road and I wanted respect. But I didn't want respect from *anybody* on the street – I

wanted respect from the people I would value their respect. So it was *my* people. So it was the people I had made that journey with, I wanted for them to say to me – the proudest thing would be for someone who I rowed with in my novices boat to say, "Oh yeah! I rowed with Martina".

For others, it was relationships that came to the fore in times of difficulty, de-selection, injury, or other hardship. Dawn, a judo player, told of the important role her mother played in helping her through the emotional disappointment of not being selected for a major event. Shauna described how while training for an Olympics there was an ethos of care and connection between the athletes:

> Well we train as an 8 – and this is 8 frightened girls all wanting to be part of the team all trying to impress. Even if girls were injured you didn't want to tell them [the coaches/selectors] they were injured because they just wanted to be part of it.

Central to all these stories is a very different conception of success: one that is based around the maintenance and valuing of relationships and connection. It is often these relationships which provide the support athletes need at critical moments in their lives. To sustain not only the relationships themselves – but also an awareness of the presence and value of relationships – requires the continued narration of a relational self which, it appears, can all too often be sacrificed in favour of the kind of performance stories we quoted previously.

Reflections

Having presented three alternative stories of success, the next question might be how might these findings inform athlete support/development initiatives? For us, a first important point to recognise is that success – in the terms of these elite and professional athletes – is a broader and more multidimensional concept than the singular conception encapsulated within the dominant performance narrative in elite sport. Beyond winning, athletes shared stories in which effort and application, embodied experience and relationships were valued as successful 'outcomes' irrespective of performance outcomes. We see this insight as critical to long-term athlete well-being, development and performance for the reasons suggested in this account from Dan, a Paralympics swimmer:

> To begin with I was very focused on the outcome, you know, like I said: I'm going to try and win this gold medal. But when I became a full-time swimmer I joined an able bodied swimming club ... so I trained with an Olympic coach and some Olympic swimmers who were getting ready to go to [the Olympics]. And I had it really, really tough. You know, physically tough – just how far we were swimming each week, just so draining. And I had another one of those moments and I suddenly thought: I've only got one reason why I'm doing this and that is trying to win a medal. And that is just not working ... I actually came up with five reasons why I did it – a gold medal was one of them ... The other things were that I enjoy being fit and healthy, that I like the lifestyle – you know, I like that I travel around the world and represent the country and normally had free time during the day and that kind of thing, I enjoyed the camaraderie of my team, and I had a respect for my coach. So those five things. So at any one time, any one of those five things would make me go to training and train to the best my ability.

This account, for us, is the nub in terms of both motivation and actually *being* successful in the world of elite and professional sport. Rather than rigidly adhering to the terms of the dominant performance narrative – which would demand dedication to the gold medal – Dan came to the realisation that *multiple* successes were not only possible but critical on his particular journey of preparing for a Paralympics Games. Within this account are elements of a performance narrative (striving for gold), a discovery narrative (the lifestyle and travel), and a relational narrative (the camaraderie of my team). As Dan explains, any one of five factors had the potential to motivate him to continue, even at those times when the performance goal may be insufficient.

This example illustrates that to remain healthy, sustain involvement and to maintain performance at the highest level, athletes need alternative and diverse conceptions of success. Indeed, work in sport (e.g. Carless & Douglas, 2009; Douglas & Carless, 2009) and other fields (e.g. Frank, 1995; McLeod, 1997; Neimeyer et al., 2006; Smith & Sparkes, 2008) indicates that problems are likely when a single story becomes dominant. In sport, it seems to be a performance narrative – which revolves around winning/beating others – which dominates, often silencing, trivialising or rejecting other story types.

As a result of the dominance of the performance narrative, those experienced athletes who *do not* subscribe to the terms of this story type must do narrative 'work' if they are to resist the cultural pressures towards a singular conception of success (or identity) to create and sustain a personal story that allows them to continue despite inevitable fluctuations in form, fitness and so on. As Carless and Douglas (2009) have argued, this process of resistance is a necessary one if athletes are to avoid the dominant monological story to, instead, sustain a dialogical and multidimensional narrative thread which supports identity possibilities that do not end when sport career ends.

We suggest that coaches, managers, governing bodies, sport psychologists, and other athletes all have a role to play in supporting alternative stories. *Supporting* in these terms means raising awareness of the presence and possibility of alternatives to performance discourse which help individuals to 'thicken' their own life story, in ways that stay close to personal embodied experience. Sharing alternative stories – in particular those of sportspeople who have achieved at elite or professional level – has the potential, we suggest, to serve as an antidote or counterbalance to the dominant stories within contemporary sport culture which prioritise winning and performance outcomes over and above all other facets of athletes' lives including – too often – long-term well-being.

Researchers also have a role to play as the assumptions, methods and language we employ shape understandings of sport. To characterise the move from initial participation to elite competition, scholars in recent years have suggested young performers move from experiencing sport as 'play' to specialisation and mastery where sport becomes 'work' (Wylleman, Alfermann, & Lavallee, 2004). Thus, it has been surmised that, 'Athletes at the mastery phase are considered to be "obsessed" by their sport' (Wuerth, Lee, & Alfermann, 2004, p. 23). This is just one way *we* (as researchers) story – and constrain – athletes' lives, their motivations and what success is. Evident, however, in the athletes' accounts above are individuals in the 'mastery phase' who maintain strong narrative links to relationships, the joy of an embodied experience, and the satisfactions of application. Stories of 'obsession' and 'work' are notable by their absence. If we continue to only listen for and research 'performance as winning' then we too contribute to an impoverished narrative thread which limits future identity options. Given the accounts presented here we ask, is it time to reconsider?

Acknowledgements

We would like to thank all the participants in this research for willingly and generously sharing with us stories of their lives. We also acknowledge and thank the UK Sport Council who funded and facilitated the research which we have drawn upon in this article.

Notes on contributors

David Carless is a Reader in Narrative Psychology in the Carnegie Research Institute at Leeds Metropolitan University. His research – which lies at an intersection of psychology, sociology, and the arts – draws on narrative and arts-based methods to explore identity and mental health in sport and physical activity contexts.

Kitrina Douglas gained her Ph.D. from the University of Bristol, UK, where she remains a visiting fellow. She played professional golf for 12 years and was English, British and twice European Champion, in 2008 she was awarded "Master Professional" by the Professional Golfers Association for her contribution to coaching. Her research interests are within the field of narrative inquiry and artistic, creative and performative methodologies. She publishes in both academic and non-academic fields.

References

Carless, D. (2010). Who the hell was *that*? Stories, bodies and actions in the world *Qualitative Research in Psychology, 7*(4), 332–344.
Carless, D., & Douglas, K. (2009). 'We haven't got a seat on the bus for you' or 'All the seats are mine': Narratives and career transition in professional golf. *Qualitative Research in Sport hand Exercise, 1*(1), 51–66.
Crossley, M.L. (2000). *Introducing narrative psychology: Self, trauma and the construction of meaning*. Buckingham, UK: Open University Press.
Csikszentmihalyi, M. (1990). *Flow: The psychology of optimal experience*. New York: Harper and Row.
Department for Culture, Media and Sport. (2008). *Playing to win: A new era for sport*. London: HMSO. Crown Copyright.
Douglas, K. (2009). Storying my self: Negotiating a relational identity in professional sport. *Qualitative Research in Sport and Exercise, 1*(2), 176–190.
Douglas, K., & Carless, D. (2006a). Performance, discovery, and relational narratives among women professional tournament golfers. *Women in Sport and Physical Activity Journal, 15*(2), 14–27.
Douglas, K., & Carless, D. (2006b). *The performance environment: Personal, lifestyle and environmental factors that affect sporting performance*. London: UK Sport Council.
Douglas, K., & Carless, D. (2008). Using stories in coach education. *International Journal of Sports Science and Coaching, 3*(1), 33–49.
Douglas, K., & Carless, D. (2009). Abandoning the performance narrative: Two women's stories of transition from professional golf. *Journal of Applied Sport Psychology, 21*(2), 213–230.
Douglas, K., & Carless, D. (2011). A narrative perspective: Identity, well-being, and trauma in professional sport. In D. Gilbourne & M. Andersen (Eds.), *Critical essays in applied sport psychology* (pp. 3–22). Champaign, IL: Human Kinetics.
Frank, A.W. (1995). *The wounded storyteller*. University of Chicago Press.
Hertz, R., & Imber, J.B. (1995). *Studying elites using qualitative methods*. London: Sage.
Lieblich, A., Tuval-Mashiach, R., & Zilber, T. (1998). *Narrative research: Reading, analysis and interpretation*. London: Sage.
McAdams, D. (1993). *The stories we live by*. New York: The Guildford Press.
McLeod, J. (1997). *Narrative and psychotherapy*. London: Sage.
Neimeyer, R., Herrero, O., & Botella, L. (2006). Chaos to coherence. Psycho-therapeutic integration of traumatic loss. *Journal of Constructivist Psychology, 19*(2), 127–145.
Pensgaard, A-M., & Duda, L (2002). 'If we work hard, we can do it'. A tale from an Olympic (gold) medallist. *Journal of Applied Sport Psychology, 14*, 219–236.
Plummer, K. (2001). *Documents of life 2*. Thousand Oaks, CA: Sage.

Reissman, C.K. (2008). *Narrative methods for the human sciences*. Thousand Oaks, CA: Sage.

Smith, B., & Sparkes, A. (2008). Changing bodies, changing narratives and the consequences of tellability: A case study of becoming disabled through sport. *Sociology of Health and Illness, 30*, 217–236.

Somers, M. (1994). The narrative construction of identity: A relational and network approach. *Theory and Society, 23*, 605–649.

Sparkes, A.C. (2005). Narrative analysis: Exploring the *whats* and the *hows* of personal stories. In M. Holloway (Ed.), *Qualitative research in health care* (pp. 91–209). Milton Keynes: Open University Press.

Sparkes, A.C., & Douglas, K. (2007). Making the case for poetic representations: An example in action. *The Sport Psychologist, 21*(2), 170–189.

Sparkes, A.C., & Partington, S. (2003). Narrative practice and its potential contribution to sport psychology: the example of flow. *The Sport Psychologist, 17*, 292–317.

Spence, D. (1982). Narrative persuasion. *Psychoanalysis and Contemporary Thought, 6*, 457–481.

Wuerth, S., Lee, M., & Alfermann, D. (2004). Parental involvement and athletes' career in youth sport. *Psychology of Sport and Exercise, 5*, 21–33.

Wylleman, P., Alfermann, D., & Lavallee, D. (2004). Career transitions in sport: European perspectives. *Psychology of Sport and Exercise, 5*, 7–20.

THOUGHT PIECE

Realising the Olympic dream: vision, support and challenge

Calum A. Arthur, Lew Hardy and Tim Woodman

School of Sport Health & Exercise Sciences, Institute for the Psychology of Elite Performance, Bangor University, George Building, Wales, Bangor LL57 2PZ, UK

The sporting arena is replete with examples and anecdotes of great inspirational coaches that have led teams to success, often in the face of adversity and against seemingly better opponents. The role of the coach in developing and motivating athletes has also been the focus of much research in sport psychology (e.g., Challaduria 1990; Smith & Smoll, 2007). Despite the ease with which one readily accepts that coaches can be inspirational, the sport coaching literature is somewhat devoid of research on inspirational coaches and the effects of such coaches on athletic success. The purpose of the current paper is to theoretically delineate the inspirational effects of coaches in sport. Given the relative paucity of inspiration-related research in sport we draw upon contemporary theories of leadership from organisational and military psychology (e.g., transformational and charismatic leadership theories). We propose a sport-specific model of leadership that centres around the vision, support, and challenge meta-cognitive model developed by Arthur and Hardy in military contexts. The model posits that 'great' coaches inspire their athletes by: (a) creating an inspirational vision of the future; (b) providing the necessary support to achieve the vision; and (c) providing the challenge to achieve the vision. The underlying proposition is that the vision provides meaning and direction for followers' effort. That is, the vision serves as the beacon around which all the sweat, pain and sacrifice involved in achieving success at the highest level in sport is directed. At the heart of this model is the notion that athletes can achieve their dreams provided they are inspired to do so; this is because all other things being equal the person who is motivated to practice longer and train harder will ultimately be the best. The current paper will delineate the coach's role in inspiring the athlete to train harder and longer.

The sporting arena is replete with examples and anecdotes of inspirational coaches that have led teams to success, often in the face of adversity and against seemingly better opponents. Indeed, the influence of the coach is summarised nicely by Dan Britton talking about the legendary basketball coach John Wooden: 'His purpose in coaching was to instil greatness in others. He was committed to teaching, inspiring and motivating people, and he empowered his players to do great things' (Dungy, Robinson, Osborne et al., 2010, p. 13). It is therefore surprising that the models of leadership and coaching in sport are either devoid of the notion of inspiration or only give it a passing mention; we still know very little about precisely why great coaches are great and how in turn they motivate their athletes to achieve Olympic greatness. For example, the sport coaching models developed by Chelladurai and colleagues, Smith, Smoll and colleagues, Horn and colleagues, and Côté and colleagues have all provided an insight into the effects of coach behaviours, some processes and mechanisms by which these behaviours exert their influence and the moderating effects of situation, context, and personality. However, there is very little mention of the inspirational effects of great coaches in these theories and models. The purpose of this paper is not to provide a review of the sport coaching models (for reviews, see Chelladurai, 1990, 2007; Chelladurai & Riemer, 1998; Riemer, 2007; Smith & Smoll, 2007); rather, we will delineate a new model of inspirational coaching based on the principles of vision, support and challenge.

Underpinned by transformational leadership theory (Bass, 1985) the meta-cognitive model of *vision, support* and *challenge* was first developed by Hardy and Arthur in a military context (e.g. Arthur, 2008; Arthur & Hardy, 2008; Arthur & Hardy, 2011; Arthur, Hardy, & Wagstaff, 2010; Hardy & Arthur, 2006; Hardy & Arthur, 2008; Hardy, Arthur, Jones, Shariff, Munnoch, & Isaacs, 2010; Hardy, Shariff, Munnoch, & Allsopp, 2004). The model posits that *great* coaches inspire their athletes by: (a) creating an inspirational *vision* of the future; (b) providing the necessary *support* to achieve the vision; and (c) providing the *challenge* to achieve the vision. The underlying proposition is that the vision provides meaning and direction for athletes' effort. That is, the vision serves as the beacon towards which all the sweat, pain and sacrifice is directed on the path to Olympic success. The premise that underpins the *vision, support* and *challenge* model is that athletes can achieve their Olympic dreams provided they are truly inspired to do so; this is because all other things being equal the person who is motivated to practice longer and train harder will ultimately be the best.

An important aspect of the vision, support and challenge model is that it makes a distinction between what the coach does (i.e. coach behaviours) and the consequences of these coach behaviours (i.e. an athlete's meta-cognitions) in the same model. That is, transformational leadership is what the coach does and an athlete's perceptions of vision, support and challenge are a direct consequence of coach

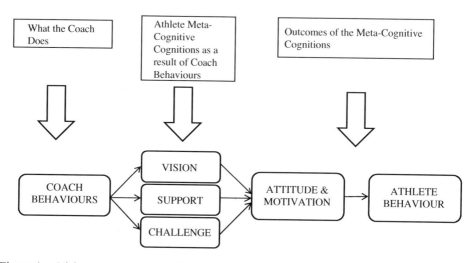

Figure 1. Vision, support and challenge model.

behaviours. In the following paper we first define the vision, support and challenge constructs in our model; we then describe the impact that vision, support and challenge will have, and finally we very briefly identify some key coach behaviours that we theorise will predict an athlete's perceptions of vision, support and challenge.

Vision

Primarily based on the charismatic and transformational leadership literatures, *vision* is defined as *the extent to which athletes have an inspirational and meaningful future image of themselves in their sport*. Whilst vision has occupied a central role in leadership theories from organisational psychology (e.g. Bass, 1985; Berlew, 1974; Conger & Kanungo, 1988; Kim, Dansereau, & Kim, 2002; Nanus, 1992) it is only recently emerging in the sport psychology literature. For example, Vallee and Bloom (2005) identified vision as one of the four higher-order themes that the expert coaches identified in their study. This finding has been replicated in other qualitative designs with vision being identified as a key component of success (e.g. Bucci, Bloom, Loughead, & Jeffrey, in press; Fletcher & Arnold, 2011). Furthermore, empirical evidence is also beginning to emerge from the sport transformational leadership literature where inspirational motivation has been shown to predict extra effort and group cohesion (e.g. Arthur, Woodman, Ong, Hardy, & Ntoumanis, 2011; Callow, Smith, Hardy, Arthur, & Hardy, 2009). The coach is thought to play a fundamental role in inspiring athletes by imparting a positive vision of the future. The strength of the athlete's vision will then be a key determinant of their motivation to work and train hard for the Olympic Games.

It is hypothesised that the transformational leader behaviours of inspirational motivation and fostering acceptance of group goals will predict vision. This is subtly different from the military model of vision, support and challenge; in the military model we also hypothesise that appropriate role modelling will predict vision. This is because in the military context the follower's vision are likely to be formulated around their direct leader because their leader is normally at the next stage of leadership in the organisation, hence the follower is likely to be promoted into that leadership role. However, in the sport context the coach is less likely to serve as the future image of the athlete. Consequently, role modelling is not theorised to predict vision in the sport model.

Support

Athletes need support in order to achieve their vision and to believe that the vision is attainable. A brief review of the social support literature (e.g. Blazer, 1982; Cohen & Wills, 1985; House, 1971; Rees & Hardy, 2000; Rees & Hardy, 2004; Rees, Hardy, & Evans, 2007; Sandler & Berrera, 1984; Sarason, Sarason, & Pierce, 1990) suggests that support is multidimensional in nature. The precise number and nature of the sub-dimensions is the subject of some debate (see, for example, Cutrona & Russell, 1990; Rees & Hardy, 2004; Rees et al., 2007), but evidence suggests that support includes emotional, esteem, informational and tangible aspects (Cutrona & Russell, 1990; Rees & Hardy, 2004). Another important consideration born out of the social support literature is the notion of received and perceived availability of support. That is, in order to capture the full spectrum of social support one needs to measure both received and perceived availability of support. Based on the literature, the definition of support is: *the extent to which emotional, esteem, informational, and tangible support is provided or is perceived as being available when needed.*

It is proposed that perceptions of support will help athletes to believe that their vision of Olympic success is achievable and that perceptions of support will contribute to athletes feeling valued and important. The relationship between support and job satisfaction is described within the social exchange theory framework (e.g. Blau, 1964; Gouldner, 1960). Social exchange theory suggests that people will respond positively to favourable treatment; that is, perceived favourable treatment (e.g. perceptions of support) will be reciprocated with positive affective outcomes (cf. Gouldner, 1960). In a related vein, organisational support theory (Eisenberger, Huntington, Hutchison, & Sowa, 1986; Shore & Shore, 1995) posits that the extent to which employees' socio-emotional needs are met will impact global beliefs that the organisation values their contributions and cares about their well-being. Supporting the above theoretical links, a meta-analysis (Rhoades & Eisenberger, 2002) found a strong positive relationship between perceived support and job satisfaction in 21 independent samples.

It is proposed that the leader behaviours of individual consideration, inspirational motivation and appropriate role modelling will load onto the support component of the model. That is, the more coaches display these behaviours the more supported their athletes will feel.

Challenge

The notion of *challenge* has received considerably less research attention. A notable exception to this is the challenge and hindrance stressor differentiation literature (see LePine, LePine, & Jackson, 2004; Podsakoff, LePine, & LePine, 2007). This theoretical perspective posits that there are two different types of stress in the workplace: *hindrance stress* and *challenge stress. Hindrance stress* includes role ambiguity, role conflict and hassles that are negatively related to performance (Beehr, Jex, Stacy, & Murray, 2000; LePine et al., 2004; Fox, Spector, & Miles, 2001; Podsakoff et al., 2007; Villanova, 1996; Woodman & Hardy, 2001). *Challenge stress* includes work demands and workload, which are positively related to performance (Beehr et al., 2000; Beehr, Walsh, & Taber, 1976; LePine et al., 2004; Podsakoff et al., 2007). It is the challenge component of the hindrance-challenge stress model that is of particular salience to the vision, support and challenge model. Podsakoff et al. stated that leaders who have high performance expectations of their followers and who set goals that stretch their followers will challenge their followers by increasing the magnitude of the discrepancy between a follower's current state and a future desired state. In Olympic terms, the gap between an athlete's current performance and the performance needed for Olympic success will be clearer to the athlete if the coach emphasises the Olympic expectations with ever more challenging goals. Consequently, the definition of challenge is: *an understanding of what needs to be done in order to achieve goals and the gap between current state and a future desired state, with the implicit assumption that the larger the discrepancy the more challenged followers are.*

Whilst the positive effects of challenge might not be as intuitively obvious as the positive impact of vision and support, there are some literatures that exhort the positive effects of challenge. For example, Seyle (1978) proposed that humans engaging in stressful and challenging activities often express enjoyment, even euphoria; McCall, Lombardo, and Morrison (1988) suggested that employees thrive when they have challenging job demands; and Campion and McClelland (1991) suggested that challenging job designs are associated with higher levels of satisfaction and involvement. Furthermore, several studies have reported a positive relationship between job challenges and affective outcomes such as satisfaction (e.g. Beehr, Glaser, Canali, & Wallwey, 2001; Cavanaugh, Boswell, Roehling, & Boudreau, 2000; Dwyer & Ganster, 1991). Consequently, there is good reason to believe that challenge will motivate athletes to train harder toward their Olympic aspirations.

It is proposed that the transformational leader behaviours of high performance expectations and intellectual stimulation will predict an athlete's perception of challenge. In other words, the more the coach displays these behaviours the greater the perceptions of challenge their athletes will have.

Summary

Olympic greatness will be achieved by the coach instilling a combination of vision, support and challenge in their athletes. The coach is at the centre of this process and will be a determining factor in creating the vision and shaping the athlete's perceptions of challenge and support. Clearly, athlete and context play a significant role. For example, athlete optimism may mediate or moderate the likelihood of athletes adopting the vision; and narcissism may impact the content of the vision to reflect some of the core personality factors associated with narcissism (e.g. personal glory). Equally, the support and the level of challenge may need to be adjusted for those athletes who have lower self-esteem. The relative quantity and quality of support and challenge will also likely have an impact. For example, very high levels of challenge accompanied by very little support will increase the likelihood of athlete burnout and withdrawal from sport. Conversely, high levels of support accompanied by low levels of challenge will likely lead to de-motivation because of boredom.

Most athletes train for the Olympic Games with dreams of Olympic glory. Coaches who can provide the right balance of vision, support and challenge will inspire their athletes to realise that dream and achieve Olympic greatness.

Notes on contributors

Calum Arthur is a lecturer in sports psychology at Bangor University, Wales and is a co-director of the Institute for the Psychology of Elite Performance. His principle research focus is the conceptualisation, measurement, impact, and training of leadership. Calum has published in sport and organizational psychology.

Lew Hardy's first PhD was in pure mathematics, he later went onto specialise in performance psychology. Lew has published over 150 full length research articles spanning broad range of psychological domains (e.g., stress and performance, self-concept, leadership, coaching, psychological skills, self-construct theory, and contexts (sport, exercise, organisational, military, and health).

Tim Woodman is head of School of Sport Health and Exercise Sciences at Bangor University, Wales, and is also a Co-Director of the Institute for the Psychology of Elite Performance. Tim's research spans a broad area of performance psychology which includes publications in, stress and performance, emotion regulation, personality, leadership, and risk taking.

References

Arthur, C.A. (2008). *Transformational leadership in Infantry recruit training in the British Army*. Wales: PhD dissertation, Bangor University.

Arthur, C.A., & Hardy, L. (2008). *Vision, support, and challenge model of transformational leadership*. Estoril, Portugal: Verbal presentation at the European College of Sports Science.

Arthur, C.A., & Hardy, L. (2011). *Vision support and challenge: Developing a measure in the military*. Hawaii, USA: Verbal presentation at the Association for Applied Sport Psychology Conference.

Arthur, C.A., Hardy, L., & Wagstaff, C. (2010). *Report on study into values based leadership, transactional leadership, and coaching on the internalisation of the core values of the British army, attitude and performance in phase 1 Army training*. Bangor, Wales: Bangor University, Institute for the Psychology of Elite Performance.

Arthur, C.A., Woodman, T., Ong, C.W., Hardy, L., & Ntoumanis, N. (2011). The role of athlete narcissism in moderating the relationship between coaches' transformational leader behaviors and athlete motivation. *Journal of Sport and Exercise Psychology, 33*, 3–19.

Bass, B.M. (1985). *Leadership and performance beyond expectations*. New York: Free Press.

Beehr, T.A., Walsh, J.T., & Taber, T.D. (1976). Relationships of stress to individually and organizationally valued states: Higher order needs as a moderator. *Journal of Applied Psychology, 61*, 35–40.

Beehr, T.A., Glaser, K.M., Canali, K.G., & Wallwey, D.A. (2001). Back to basics: Re-examination of demand-control theory of occupational stress. *Work and Stress, 15*, 115–130.

Beehr, T.A., Jex, S.M., Stacy, B.A., & Murray, M.A. (2000). Work stressor and coworker support as predictors of individual strain and job performance. *Journal of Organizational Behavior, 21*, 391–405.

Berlew, D.E. (1974). Leadership and organizational excitement. *California Management Review, 17*, 21–30.

Blau, P.M. (1964). *Exchange and power in social life*. New York: John Wiley & Sons.

Blazer, D. (1982). Social support and mortality in an elderly community population. *American Journal of Epidemiology, 115*, 684–694.

Bucci, J., Bloom, G.A., Loughead, T.M., & Carron, J.G. (in press). Ice hockey coaches' perceptions of athlete leadership. *Journal of Applied Sport Psychology*.

Callow, N., Smith, M., Hardy, L., Arthur, C.A., & Hardy, J. (2009). Measurement of transformational leadership and its relationship with team cohesion and performance level. *Journal of Applied Sport Psychology, 21*, 395–412.

Campion, M.A., & McClelland, C.L. (1991). Interdisciplinary examination of the costs and benefits of enlarged jobs: A job design quasi-experiment. *Journal of Applied Psychology, 76*, 186–198.

Cavanaugh, M.A., Boswell, W.R., Roehling, M.Z., & Boudreau, J.W. (2000). An empirical examination of self-report work stress among U.S. managers. *Journal of Applied Psychology, 85*, 65–74.

Chelladurai, P. (1990). Leadership in sports: A review. *International Journal of Sports Psychology, 21*, 328–354.

Chelladurai, P. (2007). Leadership in sports. In G. Tenenbaum & R.C. Gould (Eds.), *Handbook of sport psychology* (3rd ed., pp. 13–133). Hoboken, New Jersey: John Wiley & Sons.

Chelladurai, P., & Riemer, H. (1998). Measurement of leadership in sport. In J.L. Duda (Ed.), *Advances in sport and exercise psychology measurement* (pp. 227–253). Morgantown, WV: Fitness Information Technology.

Cohen, S., & Wills, T.A. (1985). Stress, social support, and the buffering hypothesis. *Psychological Bulletin, 98*(2), 310–357.

Conger, J.A., & Kanungo, R.N. (1988). *Charismatic leadership: The elusive factor in organizational effectiveness*. San Francisco: Jossey-Bass.

Cutrona, C.E., & Russell, D.W. (1990). Type of social support and specific stress: Toward a theory of optimal matching. In B.R. Sarason, I.G. Sarason, & G.R. Pierce (Eds.), *Social support: An international view* (pp. 19–366). New York: John Wiley & Sons.

Dungy, T., Robinson, D., Osborne, & Others (2010). *The greatest coach ever: Tony Dungy, David Robinson, Tom Osborne, and others pay tribute to the timeless wisdom and insights of John Wooden.* California, USA: Regal From Gospel Light Ventura.

Dwyer, D.J., & Ganster, D.C. (1991). The effects of job demands and control on employee attendance and satisfaction. *Journal of Organizational Behavior, 12,* 595–608.

Eisenberger, R., Huntington, R., Hutchison, S., & Sowa, D. (1986). Perceived organizational support. *Journal of Applied Psychology, 71,* 500–507.

Fletcher, D., & Arnold, R.S. (2011). A qualitative study of performance leadership and management in elite sport. *Journal of Applied Sport Psychology, 23,* 223–242.

Fox, S., Spector, P.E., & Miles, D. (2001). Counterproductive work behavior (CWB) in response to job stressor and organizational justice: Some mediator and moderator tests for autonomy and emotions. *Journal of Vocational Behavior, 59,* 291–309.

Gouldner, A.W. (1960). The norm of reciprocity: A preliminary statement. *American Social Review, 25,* 161–178.

Hardy, L., & Arthur, C.A. (2006). *Final report on study into the infantry training centre coaching and leadership initiative.* Bangor: Institute for the Psychology of Elite Performance, University of Wales.

Hardy, L., & Arthur, C.A. (2008). *A study into the section commanders' course at the Infantry Battle School Brecon.* Bangor: Institute for the Psychology of Elite Performance, Bangor University.

Hardy, L., Shariff, A., Munnoch, K., & Allsopp, A. (2004). *Can leadership development positively influence the psychological environment military recruit training? An interim report evaluation of the Royal Marine Coaching Advisory Team Leadership Innovative.* INM Report 2004.005. Alverstoke, Hants: The Institute of Naval Medicine.

Hardy, L., Arthur, C.A., Jones, G., Shariff, A., Munnoch, K., Isaacs, I., & Allsopp, A.J. (2010). The relationship between transformational leadership behaviours, psychological, and training outcomes in elite military recruits. *The Leadership Quarterly, 21,* 20–32.

House, R.J. (1971). A path-goal theory of leadership effectiveness. *Administrative Science Quarterly, 16,* 321–339.

Kim, K., Dansereau, F., & Kim, I. (2002). Extending the concept of charismatic leadership: An illustration using Bass's (1990) categories. In B.J. Avolio & F.J. Yammarino (Eds.), *Transformational and charismatic leadership: The road ahead* (pp. 35–66). Oxford: JA/Elsevier.

LePine, j.A., LePine, M.A., & Jackson, C.L. (2004). Challenge and hindrance stress: Relationship with exhaustion, motivation to learn, and learning performance. *Journal of Applied Psychology, 89,* 883–891.

McCall, M.W.Jr., Lombardo, M.M., & Morrison, A.M. (1988). *The lessons of experience. How successful executives develop on the job.* Lexington, MA: Lexington Books.

Nanus, B. (1992). *Visionary leadership.* San Francisco: Jossey-Bass.

Podsakoff, N.P., LePine, J.A., & LePine, M.A. (2007). Differential challenge stressor-hindrance stressor relationships with job turnover attitudes, turnover intentions, turnover, and withdrawal behavior: A meta-analyses. *Journal of Applied Psychology, 92,* 438–454.

Rees, T., & Hardy, L. (2000). An investigation of the social support experiences of high-level sports performers. *The Sports Psychologist, 14,* 327–347.

Rees, T., & Hardy, L. (2004). Matching social support with stressors: Effects on factors underlying performance in tennis. *Psychology of Sport and Exercise, 5,* 319–337.

Rees, T., Hardy, L., & Evans, L. (2007). Construct validity of the social support survey in sport. *Psychology of Sport and Exercise, 8,* 355–368.

Rhoades, L., & Eisenberger, R. (2002). Perceived organizational support: A review of the literature. *Journal of Applied Psychology, 87,* 698–714.

Riemer, H.A. (2007). Multidimensional model of coach leadership. In S. Jowett & D. Lavallee (Eds.), *Social psychology in sport* (pp. 7–74)Human Kinetics.

Sandler, I.N., & Berrera, M.Jr. (1984). Toward a multimethod approach to assessing the effects of social support. *American Journal of Community Psychology, 12,* 37–57.

Sarason, B.R., Sarason, I.G., & Pierce, G.R. (1990). Traditional views of social support and their impact on assessment. In B.R. Sarason, I.G. Sarason, & G.R. Pierce (Eds.), *Social support; An international view* (pp. 9–25). New York: John Wiley & Sons.

Seyle, H. (1978). *The stress of life.* New York: McGraw-Hill.

Shore, L.M., & Shore, T.H. (1995). Perceived organizational support and organizational justice. In R. Cropanzano & K.M. Kacmar (Eds.), *Organizational Politics, Justice, and Support: Managing Social Climate at Work* (pp. 149–164). Quorum Press.

Smith, R.E., & Smoll, F.L. (2007). Social-cognitive approach to coaching behaviors. In S. Jowett & D. Lavallee (Eds.), *Social psychology in sport* (pp. 75–90). Human Kinetics.

Vallee, C.N., & Bloom, G.A. (2005). Building a successful university program: Key and common elements of expert coaches. *Journal of Applied Sport Psychology, 17,* 179–196.

Villanova, P. (1996). Productive validity of situational constraints in general versus specific performance domains. *Journal of Applied Psychology, 81,* 532–547.

Woodman, T., & Hardy, L. (2001). A case study of organisational stress in elite sport. *Journal of Applied Sport Psychology, 19,* 131–141.

Developing rapid high-pressure team decision-making skills. The integration of slow deliberate reflective learning within the competitive performance environment: A case study of elite netball

Pam Richards[a], Dave Collins[b] and Duncan R.D. Mascarenhas[a]

[a]University of Glyndwr, Department of Sport and Exercise Science, Plas Coch Campus. Mold Road, Wrexham, LL12 2AWUK; [b]Institute of Coaching and Performance, University of Central Lancashire, Preston, UK

This paper explores the complexity of developing decision-making skills in elite netball. Using the attacking centre pass as a theme, we present a framework designed to develop decision-making capabilities of the coach, performers and the players collectively as a team. The paper exemplifies the integration of reflective practice principles into coaching strategies, as the cyclic link between the 'off-court' slow deliberate environment and the 'on-court' applied performance environment. Using a five-stage framework adapted from field hockey, we describe various reflective mechanisms which can be used and incorporated into coaching strategies to develop effective team decision making. The paper utilises a period of preparation from a world cup programme to demonstrate how a coach can empower players individually and collectively as a team to reflect 'on-action' which, in turn, facilitates the coach, players and team 'reflecting-for-action' and ultimately 'in-action'.

Introduction: integrating slow deliberate conscious learning to facilitate rapid team decision making

One of the key challenges for coaches in sport is developing both individual and team decision making (DM) skills. The parameters of the high-performance sporting environment mean that the difference between winning and losing has been reduced to the smallest of margins. Accordingly, coaches are required to create training environments which simultaneously integrate core components of physical, technical and tactical elements of the game into player's internalised plans, which are then capable of adapting to a variety of contextual situations (Richards, Mascarenhas, & Collins, 2009). Reflecting these concerns, the necessity to raise the performance bar requires coach-practitioners to creatively integrate and develop DM skills, simultaneously in line with the development of technical and tactical aspects. The ability to reflect and learn has therefore become an import component of elite sport (Hauw, 2009).

The dynamic environment of team sports is characterised by high intensity bouts of activity (Elferink-Gremer, Visscher, Lemmink, & Mulder, 2004) involving the integration of motor skills and cognitive functioning (Burke, 1997). Such dynamic team environments require individuals to perform skills under physical pressure (Sunderland & Nevill, 2005) and execute complex, multiple patterns of play (Richards, 2008) in order to secure success. These highly intensive activities, performed in dynamic movements of play, demand that players, individually and collectively, make decisions both quickly and accurately. This ability to execute skills and make decisions rapidly requires both tactical understanding and 'game intelligence' (Elferink-Gremer et al., 2004; Richards, 2005), and often incorporates both anticipatory and DM skills (Elferink-Gremer et al., 2004).

Reflecting this importance, a significant amount of literature over recent years has explored the nature of DM in sport. Comparison between the novice and expert performer has provided us with a wealth of literature relating to the superior performance of experts (Abernethy, Gill, Parks, & Packer, 2001; Beilock, Carr, Macmahon, & Starkes, 2002; McPherson, 1993; Starkes, 1987; Vickers, 1986), including a differentiation in DM ability. One clear conclusion to emerge is that experts identify and use different sources of information to novice performers (Abernethy, 2005; Müller, Abernethy, & Farrow, 2005). Although this literature has significantly contributed to our understanding, however, it has largely considered the development of *individual* DM skills, predominantly in a closed environment or in a perceptual training context and with little or no consideration of how individual DM can mesh effectively with group considerations such as team style. The question that appears unanswered relates to *how* we may best develop these DM skills *across* the players in a team: designing criteria with player involvement, developing elements in an integrated manner in training, then finally making them pressure resistant, enabling consistent but situation-appropriate execution at rapid speeds in the competitive environment. To date, this question has been addressed only tangentially, and then mostly in teaching environments with younger and inevitably lower level players (Light & Fawns, 2003).

Consequently, the question which remains to be addressed, and one which this paper now explores, is to consider how various 'slow time' approaches, for example, the use of team meetings, video discussion, etc., which lend themselves to elements of reflective practice, can best be exploited to drive changes in high speed/high pressure, on-pitch DM. The process of reflection also provides a framework for performers to be empowered and take responsibility for their own learning (Richards et al., 2009). Research indicates that, although such methods of delivery produce a lower level of understanding in the initial stages, this method generates long-term benefits to performance (Vickers, Reeves, Chambers, & Martell, 2004, cited in Williams & Hodges, 2004).

Team over individual DM: meeting this essential dimension for team sports

Each team is made up of different combinations of emotional states, individual personalities, playing background and experiences. It is these components that 'shape' the *trademarks* of a team and these parameters that need to be accounted for within high-performance DM. Therefore, the concept of empowering individuals through the reflective process enables the information that is required collectively, not only to be understood and internalised in relation to the team objectives but also in consideration of the wider parameters of the team (the specific of individuals). Figure 1 illustrates the process by which construction of slow deliberate conscious training environments may facilitate the development of rapid-fire action in dynamic and pressurised situations.

The model consists of three main stages with 'feedback' and 'feed-forward' mechanisms, facilitating a cyclical process for continual learning and development of constructs. Each of the three distinct stages addresses the development of cognitive structures (Mental Models, Shared Mental Models and Recognition Primed Decision Making) and the contextualisation of these structures in the specific environmental situations. The development of such knowledge structures also enables players and teams to attend to information that is significant in the display, prioritise and then order this information so that the correct course of action can be determined. The construction of such slow deliberate learning situations, whereby individuals are empowered to contribute to a solution, results in the content of these situations being internalised and stored (and also used 'off line' away from the team) by players. This provides for an increasingly robust mental model (MM) where, in future situations, information perceived in the environment is matched, enabling rapid execution of technical and tactical skills (Richards, 2005).

Reflecting these various issues, the purpose of this paper is to explore the DM process illustrated in Figure 1, which has proved to be successful in hockey (Richards, 2005; Richards et al., 2009) and football (Bate & Richards, 2011; Merola, Donovan, & Richards, 2009) to the more complex DM environment of netball. Netball provides a unique DM environment with a smaller playing area, rules of the game which restrict the ball carrier from moving with the ball to create options coupled with the pressure of having to pass the ball within 3 seconds of receiving

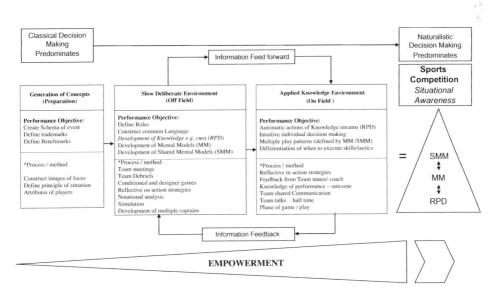

Figure 1. Cyclic decision-making model illustrating the slow deliberative conscious learning process transferred to the rapid quick fire actions (Speculative). (*Processes are examples to illustrate and not limited to those mentioned above.)

it, which results in an environment which has even greater DM challenges than most invasion sports.

The combination and interaction of 'off-court' and 'on-court' training enables the coaches to skilfully shape not only their own decisions but more importantly the team's, thus generating more effective DM in the 'applied knowledge environment' (on-court). DM development is achieved in a five-stage process. Stage 1 generates the coach's vision of performance and the development of an MM for the specific component which is the focus for development. Stage 2 empowers the players enabling them to contribute their knowledge and experience to the identified component. This second stage results in the development of a team shared mental model (SMM) and the development of a common language. Stage three builds the complexity by adding more detail to the SMM and the development of players' own internalised plans. The coach shapes the learning of the players at this stage by layering the complexity and increasing the understanding of the players. This period could range from days to months depending on performer level and the component being addressed. Stage four relates to the maintenance of knowledge when players are away from the performance setting. In some environments, stages three and four are integrated. Stage five is the application of and the transfer of learning to the ultimate performance setting.

Methods and outcomes

Background to the consultancy work

At the time of writing the first author had been working with an elite netball coach, her assistants and international players for a period of two years in preparation for the 2013 world cup. Much of this work has been adapted and transferred from the first author's experiences of working as an international coach in hockey. Over a period of 19 years of coaching hockey internationally across a range of age groups from juniors to seniors, a key challenge has been the development of a team of autonomous 'thinking' individuals who take responsibility for their actions individually, but who collectively position their decisions and actions in the context of the team. The initial desire to learn more about how *autonomous thinking players* could be developed resulted in exploring the concept of reflective practice. Over several years, various strategies which incorporated *'reflection on-action'* and *'reflection in-action'* were experimented with (Richards, 2005; Richards & Ghaye, 2004) both into the players' training/ competition and the first author's own practice (Richards & Ghaye, 2004). Therefore, the challenge faced was to transfer the experience from hockey across into the more complex environment of netball and to facilitate both players and coaches thinking, not only *'on-action'* and where possible *'in-action'* but to develop the capabilities to *'reflect-for-action'*.

Integrating reflective practice to develop team decision making: a five-stage approach

Stage 1. Development of coaches' (mental model) situational framework

Aim

The first objective of phase one was to establish the vision of the coach (coaches' MM) with regard to the particular aspect identified as the focus for development, the *attacking centre pass*.

The *attacking centre pass* relates to the action to start the game. Each team alternatively takes a centre pass, which requires the player playing the 'Centre' position to pass the ball to one of her teammates who is allowed to enter the centre third of the court. These players are the Wing Attack (WA); Goal Attack (GA); Wing Defence (WD) and Goal Defence (GD). The *attacking centre pass* is a key concept for coaches in netball, as 50% of the time any team has possession thus enabling them to control the play. The challenge then is to convert a team's attacking centre pass to a goal scoring opportunity; thus scoring a goal from your own centre is referred to as a *centre pass completion* and is one of the key objectives for any team.

In general practice, elite coaches distinguish themselves from less experienced coaches by possessing a higher level of both declarative and procedural knowledge (Elferink-Gremser et al., 2004). Coaches therefore are continually trying to develop both their declarative knowledge (*knowing what to do*) and their procedural knowledge (*knowing when and how things should be done*) about existing aspects of their sport and new components which develop. The construction of both procedural and declarative knowledge is frequently obtained from informal learning environments (Nelson, Cushion, & Potrac, 2006) and incorporates reflecting both '*on-practice*' and '*in-practice*' situations (Nelson et al., 2006). We would argue that the development of declarative and procedural knowledge in coaches can then be progressed to develop '*reflection-for-action*'; this is where there is an accumulation of knowledge which can be used to construct predictive action.

The initial objective of this first stage therefore was to construct the development of the coaches' MM for the identified situation (in this case study, *what the perfect centre pass would look like*). MMs are constructed from perception, vision, imagination and comprehension of the task and have been classified as a set of assumptions (Johnson-Laid & Shafir, 1993). MMs are only valuable to the individual who creates them (Westbrook, 2006), so it is important that the coaches, and later the players, are empowered to shape the construction of these MMs. We would argue that the MM constructed by the coach at this initial stage represents the vision of what the ultimate '*perfect*' centre pass would look like. Furthermore, they would refer to this initial vision of the centre pass as the *alpha version*, as at this stage it does not incorporate the opinions of players. This initial '*alpha version*' is subsequently adapted to incorporate the player's perspective in stages 2 and 3 (giving them ownership) and through the interaction between coach and performer will eventually become the *beta version* (the one that is performed in action).

To confirm, however, the fundamental focus of the first stage is to facilitate the coaches establishing their vision for performance (*alpha version*). Crucially, it is only when the alpha version (the coaches' vision) is established that it can then be divided into small sections or phases and then be presented to the players in more manageable chunks (a *top-down approach*) (Richards et al., 2009). For example the centre pass can be broken down into *first phase* (the first pass made by the centre player), then *second phase* (the pass from the initial receiver) before the subsequent phases, *entry into the attacking circle* and *circle play* can be discussed. Devolving the coaches' vision (*alpha version*) of performance into small sections enables the information to be presented to the players in more manageable chunks (see Means, Salas, Crandall, & Owen Jacobs, 1993). This incorporation of the player's contributions (*bottom up approach*; Richards et al., 2009) reshapes the coaches' vision (*alpha version*) and results in the formation of the new final *beta version* (reflection of coaches and players) which would be executed in matches. This process of developing individual, then team MM can drive expectations of individuals and can generate processes from which others can learn (Standifer & Bluedorn, 2006).

Method

In order to establish the mental models of the lead coach and the coaching team with regard to the *attacking centre pass concept*, a framework was designed. The framework took the format of a booklet to facilitate discussions amongst the coaches. Coaches simultaneously undertook project work (notational analysis of the game at world level) relating to *centre pass play*. This framework facilitated coaches discussing the core elements and principles of the *attacking centre pass*, the identification of a shared common language and agreement of the roles and responsibilities of players for the centre pass attacking strategies. This stage incorporated coaches developing a greater level of both declarative and procedural knowledge from engaging in discussion relating to the framework, resulting in the *alpha version* of what the *centre pass* would look like when performed on the world stage.

Outcome

The results of the interaction and engagement of the coaching team in this initial stage resulted in the establishment of a coaches' shared vision (SMM) of what the *centre passes* would look like.

Discussion

The framework resulted in the coaching team developing a shared vision (SMM) of the centre pass, an increased understanding of team member roles and an improved understanding of patterns of play (Standifer & Bluedorn, 2006). The development of this SMM not only facilitated an improved player understanding but also ensured that a consistent message from the coaching team would be presented to the players. It also reduced coaches getting distracted and trying to cover too many aspects of performance, and channelled the delivery in the direction of achieving a successful *centre pass completion*. A second benefit was the development of a shared common language amongst the coaches. This removed any confusion and simultaneously enabled the visual concept (a certain play pattern) to be identified verbally. Without this initial coaches' vision (the *alpha version*) there is no framework to build the detail of more complex play, to reach world-class performance.

Stage 2. Developing a team decision-making framework with players

Aim

The second phase of the process required the development of a team SMM relating to the *attacking centre passes*. The SMM would help to ensure that the perception and the subsequent co-ordination of activities of all team players and the coaches were the same (Thevenot, 2009). The impact of the SMM would be a greater connectivity between players and a co-ordination of 'on-court actions' to achieve the objects of team play. In addition, a core common language would develop from the team to represent aspects relating to play.

Method

The first author consulted with coaches with regard to the structure that would be implemented to facilitate the development of the players' framework for developing DM relating to the *attacking centre pass*. Stage 2 consisted of theory sessions (slow deliberate environment) and practical/match sessions (applied knowledge environment) (see Figure 1 which illustrates the interaction of these two environments). Phases 2 and 3 took place in a week's residential holding camp. This initial meeting with players (Stage 2) took place on day one of this holding camp.

Theory session (slow deliberate environment). This initial player's meeting consisted of four parts. The first part of the meeting reviewed the work which had been done to date. This would contextualise the new material the players would be learning that day.

This review revisited the establishment of team 'trademarks' (these are the qualities the squad perceived to be essential for a world-class team), which had been identified earlier in the support process. The second part of the meeting contextualised the focus for the attacking centres in context of the work which would be undertaken throughout the week in the holding camp. The third part of the meeting commenced the work relating to the *attacking centre pass*. In this part of the meeting, players were presented with a task which required them to work in small groups. The task required players to identify and analyse the principles and strategies that they considered to be important to create a successful attacking centre pass, asking them to reflect back on experience gained within this squad but also experience gained from other netball environments. Players then presented this information back to the whole team. After all had presented their thoughts back to the group and relevant discussions were held, the lead coach then presented a pre-prepared PowerPoint slideshow with her ideas on the same situation. During the presentation of information, both from players and the coach, the task facilitated

Figure 2.   An example of a decision-making clip observed by players to illustrate the centre pass. (Example taken from phase 4). Full video available online at: http://dx.doi.org/10.1080/14623943.2012.670111.

discussion and interaction between the players themselves and the players and the coaches. Although the information presented by various individuals had similar content, the discussion provided the opportunity to clarify language which would be used by the team and for a SMM (incorporating both perceptions of players and coaches – the start of the beta version of the attacking centre pass vision) to be constructed. Finally, three video clips of international netball play involving centre passes were presented to the players. This facilitated further discussion relating to key principles of play, language, playing elements, the roles of key players and attacking strategies that would be played and contributed to the organisation and began contextualisation of player knowledge (Hauw, 2009).

Practical session (applied knowledge environment). In order to contextualise these off-field activities and increase the complexity of the playing concepts relating to *attacking centre passes*, both in terms of developing existing levels of knowledge and introducing new aspects, a practical session was delivered on-court led by the coaching team. The session was a blend of interaction between players and coaches, where the coaches facilitated players exploring key concepts, roles and responsibilities that had been identified and discussed during the theory session, thus once again reinforcing a SMM.

Outcome

The main objective of this stage was to present players with the coaches' vision of the concept of the *attacking centre pass* and to empower the players to contribute to the reshaping of this vision so that ultimately a shared vision (SMM) emerged. A crucial corollary to this process was the development of a shared common language, a shared perception of the objectives to be achieved and a shared understanding of the roles which players would perform. For example, the concept of a player supporting the ball carrier in a specified tactical position was identified using a particular word.

Discussion

This second stage was crucial in establishing a team SMM for the *attacking centre passes*. The integration of reflective practice principles into coaching strategies encouraged performers to engage with their own development and developing a shared understanding of team concepts. The empowerment of the players to contribute to the development of the team SMM resulted in the players attaching greater value to the SMM (Westbrook, 2006). Furthermore, the empowerment of players to contribute to the team SMM (in the way which it was done) enabled players to contextualise the information in relation to their own performance (and that of others) and in doing so created internalised plans of performance (cf. Richards et al., 2009). The development of a shared common language also facilitated an increased understanding as players learned team concepts at an accelerated rate. This was demonstrated with a greater connectivity between players (Richards et al., 2009) during match play. Figure 3 in the next section illustrates the accelerated learning of team concepts and increased connectivity between players in relation to attacking centre performance indicators and the development over the process.

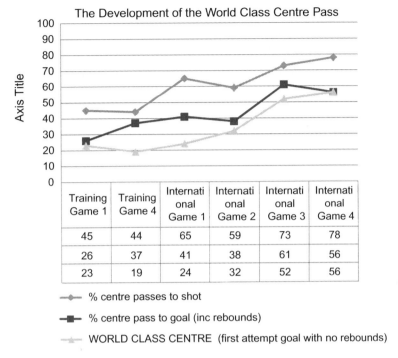

The Development of the World Class Centre Pass

	Training Game 1	Training Game 4	International Game 1	International Game 2	International Game 3	International Game 4
	45	44	65	59	73	78
	26	37	41	38	61	56
	23	19	24	32	52	56

—◆— % centre passes to shot

—■— % centre pass to goal (inc rebounds)

—▲— WORLD CLASS CENTRE (first attempt goal with no rebounds)

Figure 3. Time series to illustrate the development of connective play through the application of a developed SMM over the 31-day process.

Stage 3. Developing on-court decision making in players

Aim

The objective of this stage was to transfer the classroom generated ideas to the court. As a function of this physical practice it was anticipated that this would lead to greater detail and complexity of the team SMM and contributed to the further development of their own internalised plans of performance (Richards, 2005; Richards et al., 2009).

Method

During holding camp, four consecutive matches were played and used as a vehicle to facilitate both team and individual reflection. Games were captured and Dartfish software was used to analyse the key identified performance indicators (see Table 1 for Performance Indicators). This analysis was conducted for two reasons. First, it would enable a selection of clips to be identified for future off-court discussions, and second, to test the effect of SMM development on performance. The first author and the coaching team viewed all the clips relating to the *attacking centre pass* and identified six clips (averaging 14 seconds in length) that best represented the playing constructs which had previously been discussed. The clips represented three types of *attacking centre pass* strategies. Three clips related to strategy one, two clips related to strategy two and one clip related to strategy three. Work by Merola, Donovan and Richards (2009) and Bate and Richards (2011) in football highlighted that when players reflected on playing strategies (team tactics) there

Table 1.   Operational definitions used for notational analysis and statistical analysis.

Performance indicator	Operational definition
Number of centres	The attacking centre pass relates to the action to start the game.
P0	Passes made from the starting centre and not secured on the first pass.
P1 – pass to centre	Passes made and received in the centre third area of the court immediately following the centre pass and not progressed onto attacking third.
P2 – pass into attack1/3	Successful centre passes received and progressed onto the attacking third of the court but did not progress into the circle.
P3 – pass into circle	Successful centre passes received and progressed through the court to be secured in the attacking circle.
Centre to shot – shot missed	A passage of play where the ball moves from the first centre pass to the circle and a shot is taken. Possession is maintained by the team who took the centre pass. A goal is not scored.
Centre to goal with rebounds	A passage of play where the ball moves from the first centre pass to the circle and a shot is taken. Possession is maintained by the team who took the centre pass. A goal is scored but after the ball has rebounded from the first (or subsequent attempts) at goal.
World-class centre	A passage of play where the ball moves from the first centre pass to the circle and a shot is taken. Possession is maintained by the team who took the centre pass. A goal is scored on the first attempt at goal.

was a transfer of knowledge from the main focus of reflection to similar related areas. Based on these findings, strategy one was perceived by the coaching team to be the most important so had the main emphasis placed on it, with expected transference to other strategies which had been discussed with the team. The other strategies were not ignored but had a reduced focus at this stage.

Developing decision making by reflecting on video. Players were given a decision-making booklet, with a series of two types of sheets (sheet A and sheet B) endorsed by the coaching team. Sheet A would be used to review clips 1, 2, 4 and 5. This required the players to write their reflection at specific phases of the *attacking centre pass* based on the observation and reflection on the video. At phase one (when the centre player was standing with the ball waiting for the whistle) the players were asked to reflect on the cues in the environment which they needed to be aware of (this matched the team SMM). Phase two asked players to reflect and make a decision as to where the most effective pass should be played at certain key points in the clip. For clips 1, 2, 4 and 5 the video was played and stopped at the phases outlined above and the players wrote their responses in the decision book. After the players had written their responses, the clip was played again and the group discussed the clip in relation to cues in the environment, role of the teammates and the contextualisation of the clip in context of the team SMM. For clips 3 and 6 the same process was completed; however, additional information was asked for on sheet B at this point. This required the players to write in detail what their role was and what was the role of others in the specific situation. After the completion of clips 3 and 6 the team once again discussed the clips verbally. Finally, the players were presented with their statistics from the match they were reflecting upon. This included established on-going statistical feedback (such as turnovers, goals etc.) in addition to specific statistics relating to the *attacking centre passes*. This process was repeated for each of the four consecutive matches played during holding camp.

Outcome

Several key outcomes were identified at this stage. The immediate impact was that a higher level of connective play on the court resulted from the increased understanding of their own and teammates' roles. This is illustrated in the inferential statistical data in phase 3 and is pictorially displayed in Figure 3.

As the sessions during the week developed, players became more confident at discussing a wider variety of aspects within the team meeting. This was also translated into the increased complexity and detail written in the DM booklets and verbally discussed. Finally, changes were evident through a clear trend to comment on a wider variety of visual information which was being perceived in the playing environment and more comments that pertained to both their own roles as well as the roles of teammates. Players developed a detailed understanding of their own specific position and could contextualise this in relation to the team SMM. Team discussion also facilitated an increase in the complexity of their team SMM developed for the *attacking centre pass*. This was demonstrated with the team discussing additional information which related to the specific role of players at various phases of the centre pass. In addition, there was evidence that knowledge specifically learnt relating to one particular attacking centre pass strategy was transferred and applied to other playing contexts experienced through the game. For example, tactical play relating to the WA was directly transferred to the GA even though video footage of the GA in the same situation had not been observed.

Discussion

In tandem, these approaches enabled an increased shared understanding of the playing concepts, together with greater individual clarity on the expected roles which would be performed by individuals. As a result, team identity was strengthened, specifically in the performance context. This was evident with a greater level of connectivity between players on the court as there was a higher level of co-ordination of players' actions to achieve the teams playing objective (SMM – *beta version*). This enabled players to respond quickly to high-pressure decisions and develop the layers of complexity to incorporate a range of multiple play patterns into the team's performance. Evidence to support this was reflected in coaches' comments and statistics, as presented in Table 2 and 3, with Figure 3 displaying the initial learning at this stage and the subsequent learning which occurred. What was significant was the increasing complexity with regard to the detail and the attacking strategy, and the understanding of when specific action needed to be played in the performance context. This development facilitated a change in the '*benchmarking*' criteria by which the team assessed itself. Although traditional values that had previously been used to assess performance were maintained, additional criteria relating to 'world-class' performance (relating to the centre pass) were introduced by the consultant and are reflected in Figure 3.

Stage 4. Maintaining decision making ...

Aim

This phase was implemented with the focus of maintaining each player's knowledge in the two-week period between leaving holding camp and departing for an overseas tour.

Table 2.   Performance indicators illustrate development of SMM and team connectivity as play patterns reflect a higher percentage of centre passes reaching the circle area.

	Training Game 1 Raw data %	Training Game 4 Raw data %	International Match – 1 Raw data %	International Match – 2 Raw data %	International Match – 3 Raw data %	International Match – 4 Raw data %
P0	1	5	2	3	3	1
Ball not received on first pass	3%	19%	6%	8%	7%	2%
P1	4	1	3	5	4	1
Ball received in centre third from centre pass	13%	3%	9%	14%	9%	2%
P2	10	6	8	7	5	7
Ball progressed to attacking third from centre pass	32%	22%	23%	19%	11%	15%
P3	16	15	22	22	32	37
Ball received in circle from centre pass	52%	56%	62%	59%	73%	81%

Note: See Table 1 for definitions of performance indicators.

Method

Prior to departing on tour, the squad received a DM workbook together with three video clips through the post. Players were either assigned the 'Attackers Decision booklet' or the 'Defenders Decision booklet'. The allocation of the booklet was based on the main position the player played in the squad. Both booklets consisted of two questions relating to the clips. Question 1 required the player to reflect on the cues in the playing environment and question 2 related to the specific action of their own role and their teammates' role within the same playing unit, e.g. attacking or defensive units. Question 2 separated the *attacking centre passes* into phases. The difference between the attacking and defensive DM booklet related to the detail which was required for question 2. Attacking players made reference to the role of team members in the attacking unit while the defence players provided detail for fellow players playing in the defensive unit. The aim was to develop unit specific declarative and procedural knowledge of the players. The clips viewed by both attack and defence were identical and related to 'best practice'. Players completed the work and presented the information to the team during day one of the tour.

Outcome

Players completed the task by observing the clips and answering the related questions. Reflections from coaches indicated that a high level of the material which had been introduced at camp had been maintained and did not have to be reviewed. This facilitated players maintaining specific information relating to their own role

Table 3.   Statistics representing the progression in centre pass to completion for world-class criteria.

SUMMARY STATISTICS (%)	Training Game 1	Training Game 4	International Game 1	International Game 2	International Game 3	International Game 4
% centre passes to shot	45	44	65	59	73	78
% centre pass to goal (including rebounds)	26	37	41	38	61	56
WORLD CLASS CENTRE (first attempt goal with no rebounds)	23	19	24	32	52	56

and the role of players who played in close proximity to them, but was contextualised in the context of the team shared mental model. This was to ensure retention of information and simulate a review session at the start of the tour.

Discussion

Discussion between the first author and the coaching team with regard to the feedback of the first meeting on tour suggested that the players had engaged with the process at stage 4. Performance indicators in Table 3 illustrate that knowledge and application of centre passes was maintained from the last match of holding camp to the first international match of the tour. Centre passes reaching the circle increased from 56% in camp to 62% for match one on tour. However, the players' level of written communication on tour was not as high as previously observed in the holding camp but it was felt by the coaching team that the verbal comments presented by the players in the meeting on tour demonstrated a detailed and comprehensive understanding of the clips and team concepts.

Stage 5. Application and transfer to the world stage …

Aim

The final objective at this stage was the transfer of all the learning which had occurred in a competitive match played on the world stage. The squad played a four-game test series against a junior national squad currently ranked in the top four in the world at junior level.

Method

Replicating the procedure used in stage three, reflective activities took place after each of the four international matches. These games were video recorded and analysed for the performance indicators, as previously stated above. From analysis of the video a selection of six clips were identified and used to facilitate a team debrief / feedback session. As outlined in stage three the players viewed the clips and through a combination of verbal discussion and written information reflected back on (1) the team, (2) the unit and (3) each individual player's performance. Match statistics were also presented for team performance and specifically for attacking centre passes.

Outcome

As the team is still using the vocabulary, concepts and SMM that are presented here, in order to maintain their competitive advantage it is not possible to fully report specific examples of outcomes from each section. However, analysis of performance from both a quantitative perspective (team statistics) and qualitatively from feedback by both players and coaches during the process indicated that the integration of reflective practice and video clips facilitated a shared understanding of the team SMM with regard to the attacking centre pass. The ability of the players and coaches to reflect both '*on-action*' and '*in-action*' had facilitated the squad engaging with '*reflection-for-action*'. Playing concepts could be discussed and reflected on retrospectively and from this reflection future actions could be proposed to facilitate more effective DM in 'live' match play.

Match statistics. The development of a SMM is reflected in the performance indicators in Figure 4. Figure 4 illustrated the increasing frequency in which the *attacking centre passes* penetrated the attacking circle with a progression of 55% in the first match in camp to 87% for the fourth international game on tour (a 31-day time period). In addition, not only did the frequency of the centre pass reaching the circle increase but also, as Table 2 highlights, there were parallel improvements in quality of play. Using the world-class criteria established for *centre pass to completions* during this paper, the number of world-class centres performed in matches increased from 23% in holding camp to 56% for the final international match. This again is reflected visually in Figure 3 and statistically in Table 3. Furthermore, inferential statistics using the Mann-Whitney U (independent sample) produced a significant difference of $p = 0.35$ and $p = 0.27$, respectively, for analysis *of world class centres* and *centre passes penetrating the circle* when analysed in a ratio of centre passes performed in the training camp compared to the international stage.

Discussion

The ability of the team to incorporate '*reflection on-practice*' at a team and individual level allowed '*reflection-for-action*' by coaches and players. This accelerated the transferring of team SMMs into more effective DM on the court against superior opposition on the world stage. In addition, '*reflection-in-action*' and '*reflection-on-action*' from the players' perspective (and also from the coaches) had increased their understanding of team concepts. The reinforcement of reflecting on individual and team performance has developed the complexity of the playing concept and exposed the players to new experiences.

Global results and discussion

This section can only briefly highlight and explore some of the key issues identified in the paper, but it is hoped it will contribute to informing the development of DM within coaching practice.

Development of coaches

It is essential that in the process of developing DM in teams that the initial version of what performance will look like is perceived by the coach and their coaching

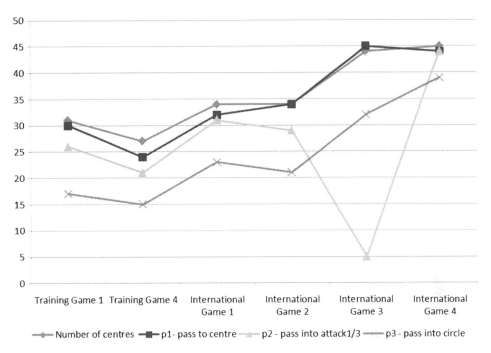

Figure 4. The connectivity of players owing to SMM is reflected in the increase frequency of the centre pass reaching the attacking circle.

team. This *alpha vision* as referred to in this paper provided the foundations for the building of more complex layers. It is only when this *alpha version* exists that it can be broken down to chunks and presented to the players. The empowering of the players to contribute to the discussions relating to the alpha version results in the development of a SMM and shared common language amongst coaches and the team. The establishment of this new *beta version* then enables criteria to be developed that can be used to benchmark criteria to assess both current and future performance. At this stage it is critical that the correct criterion is applied as this will establish the performance bar.

Furthermore, the layering of information as the concepts are rebuilt gradually increases the complexity of the playing component being developed. The interaction of the slow deliberate 'off-field' environment and the applied playing context of 'on-field' allows the player, and team collectively to 'reflect-on-performance'. This interaction of these two environments enables the players and team to 'reflect-for-action' which accelerates the transferring of knowledge to the performance context. This in turn produces a greater ability to '*reflect-in-action*' as the team and each individual takes increasing responsibility for their own learning and 'on-field' DM is improved.

Developing team DM

A key component of team DM is the development of a SMM. This cannot be developed in isolation of the players but in conjunction with them. It is only when the players are empowered to contribute to the vision will they value it (Westbrook,

2006). This is vital in the processing of information as not only will it 'shape' and define their own role but it will result in a greater understanding and appreciation of the contribution of team members. This will increase the connectivity between players and facilitate more effective play, especially in complex and pressured situations as illustrated in the paper.

In addition, we would argue that the 'owning' of the vision will place a value on information which is received and this will have a 'weighting' of importance attached to it (Richards et al., 2009). The value attached to incoming information will determine how it is attended to and what priority is given to it, but, more importantly, where it will be placed in cognitions of the player in context of performance.

Implications for coaching

One of the major impacts of the processes outlined in this paper is that it provides a framework for the development of an identified component of performance. This channels the coaches' attention to the key issues which need to be addressed and prevents a coach becoming distracted with trying to address too many issues. This focus enables a more effective coaching delivery and reduces isolation of the coach, as the process requires the engagement with the rest of the team and performers. The implication for coaches is that it does require additional time in planning, which as we know in coaching is a precious commodity. In order for a coach to develop the skills of '*reflecting-for-action*' with the desire to influence future performances there needs to be the ability to proactively reflect both on previous performances and on-going performances.

Another implication lies with the challenge which coaches face in exploring innovative but effective methods of engaging the players with the combination of 'slow deliberate environments', where knowledge will be layered and shaped by athletes and coaches simultaneously, and the transferring of this knowledge to the performance setting. The skill of coaches to establish the alpha version and the ability to empower the players to contribute to the reshaping of the vision is fundamental in the development of team DM. Without this shared vision, the infrastructure of role clarity and a shared common language will not be established.

Notes on contributors

Pam Richards is an international hockey coach and FIH coach. Pam is a Senior Lecturer at Glyndwr University and is studying for her PhD in performance intelligence and decision making in sport. Pam is actively involved in researching decision making in hockey, football and netball. Pam provides consultancy support to an elite netball squad.

Dave Collins is Professor and Director of the Institute of Coaching and Performance. An experienced coach, coach educator and sport psychologist, he has recently returned to academe after three years as Performance Director of UK Athletics.

Duncan Mascarenhas is a BASES Accredited Sport & Exercise Psychologist and Senior Lecturer at Glyndwr University with a PhD in referee decision making. He has a range of experience in decision-making training for national governing bodies in the UK, USA and New Zealand.

References

Abernethy, B. (2005). *Sport expertise: From theory to practice [Abstract].* AIS, Australia: Applied Sport Expertise and Learning Workshop.

Abernethy, B., Gill, D., Parks, S.L., & Packer, S.T. (2001). Expertise and the perception of kinematic and situational probability information. *Perception, 30,* 233–252.

Bate, B., & Richards, P. (2011). *Developing team decision making capabilities in a professional football team.* Paper presented at the British Association of Sport and Exercise Sciences National Student Conference, Chester.

Beilock, S.L., Carr, T.H., Macmahon, C., & Starkes, J.L. (2002). When paying attention becomes counterproductive: Impact of divided verses skilled focused attention on novice and experienced performance of senorimotor skills. *Journal of Experimental Psychology: Applied, 8,* 6–16.

Burke, L.M. (1997). Fluid balance during team sports. *Journal of Sport Sciences, 5,* 45–88.

Elferink-Gemser, M.T., Visscher, C., Lemmink, K.A.P.M., & Mulder, T.W. (2004). Relation between multidimensional performance characteristics and level of performance in talented youth field hockey players. *Journal of Sport Sciences, 22,* 1053–1063.

Hauw, D. (2009). Reflective practice in the heart of training and competition: The course of experience analysis for enhancing elite acrobatics athletes' performances. *International Journal of Reflective Practice, 10*(3), 353–363.

Johnson-Laid, P., & Shafir, E. (1993). Reasoning and decision making. Amsterdam: Elsevier. Cited in R. Hoffman (2007). Expertise out of Context. Proceedings of the Sixth International Conference on Naturalistic Decision Making (219–62). New York: Taylor and Francis.

Light, R., & Fawns, R. (2003). Knowing the Game: Integrating speech and action in games teaching through TGfU. *Quest, 55,* 161–176.

McPherson, S.L. (1993). Knowledge representation and decision making in sport. In J.L. Starkes & F. Allard (Eds.), *Cognitive issues in motor expertise* (pp. 159–188). Amsterdam: North Holland.

Means, B., Salas, E., Crandall, B., & Owen Jacobs, T. (1993). Training decision makers for the real world. In G.A. Klein, J. Orasanu, R. Calderwood, & C.E. Zsambok (Eds.), *Decision-making in action: Models and methods* (pp. 306–326). Norwood, NJ: Ablex.

Merola, T., Donovan, T., & Richards, P. (2009). *Developing decision making skill in youth footballers.* Paper presented at the British Association of Sport and Exercise Sciences National Student Conference, Aberystwyth.

Müller, S., Abernethy, B., & Farrow, D. (2005). How do world class cricket batsmen anticipate a bowler's intention? Manuscript for publication, cited in B. Abernethy, (2005).

Nelson, L., Cushion, C., & Potrac, P. (2006). Formal, nonformal and informal coach learning: A holistic conceptualisation. *Journal of Sports Science and Coaching, 1*(3), 247–254.

Richards, P. (2005, June). *Empowering the decision-making process in the competitive sport environment through using reflective practice. Can performance intelligence be taught?* Paper presented at the 4th Carfax International Conference on Reflective Practice, Gloucester.

Richards, P. (2008). *Empowering the team: Is it an effective way to facilitate an autonomous performance environment?.* Paper presented at the Sports Coaching and the Sociological Imagination Conference, Manchester Metropolitan University, Manchester.

Richards, P., & Ghaye, T. (2004). Thinking teamwork: Being the best through reflective practices. *Sport and Exercise Scientist, 2*(December).

Richards, P., Mascarenhas, D., & Collins, D. (2009). Implementing reflective practice approaches with elite team athletes: Parameters of success. *International Journal of Reflective Practice, 10*(3), 353–363.

Standifer, R., & Bluedorn, A. (2006). Alliance management teams and entrainment: Sharing temporal metal models. *Human Relations, 59*(7), 903–927.

Starkes, J.L. (1987). Skill in field hockey: The nature of cognitive advantage. *Journal of Sport Psychology, 9,* 146–160.

Sunderland, C., & Nevill, M.E. (2005). High intensity intermittent running and field hockey skill performance in the heat. *Journal of Sport Sciences, 23*(5), 531–540.

Thevenot, C. (2009). Arithmetic word problem solving: Evidence for the construciont of mental models. *Acta Psychological, 133*, 90–95.

Vickers, J.N. (1986). The resequencing task: Determining expert-novice differences in the organisation of a movement sequence. *Research Quarterly for Exercise and Sport, 69,* 111–128.

Vickers, J.N., Reeves, M.A., Chambers, K.L., & Martell, S. (2004). *Decision training: Cognitive strategies for enhancing motor performance* (pp. 103–120). London: Routledge.

Williams, M., & Hodges, N.J. (2004). *Skill acquisition in sport – Research, theory and practice*. London: Routledge.

Westbrook, L. (2006). Mental models: A theoretical overview and preliminary study. *Journal of Information Services, 32*, 563–579.

Reflections on a dream: towards an understanding of factors Olympic coaches attribute to their success

Janet L. Currie[a] and Shelley Oates-Wilding[b]

[a]*Learning Cultures & Practices, University of Technology Sydney (UTS), Sydney, Australia;* [b]*Hawaii Canoe and Kayak Team (HCKT), Honolulu, USA*

When coaches watch our athletes in the Olympic Games competing as the best in the world, we fill with pride in what we have nurtured and produced as a nation. However, often less visible, yet no less integral to this success is the Olympic coach. While defining what it means to be an effective coach is quite difficult and controversial, most would agree that to have reached Olympic coaching level is to have reached the pinnacle or ultimate level of your sport. What sets these coaches apart enabling them to be the best in the world, emerging to become leaders in their chosen field? This paper fills a gap in the current literature by identifying the most significant factors eight Olympic coaches attribute to their own success and fulfilment of goals. Analysis revealed that having a passion and commitment to wanting to succeed, past experience as an athlete, learning from other coaches/mentors, focusing on the needs of the athlete and a need to contribute were the key factors identified as helping them reach their dream of becoming an Olympic coach.

Becoming a high-performance sports coach

Sports coaches today are required to use an effective mix of organisational skills, teaching strategies, communication skills and group management practices, based on a sound understanding of sports science (Schembri, 2001, p. 3). While the precise role of elite or high-performance coaches is often varied (Robinson, 2010), it has been established that this group usually undertakes a range of tasks aiming to produce gold-medal winning performances by athletes competing in international competitions such as the Olympics (Mallett, 2010; Saury & Durand, 1998). The role of a high-performance coach normally involves a more intensive personal and professional commitment, extensive interpersonal contact with athletes, and greater focus on intense preparation and competition involvement, focus on performance standards, variables and competition outcomes, including longer-term goals, compared with colleagues working at the non-elite or participation level (Lyle, 2002, p. 53). Figure 1 highlights some of the main roles of the sports coach, with those

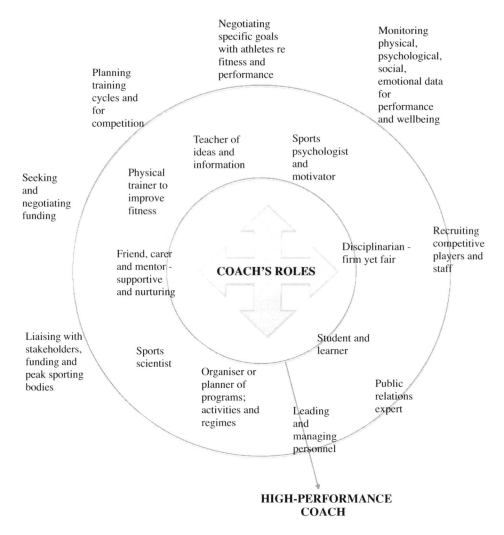

Figure 1.   Roles and responsibilities of the coach.
Sources: Banks (2009); Lyle (2002).

aspects more likely to be associated with the high-performance coach located towards the outer circle.

To further develop the professional standards of one's coaching towards the 'elite' level or meeting the needs of the high-performance athlete, a number of avenues are recommended (Banks, 2009; Lynch & Mallett, 2006). Figure 2 illustrates major sources often used for the development of individual coaching expertise. Gilbert, Côtè, and Mallett (2006) listed a coach's past participation as an athlete and accumulation of coaching experience as primary factors, whereas Schempp and McCullick (2010) stated the need for coaches to build a profile combining an extensive knowledge base with highly developed coaching skills. The individual might be encouraged to further their career by engaging in educational programmes and coaching courses (Banks, 2009; Gilbert et al., 2006; Martens, 1997; Zakrajsek, 2010).

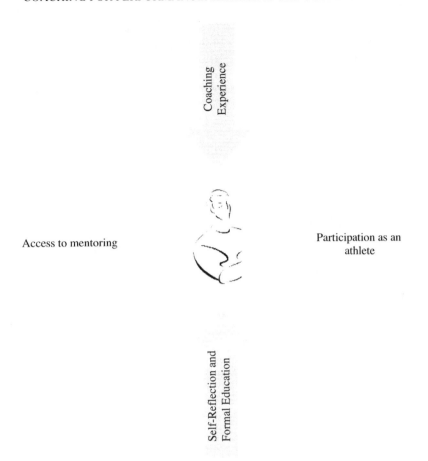

Coaching Experience

Access to mentoring

Participation as an athlete

Self-Reflection and Formal Education

Figure 2.   Major sources of developing coaching expertise.
Sources: Lynch and Mallett (2006); Mallett (2010).

This developmental process is often ongoing throughout the coach's career (Cross & Lyle, 1999; Martens, 1997). However, at the end of the day, the criteria for meeting the status of 'elite coach' may include being recognised as being effective or successful at the international level of competition (Saury & Durand, 1998; Tan, 1997). This is generally measured by the performance attainment of athletes at recognised international competitions and the number of medals won at those events (Bicycling Australia., 2008; Gilbert & Trudel, 2005; Gould, Guinan, Greenleaf, Medbery, & Peterson, 1999). As Lyle (2002, p. 254) stated: 'Coaching success is measured by association with successful performers'.

A further personal measure of a coach's ultimate success might include her/his individual selection as a coach at the Olympic level (McCain, 2008). Research investigating the Olympics has tended to focus on the performance of athletes, yet coaches are also performers directly influencing athletes' success at the Games (Gould et al., 1999). For example, negative aspects of an Olympic coach's performance at the Games or 'coaching issues' are often only noted by groups of teams who fail to meet performance expectations, in contrast with those who succeed (Gould et al., 1999).

Once they have reached the pinnacle of their profession, that is, to Olympic level, it is less clear what factors coaches themselves attribute to reaching this goal. There is a paucity of research available helping to understand those factors from the coach's own point of view. Past research has tended to focus on examining factors attributed to athlete success at the Olympics (Dieffenbach, Gould, & Moffett, 2008; Dunphy, 2008; Gould, Guinan, Greenleaf, & Chung, 2002; Gould et al., 1999; Riewald & Peterson, 2003; Sweetenham, 2008). Therefore, to help gain a greater understanding, we held a reflective conversation with eight Olympic coaches.

Procedures

This exploratory study used in-depth interviews to focus on the participant's perception of how they reached their goal of becoming an Olympic coach. In-depth interviewing was used because it is a useful technique for gaining an oral life history to help access and understand the significant experiences and events in the informant's life and career (Minichiello, Aroni, Timewell, & Alexander, 1990). A sample of convenience consisting of eight male Olympic coaches participated in unstructured conversations between the researcher and informant, focusing on the coach's perceptions of life, sport and experiences, expressed in his own words (Minichiello et al., 1990, p. 87). Using the open-ended interview techniques outlined by Robson (2011, pp. 283–289) we asked the coaches the main focus question: 'What main factor do you feel helped you to reach your goal of becoming an Olympic coach?' Coaches represented Beach Volleyball (n = 1), Fencing (n = 1), Modern Pentathlon (n = 1), Water Polo (n = 3), Kayaking (n = 1) and Volleyball (n = 1). The participants had been coaching in their chosen sport for an average of 15 years and had represented as a coach on average at two Olympic Games. Interview transcripts were audio-recorded then transcribed verbatim. Using the procedures outlined by Robson (2011, p. 469), an analysis was conducted to identify the major themes to emerge from the qualitative data. In this thematic coding approach, all the data were coded, or identified as representing a concept of interest, and labelled. Codes with similar or related labels were grouped together as themes. The following sections describe the main themes to emerge from the qualitative data.

Reflections on an Olympic Dream: how did I get here?

The participants identified a broad range of factors they feel helped them to reach their dream and pinnacle of their sport, that is, to be an Olympic coach. All but one coach would not narrow the reasons down to a single contributory factor; they felt there were many reasons. As Rob said, 'I don't believe there is only one thing'. The range of factors presented might reflect the fact that the coaches represented varying Olympic sports. Burt immediately thought of many factors:

> That is quite a tough question to limit it to one main thing. Many things cross my mind when thinking about this, early playing and coaching experiences, learning from other coaches, family support, commitment to my dreams/goals, the incredible help from coaching and support team members, opportunity, luck etc.

Interestingly, Hans also stated that it was a question that could only be answered on reflection, at the end of one's coaching career:

I imagine it won't be until after retirement and reflection, much like we did as players, that you can honestly answer this, because I can't pinpoint one major factor.

Passion, commitment and persistence

The most common theme to arise was the belief held by four of the eight coaches that an individual passion or commitment was considered necessary for what they were attempting to achieve. John, an Olympic coach of many years standing replied to the question in just one word, 'Passion'. Hans' response was characterised by having a drive or passion to succeed: 'I suppose that sums it up – the desire and drive to be successful'. Rob felt that 'Wanting to become a better coach, having passion, knowledge and belief that you can do the job while backing your gut feelings'.

To be successful, Burt explained that a major personal commitment was also considered necessary:

> To narrow it to one, I think that I would have to say that having the commitment would be number one. To even have the opportunity to be at the top of your sport you have to be prepared to do the years of volunteer coaching which brings a big time and financial commitment. Then as you move to higher level coaching you have to be prepared to be away from home for 4–6 months per year. For me it was over 20 years of coaching before I became Head Coach of the National Team. But commitment is also a commitment to keep learning and improving, putting the team first etc. (Burt)

According to Lyle (2002, p. 238), commitment is a major characteristic of performance coaching as 'the intensity of commitment required for success is considerable'. Zakrajsek (2010) recalled his journey to being an Olympic coach and cited commitment as a major 'ingredient' along with talent/work ratio and education. Just like the situation explained by Burt, commitment to Olympic coaching does not come without personal sacrifice, as Zakrajsek (2010, p. 2) explained:

> Unfortunately, in the process of making commitments to our athletes we sacrifice part of ourselves as well as time spent with our significant others and family members. This is a huge part of getting to the Olympic Games. Even if you strive for balance in life as we all do, you will find that life is made up of tough decisions between two important values that are in conflict with each other such as family time versus coaching time. You must make sacrifices to coach at the Olympic Games.

Another participant explained that for him, 'the factors needed to be an Olympic athlete are very similar to coaching' and persistence was required:

> I would say the single most important factor would be persistence towards a focused goal. (Ron)

Gary's reflection was similar, citing that 'Resilience and humility towards the craft, the players and the staff' was required. Holt and Dunn (2004) studied psychosocial factors associated with soccer success at the professional level and noted resilience as being a critical factor, in addition to discipline and social support. Resilience includes the ability to 'bounce back' from adversity. Bass (2010) reported how during the 2010 Winter Olympic Games there was an extraordinary amount of adversity faced by athletes in a number of disciplines and by specific athletes, the most noteworthy being the tragic circumstances surrounding the death of Joanie Rochette.

Many other athletes faced adversity as well, ranging from extremely bad weather conditions (Cypress), significant changes to venues (Luge and Alpine), and a lack of training opportunities based on schedule and/or weather issues. Bass (2010, p. 19) concluded that resilient methods of coping as lead by coaches can actually create a competitive advantage:

> Well-prepared teams with strong leadership were able to respond to adversity effectively, thus creating a competitive advantage for their athletes ... it was clear that teams who made a long-term commitment to developing appropriate staff [coaching] behavior were able to respond to adversity effectively.

Ron also added that he was able to 'Learn from setbacks along the way'. Similarly, Schempp and McCullick (2010, p. 222) concluded that the process of gaining extensive coaching experience offers an 'unparalleled opportunity to learn'. They stated that the difference amongst coaches who 'consistently reach the pinnacle of success' is due, in part, because this group have mastered the skill of continual improvement gained from learning from one's experiences. Burt wished to also add that:

> In the end even having all this commitment doesn't guarantee anything you also need an element of luck (right place at the right time).

Past experience as an athlete

Two of the eight participants nominated athletic participation experience as a contributing factor. For example, Max offered five reasons for how he felt he achieved his goal of being an Olympic coach; however, he strongly highlighted the fact he was able to draw on his 'past experiences as an Olympic athlete'. Past experience gained as a participating athlete has been reported in the wider literature as an important source of coaching knowledge (Irwin, Hanton, & Kerwin, 2004; Jones, Armour, & Potrac, 2003). Mallett (2010, p. 122) stated, 'It makes sense that coaches are likely to coach in a sport which they have significant playing experience'. Robinson (2010, p. 25) concluded that ex-international athletes are often fast-tracked towards high-performance coaching roles because 'they have a wealth of experience and knowledge to impart'. The successful coaches in Gilbert et al.'s (2006) investigation were characterised by having a minimum of several thousand hours of athletic participation for an average total of 13 years. For the 10 Olympic athletes interviewed in Dieffenbach et al.'s (2008, p. 64) study, the athletes felt that having a coach who had competed at national, world or Olympic level was an important aspect of the coach's 'credibility'. Mallett (2010, p. 123) examined the benefits to the high-performance coach of having previously played the sport as primarily being (a) knowledge of the skills, rules, strategies and tactics; (b) understanding the sport's culture; and (c) an increased sense of belonging, and confidence or self-efficacy in one's role.

Mentors

'Learning from other coaches' through mentoring was nominated by two participants as having helped them reach their goal. Ron explained this factor as 'continuing to look to others that have achieved the goal you are striving for'. The nine elite coaches taking part in the study by Nash and Sproule (2009) attributed access to mentors at the initial stages of their coaching careers as vital. Gilbert and Trudel (2005) similarly concluded that access to mentors is critical for a coach's development. Even at the elite level, Irwin et al. (2004) noted that 91% of coaches in their study felt mentoring was still very important to their success. Likewise, once they reached the elite level, the coaches in Nash and Sproule's (2009) study believed that continual networking with other coaches of 'like mind' as being essential to one's progress and growth as a coach. All of the five elite coaches participating in Lynch and Mallett's (2006, p. 19) study acknowledged the important influence of mentors in their 'becoming a successful high performance track and field coach'. However, Gilbert and Trudel (2005) warned that some coaches may have limited contact with their peers due to the competitive nature of sport. Some coaches are therefore hesitant to share information with other coaches who are viewed as competitors. The more elite or senior a coach becomes, the more restricted the number of suitable mentor coaches at the Olympic level or above is potentially available to assist him or her.

Knowledge and understanding of the sport and focus on needs of athlete

Max noted 'knowledge and understanding of the sport' as a factor contributing to him becoming an Olympic coach. Expert coaches generally have an extensive knowledge base (Gilbert & Trudel, 2005), and Martens (1997) described it as an essential attribute. Schembri (2001, p. 3) described the foundation of good coaching as having an extensive knowledge of the sport's techniques and tactics. However, Cassidy, Jones, and Potrac (2009, p. 10) cautioned against this factor being over-emphasised, whereby the coach becomes a mere technician involved in constant knowledge transfer, and their athlete a mere robot. 'Let's not ever forget that a great coach is somebody that gives people a great experience' (Schubert, 2010, p. 29). Enjoyment gained through a positive, innovative team environment and culture has been noted as helping improve player performance and ability to think clearly under pressure (Lee, Shaw, & Chesterfield, 2009b). Max also explained how this athlete-centred approach was vital for him succeeding at becoming an Olympic coach:

> I believe that the main factor that helped me to become an Olympic coach was the combination of a genuine interest in the athlete, the ability to empathise, an acute understanding of the individual style and technique best suited to the athlete and knowledge and understanding of the sport.

In this approach, empowerment of the athlete is the central concern and focus (Lee et al., 2009b, p. 306). In investigating what factors eight national and international coaches felt had made them successful, all participants in a study by Jones et al. (2003) highlighted the importance of social relations with the athletes and adopting a holistic perspective of coaching – getting to know them as individuals and not just as performing physical machines. A 'quality coach-athlete relationship' has been stressed by Olympic coaches as a critical influence on their athlete's success at the Games (Dieffenbach et al., 2008). Essentially, 'If the athletes feel valued, they are more likely to want to train hard and play well for the coach' (Cassidy et al., 2009, p. 49). The Olympic coaches taking part in Dieffenbach et al.'s (2008) investigation said they were most successful at the Olympic Games when they based their coaching strategies on the individual needs and goals of athletes:

> A good relationship was characterized by mutual trust, confidence in each other's abilities, good communication (especially good listening skills) and a sense of collaboration or working together. A coach's display of interest and respect for the athlete beyond his/her athletic identity was also important … A main aspect of a good coach-athlete relationship was the coach's ability to understand each athlete as an individual and to individualize his/her coaching style to meet the athlete's needs. (p. 63)

Furthermore, coaches are 'performers' in their own right. To reach the Olympic level, coaches may have to have developed sports psychology skills and have a cool-headed approach (Gould et al., 1999). For example:

> In an interview with legendary Olympic swim coach, James Counsilman, it was revealed that he was often nervous at major competitions but worked hard to not let his swimmers recognize his own stress. Counsilman felt that this was of utmost importance because he had learned that athletes model their coaches' anxiety levels, become more nervous than usual, and perform poorly. In Olympic competition, being in control of one's emotional state and masking certain emotions from athletes are just some aspects of a coach's performance. Coaches must also deal with crisis situations, make tactical decisions, and interact with officials. (Gould et al., 2002, p. 231)

The way a coach generally behaves and delivers practice sessions, including coach or athlete-centred approaches is ultimately dependent on his/her philosophy of coaching (Martens, 1997; Robinson, 2010, p. 51). One's coaching philosophy will encompass an individual's set of values, beliefs and principles guiding the individual's behaviours, coaching practice and adaptation to changing circumstances, contexts and environments (Cassidy et al., 2009; Jenkins, 2010; Robinson, 2010). A focus on quality coaching also involves the individual exploring ways their role can be made more meaningful and purposeful (Cassidy et al., 2009), probably best described by the reasons given in the next section.

Wanting to make a contribution

For Erik, there a main reason given for reaching the goal of becoming an Olympic coach was his expressed need 'to make contribution and create something great':

> The fulfilment that comes from being of service. Parents, great teachers, great coaches, mentors all know what it means to be of service. Our greatest contribution to the world and most satisfying to self is contributing to someone else's greatness. We believe in people and most likely that is because we have experienced the power of someone believing in us. We are driven to pay it forward out of respect and appreciation and to keep the golden gift we received alive passed into the next generation of champions/champion builders. I'm not a perfectionist so doing something right isn't a significant part of my framework, however creating a result from the materials that you have access to truly fascinates me. It shows the power of human potential to build yourself, your systems, your performance into something that can achieve a tangible measurable result. The Olympic Games is the highest arena in sport so naturally for me it was logical choice as a testing ground for the champions' journey.

Greg proposed similar ideas, feeling a combined challenge and need to contribute to his sport:

> If I can contribute and help Australia achieve this from a coaching perspective, then that challenge can be ticked off and I can sit back happily until something else presents itself.

Looking back down from the mountain top: discussion and implications

This group of coaches felt that the passion and commitment to want to succeed, experience as an athlete, learning from other coaches/mentors, focusing on the needs of the athlete and a need to contribute were key factors in how they reached their dream of becoming an Olympic coach (see Figure 3). The range of responses may reflect the variability in playing and coaching backgrounds experienced on high-performance coach pathways, such as to the Olympic Games (Mallett, 2010).

Interestingly, only Max highlighted his ability to empathise with and attune into the needs of his athlete as helping him succeed at becoming an Olympic coach. Research points to one's emotional intelligence ('EI'), or the ability to perceive, comprehend, detect and decipher emotions in faces, pictures, voices and in one's

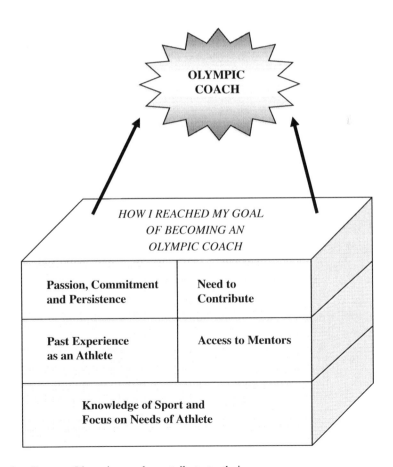

Figure 3.   Factors Olympic coaches attribute to their success.

self, the ability to harness emotions to facilitate efforts and decision making and manage emotions effectively, as being associated with leadership success and ability to influence others in leadership roles (Côté, Lopes, Salovey, & Miners, 2010). Sports coaches have noted that characteristics such as supreme self-confidence, mental toughness, unshakeability and strong will are now related to EI and aspects of the best performing athletes (Morgan, 2003; Stough, Clements, Wallish, & Downey, 2009). Likewise, coaches who cannot only control their own, but are also able to help their athletes manage emotions may help prevent inappropriate outbursts of rage or aggression and lead to productive channelling of emotions towards motivation and drive, may find this contributes towards overall success. Successful coaches reaching the Olympic level may have higher levels of emotional management whereby s/he is more effective in being able to maintain beneficial moods, manage stress in themselves and their athletes, aiding with task focus and avoiding distraction (Stough et al., 2009).

One factor that was not highlighted included the contribution of one's support team and trainers. As Zakrajsek (2010, p. 2) noted, 'teamwork makes the dreamwork'. It may take time to build up considerable trust and ensure that trainers are loyal to the coach's personal values and vision for the athlete. Cultivating long-lasting professional relationships with an effective support team will help a coach 'reach the top' Zakrajsek (2010).

Extensive coaching experience gained through long years of effort and work (approximately 10 years or 10,000 hours of deliberate practice) is frequently reported in the wider literature as an essential element in the development of coaching expertise (Bell, 1997; Lynch & Mallett, 2006). Mallett (2010) concluded that accumulated hours from coaching experiences contributes most to the coach's development. Therefore, it was surprising that, in contrast, none of the participants in our study nominated experience as assisting them to reach their dream of becoming an Olympic coach. Many international-level coaches have been coaching for an average of 10 years (Mallett, 2010), with Schempp and McCullick (2010, p. 221) concluding that there is no substitute for experience when it comes to developing expertise:

> Simply put, no one achieves expertise in coaching without substantial experience. There is no empirical evidence to support the notion that an inexperienced coach can consistently outperform a coach with extensive experience. To the contrary, research has repeatedly revealed that it takes extensive experience – a minimum of 10 years in most fields – to reach the level of expert. While it takes more than just experience, clearly one cannot become expert without substantial experience in one's craft.

However, Kidman and Hanrahan (2011, p. 4) have argued that experience alone is insufficient for developing the expertise considered necessary to become an elite coach. They have stated, 'Coaches do not just complete a coaching course, coach for a specified time and then, presto, become perfect coaches'. Gilbert et al. (2006) found that the level of time a coach spent in formal education decreased as a coach progressed to elite level. This may explain why education was not reported as a critical factor for the coaches in our study. Gilbert and Trudel (2005) also discovered that more experienced coaches relied less on coaching materials and resources than others and tended to prefer self-reflection. According to Lee et al. (2009b, p. 302), coaches and players can become proficient through asking 'why-type' questions, helping to decipher what went well, and why. The simple accumulation of years of experience does not guarantee that one will be an effective coach. Effective coaches transform their experience into knowledge through a process of reflection (Gilbert & Trudel, 2005; Jenkins, 2010).

Coaching is also completed within a dynamic, complex, uncertain and fluid environment (Bowes & Jones, 2006; Mallett, 2008; Saury & Durand, 1998). Although the group of coaches participating in this study were obviously skilled at engaging in highly structured coaching plans to reach the level of Olympic coach, they did not mention having highly effective improvisory skills. This might include responding effectively to the dynamic sporting environment often with limited control and the ability to reflect, work, dynamically adapt to variations and respond in a highly turbulent environment (Lyle, 2002; Mallett, 2010). Lee, Chesterfield, Shaw, and Ghaye (2009a, p. 286) argued that improvisation is at the heart of the creative process and having that competitive 'edge':

> We can, however, relate it simply to being able to re-frame what is happening in front of us, and to use the power of the positive question to lead individuals and teams into a space where they can think differently about what they are doing and do different things.

Another important factor associated with Olympic coaches reaching their dream not particularly highlighted by the coaches in this study is that successful coaches appeared to have strong, positive, open and professional relationships with their athletes. Issues are discussed and solved in a timely fashion thus reducing any extra stress. In addition, there is strong evidence from reviews of performance at Olympic Games that the top coaches created effective communication strategies with their athletes. Daily athlete meetings occur ensuring each athlete had a complete understanding of their plan leading into and at the Games (Bass, 2010).

Through the process of reflection involved in taking part in our research, the Olympic coaches may have focused more on those philosophical aspects of their practice that have provided them, in retrospect, with feelings of fulfilling a greater purpose and finding meaning (Cassidy et al., 2009, p. 49). Focusing on those quality aspects of one's own career through a personal reflective process may have helped the participants to explore ways in which their coaching practice is meaningful, purposeful and enjoyable (Cassidy et al., 2009). The importance of self-reflection, to reflect on one's success and failure, to process experiences and emotions, is how a coach will draw meaning from and learn from their experiences (Ghaye, 2001; Gould et al., 1999; Mallett, 2004):

> A 'reflective practitioner' is someone who, at regular intervals, looks back at what they do and considers how they can improve. They 'reflect' at what they have done. They are not happy to cruise along ... Looking backwards enables those involved to get a sense of where they have come from, a sense of development and progress. In addition, part of the reflective process entails looking forward and therefore towards future goals. So taken together refection can be said to involve both projection and review. (Lee et al., 2009a, p. 286)

It is not known if similar responses would have been reported if participants representing 'higher-profile' or mainstream Olympic sports such as athletics or swimming had also participated in our study. Due to the significant variability in the roles of coaches for every sport, defining 'effective 'behaviours' may be problematic (Côtè & Sedgwick, 2003; Mallett, 2010). 'Typical' pathways to the Olympic coaching level may be unique to each sport and each individual's unique circumstances. Future research could explore success factors attributed by coaches 'intra-sport', and across the full range of Olympic sports, to examine the role, nature and effect of specific sporting contexts and varied environments (Côtè & Sedgwick, 2003; Gilbert & Trudel, 2005). A series of follow-up and subsequent interviews is also recommended to help develop rapport with the participant, and to also allow for capturing any new 'memories' that may have been triggered or arisen between conversations. Due to the incidental nature of the sampling technique used in this study, incorporating larger numbers of coaches in future studies may help increase generalisability (Minichiello et al., 1990; Robson, 2011).

While there are limitations to the generalisation of the findings due to the small sample involved and retrospective nature of the data, the findings suggest the importance of coaches accessing appropriate mentors, establishing effective rapport and recognising individual differences in athletes. Due to the recent transformations in the nature of coaching work and its participants, it is also recommended that future research explores the changing nature of career pathways and those factors attributed as most important to reaching the dream of becoming an Olympic coach.

Notes on contributors

Dr Janet Currie has a background in school teaching, university lecturing, community health promotion and health policy. She has qualifications in education and health promotion. Her research interests focus on investigating the perceived benefits of participation in leisure and physical activity, health promotion policy, marketing and promotion of healthy lifestyles and social and emotional well-being. Dr Currie has designed numerous educational materials in the area of health promotion and exercise including books, videos, teacher and community resources. A past national level netballer and athlete, Janet enjoys creating effective health education messages designed for engaging students in the school classroom setting, using sport as the key focus. Most recently, Janet authored the national high school teaching resource, *Dream, Believe, Achieve* for the National Rugby League of Australia. Dr Currie is a past National President, Vice-President and State representative of the Australian Health Promotion Association. She is a Director of Health Education and Promotion International and in 2003 was awarded the Outstanding Community Engagement Award by Australian Catholic University.

Shelley Oates-Wilding is one of Australia's top sportswomen and motivational speakers. A dual Olympian, World Champion, and Australian Representative in three sports, she is also a successful keynote speaker, university lecturer, businesswoman and mother. Her life's goal is to ensure others get a chance to enjoy the same benefits from achieving their goals as she does from hers. As a child, Shelley's dream was to represent her country and wear the Green and Gold at the Olympics. As a youngster she played and enjoyed all sports and represented Australia in Track & Field, Netball and Surf Life Saving. At 24 years of age, a full knee reconstruction sidelined her netball career. Not one to shy away from a challenge, Shelley never gave up on her dream and found a sport that she could do without using her legs. With her trademark discipline and determination, Shelley has become one of the world's best paddlers. She has achieved the title of World Champion in Surf Ski and Outrigger Canoeing and has represented Australia in kayaking at the Atlanta and Sydney Olympic Games. Shelley now lives in Honolulu, Hawaii and is Head Coach of HCKT.

References

Banks, J. (2009). The role of the coach. In N. Goodman (Ed.), *Beginning coaching* (4th ed.). (pp. 1–26). Canberra: Australian Sports Commission.

Bass, N. (2010). Vancouver Olympic and paralympic summary. *Coaches Plan/Plan du Coach, 17*, 18–19.

Bell, M. (1997). The development of expertise. *Journal of Physical Education, Recreation and Dance, 68*, 34–38.

Bicycling Australia. (2008). Poor Olympics heralds changing of the guard. *Bicycling Australia, 154*, 22.

Bowes, I., & Jones, R.L. (2006). Working at the edge of chaos: understanding coaching as a complex, interpersonal system. *The Sports Psychologist, 20*, 235–245.

Cassidy, T., Jones, R., & Potrac, P. (2009). *Understanding sports coaching* (2nd ed.). Abingdon: Routledge.

Côtè, J., & Sedgwick, W. (2003). Effective behaviours of expert rowing coaches: A qualitative investigation of Canadian athletes and coaches. *International Sports Journal, 1*, 62–77.

Côtè, S., Lopes, P.N., Salovey, P., & Miners, C.T.H. (2010). Emotional intelligence and leadership emergence in small groups. *The Leadership Quarterly, 21*, 496–508.

Cross, N., & Lyle, L. (1999). *The coaching process: Principles and practices for sport*. London: Butterworth Heinemann.

Dieffenbach, K., Gould, D., & Moffett, A. (2008). How coaches molded Olympians. *Soccer Journal, 53*, 63–65.

Dunphy, M. (2008). Reflections on the U.S. men's team's run to the Olympic gold medal. *Coaching Volleyball, 26*, 14–17.

Ghaye, T. (2001). Reflective practice. *Faster Higher Stronger, 10*, 9–12.

Gilbert, W.D., & Trudel, P. (2005). Learning to coach through experience. Conditions that influence reflection. *Physical Educator, 62*, 32–44.

Gilbert, W., Côtè, J., & Mallett, C. (2006). Developmental paths and activities of successful sports coaches. *International Journal of Sport Science and Coaching, 1*, 69–76.

Gould, D., Guinan, D., Greenleaf, C., & Chung, Y. (2002). A survey of Olympic coaches: Variables perceived to have influenced athlete performance and coaching effectiveness. *The Sports Psychologist, 16*, 229–250.

Gould, D., Guinan, D., Greenleaf, C., Medbery, R., & Peterson, K. (1999). Factors affecting Olympic performance. Perceptions of athletes and coaches from more and less successful teams. *The Sport Psychologist, 13*, 371–394.

Holt, N.L., & Dunn, J.G.H. (2004). Toward a grounded theory of the psychosocial competencies and environmental conditions associated with soccer success. *Journal of Applied Sport Psychology, 16*, 199–219.

Irwin, G., Hanton, S., & Kerwin, D.G. (2004). Reflective practice and the origins of the elite coaching knowledge. *Reflective practice, 5*, 425–442.

Jenkins, S. (2010). Coaching philosophy. In J. Lyle & C. Cushion (Eds.), *Sports coaching. Professionalism and practice* (pp. 223–242). London: Churchill Livingstone Elsevier.

Jones, R.L., Armour, K.M., & Potrac, P. (2003). Constructing expert knowledge: A case study of a top-level professional soccer coach. *Sport Education & Society, 8*, 213–229.

Kidman, L., & Hanrahan, S.J. (2011). *The coaching process. A practical guide to becoming an effective sports coach* (3rd ed.). Abingdon: Routledge.

Lee, S., Chesterfield, G., Shaw, D.J., & Ghaye, T. (2009). Editorial. Exploring the potential of reflective learning in sport. *Reflective Practice, 10*, 285–293.

Lee, S., Shaw, D.J., & Chesterfield, G. (2009). Reflections from a world champion: An interview with Sir Clive Woodward, Director of Olympic Performance, the British Olympic Association. *Reflective Practice, 10*, 295–310.

Lyle, J. (2002). *Sports coaching concepts*. London: Routledge.

Lynch, M., & Mallett, C. (2006). Becoming a successful high performance track and field coach. *Modern Athlete & Coach, 44*, 15–20.

Mallett, C.J. (2004). Reflective practices in teaching and coaching: Using reflective journals to enhance performance. In J. Wright, D. Macdonald, & L. Burrows (Eds.), *Critical inquiry and problem-solving in physical education* (pp. 147–158). Sydney: Routledge.

Mallett, C.J. (2008). Modelling the complexity of the coaching process: A commentary. *International Journal of Sport Science and Coaching, 2*, 419–421.

Mallet, C.J. (2010). Becoming a high-performance coach: pathways and communities. In J. Lyle & C. Cushion (Eds.), *Sports coaching. Professionalism and practice* (pp. 119–134). london: Churchill Livingstone Elsevier.

Martens, R. (1997). *Successful coaching* (2nd ed.). Champaign, IL: Human Kinetics.

McCain, C. (2008). At the Olympics, everything is a performance issue. *International Journal of Sport & Exercise Psychology, 6*, 267–276.

Minichiello, V., Aroni, R., Timewell, E., & Alexander, L. (1990). *In-depth interviewing: Researching people*. Sydney: Longman Cheshire.

Morgan, L. (2003). Enhancing performance in sports: What is morally permissible? In J. Boxill (Ed.), *Sports ethics: An anthology* (pp. 182–188). Maldin, MA: Blackwell.

Nash, C., & Sproule, J. (2009). Career development of expert coaches. *International Journal of Sports Science and Coaching, 4*, 121–138.

Riewald, S., & Peterson, K. (2003). Understanding the path to the podium: Reflections from Olympians on the process of success. *Olympic Coach, 14*, 4–8.

Robinson, P.E. (2010). *Foundations of sports coaching*. Abingdon: Routledge.

Robson, C. (2011). *Real world research. A resource for users of social research methods in applied settings* (3rd ed.). Chichester: John Wiley & Sons.

Saury, J., & Durand, M. (1998). Practical knowledge in expert coaches: On-site study of coaching in sailing. *Research Quarterly for Exercise and Sport, 69*, 254–266.

Schembri, G. (2001). Roles and responsibilities of the coach. In F.S. Pyke (Ed.), *Better coaching* (2nd ed.). (pp. 3–13). (Canberra: Australian Sports Commission.

Schempp, P.G., & McCullick, B. (2010). Coaches' expertise. In J. Lyle & C. Cushion (Eds.), *Sports coaching. Professionalism and practice* (pp. 221–231). London: Churchill Livingstone Elsevier.

Schubert, M. (2010). Coaching excellence. *American Swimming, 2010*(4), 20–29.

Stough, C., Clements, M., Wallish, L., & Downey, L. (2009). Emotional intelligence in sport: Theoretical linkages and preliminary empirical relationships from basketball. In J.D.A. Parker, D.H. Saklofske, & C. Stough (Eds.), *Assessing emotional intelligence theory, research, and applications* (pp. 291–306). London: Springer.

Sweetenham, B. (2008). Lessons learned from the Olympic experience. *Swimming in Australia, 25*, 20–24.

Tan, S. (1997). The elements of expertise. *Journal of Physical Education, Recreation and Dance, 68*, 30–33.

Zakrajsek, T. (2010). *My Vancouver 2010 journey*. Retrieved from http://tomzak1.blogspot.com/2010/02/becoming-olympic-coach.html.

Sacrifice: the lonely Olympic road

Amanda J. Wilding[a], Laura Hunter-Thomas and Roger Thomas

[a]Bournemouth University, School of Tourism, Dorset House, Fern Barrow, Poole, BH12 5BB, UK

The rarity of the Olympic Games makes it, for those who can compete, the ultimate sporting event. Whilst the common pressures experienced by athletes are well understood, the unique sacrifices made by elite adolescents in their pursuit of sporting excellence are less clear. Through a case study approach using analysis of conversation and reflections on practice, the paper aims to document the experiences of an elite adolescent female athlete's journey to qualify for the 2012 Olympic Games. The aim of the paper is therefore twofold. It will first raise awareness and understanding of the non-competitive sacrifices which ultimately became pressures experienced by the athlete in their pursuit of an Olympic dream. Second, the paper outlines the coping mechanisms employed to manage and overcome the issues created by the pursuit of an Olympic dream. Findings revealed organisation and personal stressors as a source of stress. However, developing clear roles and responsibilities offered a buffering effect, alleviating negative implications. In addition, burnout appeared to be a natural consequence of the intense lifestyle but structured interventions led to a positive return to sport. The parents' journey transpired as an area warranting further investigation.

Introduction

The elite competitive arena is like no other; it is an environment which provides unique experiences for those competing at the top level of sport (Sun & Wu, 2011). Moreover, for certain disciplines, the Olympic Games are the ultimate competition (Williams & Ford, 2009). After years of investment in intensive training programmes, athletes from around the world compete in an event that runs for less than one calendar month every four years (Stotlar & Wonder, 2006; Williams & Ford, 2009). It is this rarity of the occasion that Gould and Maynard (2009) claimed magnifies the importance of the Olympic Games for elite athletes. Sun & Wu (2011) proclaimed that many athletes have fallen foul to the enormous pressures associated with such an environment. Thus, for many athletes the 'extended engagement in practice' (Williams & Ford, 2009, p. 1381) which involves a high consumption of time and resources (Abernethy, 2008; Scanlan, Stein, & Ravizza, 1991) will actually be wasted. Hence, elite sport is a complex web of sensitive interactions, often resulting in athletes preparing for high level sporting events under stressful circumstances.

Consequently, over the past 20 years or so the stressors experienced by elite athletes have emerged as a common area of interest for many researchers (Fletcher, Hanton, & Wagstaff, 2012; Gould, Jackson, & Finch, 1993a; Hanton, Fletcher, & Coughlan, 2005; Kristiansen & Roberts, 2010; Scanlan et al., 1991; Woodman & Hardy, 2001). This area of interest is now commonly referred to as organisational stress, the field is attracting a considerable amount of interest from both the coaching and academic worlds (Fletcher & Hanton, 2003; Hanton et al., 2005). As a result there is an increasing body of literature discussing and examining the factors impinging upon the psychological and emotional well-being of an athlete due to the challenging mental and physical ramifications of engagement in sport (Adie, Duda, & Ntoumanis, 2008; Hanton, Wadey, & Mellalieu, 2008; Kristiansen & Roberts, 2010; Mellalieu, Neil, Hanton, & Fletcher, 2009). Previous literature (Fletcher & Hanton, 2003; Hanton, et al., 2005) has established a framework for categorising stressors and suggests that there are commonalities in the pressures experienced by athletes. However, the environment in which each one operates has its own intricacies that need consideration if the athlete is to flourish. Much of the early work from authors such as Gould et al. (1993a; 1993b) and Scanlan et al. (1991) was based on US national figure skating champions, whilst the more recent work from the UK has been dominated by Fletcher, Hanton and colleagues. Thus more research is needed to investigate UK athletes' experiences and from new perspectives. To this end, Kristiansen and Roberts (2010) highlighted that little is known about the adolescent elite athlete and more specifically the organisational stressors they experience. Thus whilst past research has uncovered the broad spectrum of stressors (Gould et al., 1993a; Scanlan et al., 1991; Woodman & Hardy, 2001) in elite sport, as potential Olympians we still need to understand the plight of the adolescent elite athlete and their journey beyond that of the competitive arena. The purpose of the current paper is therefore to extend the current literature base by examining and thus gaining an understanding of the athlete's experience. Specifically, this paper aims to provide a personal insight into the challenges and sacrifices faced by one 2012 Olympic hopeful and their immediate family. In particular, the paper documents the journey of the athlete in their pursuit of excellence and the consequences of the key decisions and actions made in the quest for success. Unlike previous research, the current study also documents the coping strategies employed.

In line with suggestions of Hadjistavropoulos & Smythe (2001), third parties in the following paper have been protected in order to preserve their anonymity, but a pseudonym has not, however, been utilised for the athlete involved as she wanted her story to be told. Laura, now a 19-year-old athlete from the UK, took to her chosen sport as a shy, withdrawn adolescent (as defined by Smoll, Cumming, & Smith, 2011). Her aim at this point was primarily to establish a restoration of a level of self-confidence after her experiences of bullying at school. It was these experiences that motivated her specifically to compete in what ultimately has become her sport of choice due to the martial art/self defence nature of the activity. Within a relatively short period of time Laura made the Great Britain (GB) team and began investing heavily in the sport on a number of fronts in order to pursue what had become her 'Olympic Dream'. However the dream drifted into a nightmare as the costs slowly began to outweigh the benefits. Eventually, in 2009 prior to the World Championships, Laura and her family sought the advice of a sport psychologist. In an attempt to better understand and manage what they at the time perceived to be peripheral issues, Laura's Olympic road was examined in detail and as a team they unpicked the sacrifices experienced by the athlete in the quest for Olympic success.

Whilst some see analysis of conversation as restrictive (Smith & Sparkes, 2005) due to the lack of understanding surrounding the sacrifices made by elite athletes in the sporting environment, this paper takes a case study approach which is grounded in actual conversations and reflective practices of participants. This provides a frame for the understanding and explanations not described by the participant themselves, thus it will report what the participants displayed as pertinent (Smith & Sparkes, 2005). Through this form of inquiry the paper addresses the organisational stressors experienced by Laura in order to provide a greater understanding of the role they play in the life of an elite athlete. It will thus help to address the need for a better understanding of the sacrifices elite adolescent athletes make in their quest for sporting prowess.

Getting into the sport: the athlete's story

Laura's sport consists of three categories or disciplines in which both men and women can compete, albeit separately. Components of success have been recognised as, amongst others, speed, skill, dexterity and the ability to think fast, hence requiring fighters to possess a multitude of elements to be successful due to the complex nature of the sport (Barth & Beck, 2007).

In a small green-floored gym after school, Laura worked under the tutelage of an independent coach who, although qualified to instruct students in any of the three disciplines associated with the sport, chose to introduce Laura to the quicker, more dynamic, and previously, mostly male-dominated discipline. Laura found the sport exciting, and her parents soon saw her involvement and talent flourish. Soon after this, Laura was the owner of her own set of equipment and began attending small age-specific national competitions. As she became more serious about her sport and moved from recreational to competitive status, she aspired to a place on the national World Championship team, and began to make changes to her lifestyle accordingly.

Laura's choice of coach was to be the first significant change; Laura's parents found a coach with a good reputation for developing athletes of Laura's age and who implemented a style of fighting pioneered by the current American National & Olympic coach. One of the immediate implications of this change was to be the first significant sacrifices of many, being that of time and effort, as discussed by Abernethy (2008). Two or three times a week, Laura would now remain at school to complete homework before being collected and taken to training. Laura's parents dutifully drove her the two hours each way to the coach's training arena for sparring and private lessons, often getting home after midnight. With this increased structured training regime also came a fitness programme that added additional nights of intensive training. This parental system began to be affectionately referred to as 'the taxi service', which drove Laura the length and breadth of the country every weekend, as she additionally began attending more competitions. Such actions fall under what Smoll et al. (2011) have considered to be a natural obligation of the parents' role, and for Laura a year round requirement of elite adolescent sport (Gustafsson, Hassmen, & Lundqvist, 2007). Examples of such intensified commitment in the form of time and effort are commonly discussed in the literature (Abernethy, 2008; Norris & Kaniasty, 1996) and, moreover, are displayed as accepted and necessary sacrifices in elite level sport. To this end, Laura and her parents engaged fully, positively and productively in this process by being open and honest about the time they were able and willing to commit (Smoll et al., 2011). Furthermore, her parents sought to gain an appreciation of the sport in order to improve their own enjoyment by gaining an understanding of the sport's format, rules and strategies, as suggested by Smoll et al. (2011).

Tipping point

As a result of this sacrifice, Laura began to make a name for herself in the national division and was soon named in the national squad. As part of the national team, in addition to the UK tournaments, Laura began travelling with her parents to foreign locales such as France and Germany to compete for her country. She reflects positively on even making the finals for her age group in her first international tournament. As a result, Laura's aspirations to become an Olympic champion began to grow. Soon realising the level of input required to reach her dream, Laura, a then 15-year-old participant, attended a training camp, which took place in the American city of Portland, Oregon. Hosted by the US National and Olympic coach whose style she and her parents had previously 'admired' the camp was held at his club, which had given rise to the successes of arguably some of the most renowned women in the sport and, specifically, Laura's discipline, including the 2004 and 2008 Olympic Champion.

At the end of the camp, which served to give what Laura describes as 'a brutal taste of what life as a truly elite athlete is all about', the head coach asked her what she really wanted from her athletic career. Laura responded by outlining her two main goals: (1) to make it to the World Championships and (2) attend the Olympic Games, to which the coach's reply was that if this was something she really wanted he could coach her to achieve her goals:

> For me, I always aim to improve young fencers who are dedicated to championship level. That's how I like to work, that's where I start from, and that is my commitment. With Laura, I saw her skill level and that she was willing to work hard, so I offered to train her.

For the next year, Laura and her parents say they were 'impotent to fully act on this offer, as she was still in full-time, compulsory education'. Laura and her parents did, however, make what they saw to be 'the best of the situation', flying out to Portland every school holiday, no matter how brief, so that Laura could train with the man who was now her full-time, and only, personal coach. Through initial exploration of Laura's story it was apparent that many of the initial sacrifices surrounding time, money and effort both Laura and her parents embraced positively and were accepted as part of the athletic lifestyle.

The decision

During this period of a year, Laura describes having 'many long and often emotionally charged family meetings' in which she discussed the pursuit of her athletic dreams whilst her parents tried to evaluate the practicality of the situation. It was during one such meeting that it was decided to make what they called 'a leap of faith' so that Laura could, in her words, 'train full time for the 2012 Olympics while studying for her A-levels'. The plan was that after completing her GCSEs, Laura and her mother would move to the US where they would rent an apartment in Portland and stay in the US for as long as their visas would allow at any one time, returning to the UK only when domestic competitive events, or their visas, required. Laura's father would remain in the UK to work in order to fund this venture. Meanwhile, Laura would also study for her A-levels independently with the hope of securing an athletic scholarship from an American University, thus allowing her mother to return to England. Eventually the time came after Laura had completed her GCSEs achieving 7 A∗s and 3 A's. Leaving school signified the start of the new sacrifice. The family began the process of arranging their affairs in order to lead a life split by 'the pond' as they now reflect. It was here that the floodgates really opened, and the meaning of the words 'challenge' and 'sacrifice' became known but maybe not fully understood.

Sacrifices became stressors

It is commonly accepted that the competitive environment is challenging and often results in stress (Mellalieu et al., 2009). In relation to the competitive environment many researchers (Hanton et al., 2005; Kristiansen & Roberts, 2010) have recognised the distinction between two types of stressors defined as competitive and organisational. Mellalieu et al. (2009) described competitive stressors as those relating directly to athletic performance whilst in turn they classified finances as an example of organisational stress. Previously referred to as 'work-related social psychological stress' (Shirom 1982, p. 21), organisational stress can be interpreted as the interaction between an individual and their work environment (Woodman & Hardy, 2001). A study by Fletcher and Hanton (2003) highlighted the need for sport psychologists to limit their concentration on those stressors that are considered competitive in nature. Interestingly, the literature from Hanton et al. (2005) suggested that many elite athletes experience a wide variety of organisational stressors and often up to four times more frequently than those of a competitive nature (McKay, Niven, Lavallee, & White, 2008) yet Fletcher, Hanton, and Mellalieu (2006) claimed that organisational stressors are less understood. Moreover, furthering Scanlan et al's. (1991) work which studied 26 elite figure skaters, Fletcher and Hanton (2003) proposed that competitive stressors are not only more likely to be similar between athletes but also stable across sports and over time. In contrast, organisational stressors are thought to be diverse and often arise in combination rather than isolation, and as a result Hanton et al. (2005) called for the sport psychologist to widen their scope of work beyond that of mental skills training interventions. This supports the earlier work Gould et al. (1993a), who had previously called for athletes, coaches and sports science specialists to increase their awareness surrounding the norms of elite performance as this would in turn increase understanding about how to help elite athletes better prepare and cope with elite life.

Recently, McKay et al. (2008) added a third category of personal stress (interaction between the athlete and personal life events that occur within their environment). In relation to stressors, Kristiansen & Roberts (2009) discussed that how one deals with such stressors often relates to, amongst other factors, what the person aspires to achieve, which in Laura's case is a place on the 2012 Olympic team. In addition, Mellalieu et al. (2009) also acknowledged the need to consider athletes' responses to organisational stress and thus that having an awareness of their individual sporting demands is required. In relation to Laura and her experiences, in line with the literature organisational and personal stressors were indeed not only more common but also more pertinent as they were named by Laura and her parents as sacrifices, and were a key reason for consulting with a sport psychologist.

Personal stressors: the total lifestyle change

For Laura her initial unexpected struggles were in her personal lifestyle changes with regard to feelings of isolation. Although her new club-mates made her feel welcome, she had left behind and, she felt lost, lasting friendships, as she found her training schedule and A-Level workload left her with few opportunities to make social arrangements with her new circle of friends, which left her feeling somewhat isolated. In her words, she 'no longer lived any semblance of a "typical" teenager's life', and she struggled with this.

Consequently both at the time, and upon reflection, Laura states that 'immediate challenges were presented by the relocation and that the initial sacrifice of moving away from family caused some fundamental issues'. Despite describing herself as being a 'hardworking and organised teenager', in the first instance Laura struggled with the workload of A-Levels and the responsibility of having to micromanage her time. She had no tutor to help her face-to-face; her father (who had previously always been there to assist with school projects and homework) was thousands of miles, and an eight-hour time difference away. Given Laura's educational aim, it was imperative that her studies continued alongside her training, but training in the US meant sacrificing a structured education system, which she was happy to do at this point in time. In relation to the road towards the 2012 Olympics Laura had to therefore establish and develop a new personal and educational lifestyle.

Such lifestyle changes have not gone unnoticed in the literature, Thiel et al. (2011) reported on the notion of support being specific to the athlete's perception and suggested that all at the same time elite athletes must protect but also risk their health, thus constantly balancing the benefits and sacrifices of elite sport. Hence, they suggested elite athletes should work within a fine line of pushing their body and mind to the edge but without damaging their emotional well-being. Furthermore, and of specific relevance to Laura's situation, they stated that elite adolescent athletes are also challenged with the need to cope with what they called 'substantial physical, psychological and social transformations' (p. 1471) such as those demonstrated in first, taking the step from the amateur to elite status, second, changing her lifestyle and third, becoming a distance learner. Thus the changes experienced by Laura are not uncommon in sport but are exaggerated by the move between two different countries and cultures. Overall, it appears that whilst there were pockets of advice for and from the family there was a lack of structured education surrounding the benefits and drawbacks of such a life-changing move. This raises the question of who should provide guidance in this type of situation and how athletes and their families should access this.

After these events had occurred as part of the initial assessment and in order to rationalise their circumstances, the family discussed this change at some length with the sport psychologist. A form of lifestyle profiling (Jeffreys, 2006) was undertaken by the family. Investigating areas such as social relationships, education and overall lifestyle management led to action planning in order to aid Laura to micromanage the different aspects of her new life, thus relieving some of the initial stresses and reducing feelings of isolation.

In their new life, responsibility also emerged as a major theme surrounding life in America whereby new roles and the functions of such roles had to be redefined and negotiated. Explanations for such behaviours can be found in the work of Frone, Russell, & Cooper (1992) who evidenced that undertaking multiple roles is associated with both psychological and physical costs. For Laura and her mother this was demonstrated in their mother/child, athlete/manager roles. They found switching between such roles was exhausting and frustrating as they would 'step on each other's toes' and had nowhere to escape to. However, to overcome this stress together the team defined each role and the responsibilities which accompanied it, and days were highlighted for when the mother and Laura would have 'separate' time. A major underpinning purpose to this exercise was to develop Laura's personal responsibility, which is claimed to be the aim of educating most young people (Long, Pantaleon, & Bruant, 2008).

Organisational stressor: training

An expected aspect of the move was an increase in training load. However, despite having come from what she perceived to be a relatively good national standing (by the time she moved to Portland she had been ranked number one in the nation in her division), Laura reflects that:

> in America, that meant nothing ... I found myself surrounded by National, Olympic and World Champions and struggled to hold my own against such fierce competitors.

Often exhausted by the twice-daily sport specific and fitness sessions she attended regularly with her new coach and trainer respectively, Laura reflects that the biggest surprise was that, compared to her club-mates, she was unfit. It quickly became sharply apparent that in her own words she had been 'living the life of an amateur, and that this was the elite division'. Laura describes her coach having to 'un-train' her in order to eliminate a number of bad habits, a process which Laura found frustrating as her performances failed to 'improve as fast as [she] had impatiently hoped they would'.

Organisation stressor: travelling and training

Laura regularly returns to the UK due to visa and competition requirements, which means she experienced training difficulties when in the UK as an appropriate venue is a five-hour drive away, which 'was not a practical commute'. She goes on to say:

> this presented a great deal of difficulty, particularly when the competitive calendar, which often presents a schedule of international and national competitions separated only by five working days, kept me in Britain for long periods of time, without a club or training partners in the interim, and without a coach at the events themselves.

Hence, whilst training in America presented many opportunities it also caused challenges and sacrifices in its own right as it made it difficult for her coach to travel to many competitions with her. Thus, for the sport psychologist working with Laura 'understanding her visa, financial and schooling demands was essential to relieving organisational stress'. More widely, such insights extend our understanding of the current literature by providing a working knowledge of organisational stressors which in turn highlights the need for practitioners, coaches, parents and National Governing Bodies to understand and address the individual stressors of elite athletes.

Organisational stressor: finance

With all this change it is clear that one sacrifice is that of money. This is regularly discussed in the literature, for example, by Scanlan et al. (1991) who specifically referred to finance as a sacrifice. In addition, Stotlar and Wonder (2006) referred to funding as a key infrastructural component for developing athletes. Laura's parents reflect that 'attempting to achieve the Olympic dream was anything but cheap'. So, before making the decision to commit to 'the Portland plan', Laura's parents 'crunched the numbers, and found that they might, they just might, be able to manage it'. Laura's father reflects:

> The financial investment was scary but do-able, especially if only for two years. There would be debt but interest rates were low and we had some capital so, like a first-time bungee-jumper, I closed my eyes and dived off the platform.

However, in time the economic landscape changed and their 'financial safety net plummeted'. Relationships with management within Laura's club became strained and difficult and the recession began to take what the family described as:

> A real toll, as Laura went from number one Cadet to number one Junior to a national Senior team member without seeing a penny of funding from outside aid.

The Talented Athlete Scholarship Scheme (TASS) was only available to UK athletes still in full-time education; consequently the whole financial burden of the pursuit of Laura's dream fell upon her parents, thus making it a pertinent family sacrifice.

Support systems

Intertwined in the stressors were issues linking to the concept of support systems. It became apparent that the existing framework of support was ad hoc, sporadic and unmanaged. According to Kristiansen and Roberts (2010), support systems are thought to be those behaviours that improve well-being in the athlete's eyes. Furthermore, they propose that support can thus be provided by, for example, parents, who are reported by Norris and Kaniasty (1996) as a received system whereby support occurs naturally, in contrast to medical staff who they refer to as a perceived system because the athlete believes this person would be there as required. When implemented appropriately support systems can serve as emotional (being loved and cared for), tangible (for example, driving the athlete to venues) or informational (which is advice and feedback orientated) functions (Schaefer, Coyne, & Lazarus, 1982).

Coach-athlete relationship

Laura's relationship with her new American based coach was in her and her family's eyes 'pivotal to her development and success'. Her coach, as described by Laura, is:

> a gifted teacher in that he trains no two students alike ... he has an uncanny knack of understanding just where a student's particular strengths and weaknesses lie, and training them to improve both.

To Laura, her coach also seems to reciprocate the respect in that she says he recognised and often acknowledged that Laura has an 'excellent brain for the sport', further remarking to her on many occasions that she is 'an extremely fast learner with perfect technique'. Building upon these strengths, Laura says that it was clear to her that, as her coach, he realised that to improve her, and hopefully develop her into a champion, they had to work on the mind games and strategy of the sport. Instilling such knowledge of the game into Laura has to her had a:

> great impact on my performance, affording me confidence on the sporting stage and equipping me with tools that I can use to alleviate performance anxiety, as well as bring about victory.

To this day, Laura and her coach continue to emphasise the importance of working on tactics in Laura's development. This relationship and knowledge of each other's strengths has evidently provided the foundations for a strong relationship of trust and respect. Such positive remarks regarding the coach provide support for the athletic triangle described by Smoll et al. (2011), which posits that when athletes and parents feel that the coach is aware of and considers their concerns it results in closeness, commitment and alleviation of hassle for all those involved despite the complex interactions which occur in the triangle (Smoll et al., 2011). Such recognition is important for other coaches, athletes, parents and practitioners to consider as a way of indirectly enhancing performance.

Medical and mental performance staff

The creation of a positive environment can be challenging because adolescent athletes often find themselves surrounded by a host of different people who are all intertwined with the athlete, yet belong to different support systems representing the varied interests of the athlete (Thiel et al., 2011). Medical support was a key priority to Laura. Upon arriving in America, she and her parents sought out a host of reputable professionals to augment those already identified in the UK. As Laura states:

> Suffering injuries is a part of any athlete's life, but without the intelligence and creative ideas of the right people at the right time, they can be debilitating ... finding such people was instrumental to preventing my development from reaching a plateau.

Over time Laura has assembled a go-to support system. Upon reflection, perhaps one of the most invaluable aspects of these systems was Laura's partnership with her sport psychologist. Specifically, she fulfilled one aspect of the information function within the social system, advice and feedback. Developing productive support systems according to the sport psychologist:

was an essential part of Laura's journey ... increasing Laura's awareness, understanding and questioning of the role and function of each person or group around her (in much the same way as they had previously done within the lifestyle section) alleviated many stressors.

Consequently, she and her family surrounded themselves with people who had a specific purpose for the good of the team rather than simply because of their reputation. Through the work undertaken, the sport psychologist learned that, whilst support systems can be a source of stress, the development of clearly defined roles ensures they have a buffering effect (Carlson & Perrewe, 1999) thus alleviating the negative impact of stresses such as isolation.

The parents' experience

Although repetitive in places, the story of Laura's parents provides new insights into elite performance. An important aspect of the journey is that of Laura's parents. Whilst they witnessed many of Laura's trials and tribulations they additionally faced many challenges and sacrifices of their own which, according to Smoll et al. (2011), warrant attention as they can have a significant influence on an athlete's psychological state. They referred to the athlete-parent relationship as the athletic triangle and posited the importance of examining this triad owing to the complex interactions between athletes and their parents because, if nurtured correctly, the triad can contribute positively to the encounters adolescents experience in their sporting environment, which is something that was of essential concern in Laura's situation.

Laura's mother's story is one of emotion and sacrifice. For example, whilst in the UK, she saw her role as 'the taxi driver' as a normal part of many parents' life irrespective of sports participation. However, the true reality of her sacrifice was felt:

> The day I watched my husband drive away from our Portland apartment for the first time ... suddenly, the man I had never been apart from for much longer than a week at a time was gone, leaving Laura and I alone for several months.

Although she had a close relationship with her daughter, she reflects:

> All at once I felt like a newly single mother of a 16 year-old, who could be expected to be as difficult as any 16 year-old might, and who suddenly lacked a paternal figure in her life.

In her new role Laura's mother describes feeling:

> Under enormous pressure, taking on the role of mother, father, teacher and manager to Laura ... there was such responsibility to ensure Laura's academic, as well as athletic, success, especially now that Laura had been removed from school, without even the safety net of a tutor, combined with the new time pressures of extra hours of training every day.

Without training or guidance she was responsible for 'structuring and managing Laura's day', and she felt the 'pressure of that cloak of responsibility on her shoulders'.

Back in the UK, Laura's father's main concerns centred on ensuring the funds were available each month to pay the bills both at home and in the US, together with funding for Laura's participation in the sport. In his words, 'this has required a considerable amount of financial plate-spinning'.

Triad support for competitions

The sport psychologist also provided support with regard to Laura's parents. In line with the recommendations from Rynne and McLean (2011), it was important to ensure that her parents' responsibilities were aimed at enhancing Laura's experience of sport. Thus it was essential that the support structure put in place for the parents created a team serving bias, whereby the 'I's' were taken out of team decisions and they were made for the good of the team and self-interest suspended (Sherman & Kim, 2005). Whilst Laura was always central, their needs also had to be satisfied to a degree. Thus it was important to develop clear communication channels between the 'core team players' so that an understanding of each person's role could be developed, thereby ensuring everyone was valued (Rynne & McLean, 2011). In addition, Mageau and Vallerand (2003) suggested that explaining decisions helps to change focus from outcome to process, which in turn can reduce parental stress. In line with their work, the team introduced broad guidelines of 'dos' and 'don'ts' of the competitive day.

The family reflected upon such actions and consider the development of the triad as:

> The most crucial support system of all was one that our sport psychologist taught us, how to create the family "Team" identity ... functioning as a team, rather than as a family, was critical to Laura's athletic success in many ways: adopting "roles" while at competitions allowed the family to deal with pressure and, sometimes, failure, in a constructive manner, and helped the family to successfully deal with challenges out-side of competition by teaching them to rely on each other ... the key outcome of this intervention of forming the family Team, most importantly, gave us a framework for successes.

Hence, on a competition day the family achieved a better balance between the emotional and tangible functions of the team.

Consequence: burnout

The pertinence of those stressors raised previously can be seen in the work of Gould et al. (1993b) who found burnout to be a result of stress accumulation, which was where Laura's journey came to an abrupt head. Specifically, in support of this Goodger, Gorely, Lavalle, & Harwood (2007) reported that the term 'burnout' began to be utilised as a way of describing the 'gradual process of exhaustion' (p. 127), making it pertinent to sport and Laura's situation in particular as she began to suffer the effects of burnout towards the end of the 2010/11 season. Along with others such as Lonsdale, Hodge, & Rose (2009), Goodger et al. (2007) highlighted Raedeke's (1997) three aspects of burnout: emotional exhaustion, depersonalisation and decreased performance, all of which were experiences Laura described, albeit to differing extents. In-depth examination of Laura's schedule provides a clear understanding for the genesis of these experiences.

Laura's competitive season runs from September to June. All year round she attends two 2½-hour practice sessions five days a week and four 2-hour fitness sessions each week (as outlined previously). In addition, to comply with visa restrictions, she must travel out of America and its contiguous states of Canada and Mexico, at least once every 90 days. In 2011, Laura reacted to these stresses by temporarily withdrawing from the sport, which is a phenomenon discussed in the athlete-specific description of burnout in Raedeke et al. (2002). In Laura's case this was in part due to exhaustion but also due to the fact that it was the end of the season, making a short-term withdrawal inevitable in any event. However, it may well be the fact that the season coming to an end was in itself a contributing factor as Laura experienced emotional exhaustion, which is said to be 'associated with intense training and competition' (Goodger et al., 2007, p. 128). Furthermore, the 2012 'Olympic Dream' was over.

In contrast to these explanations of burnout, a perspective taken by Coakley (1992) also sheds light on Laura's experiences in that he described burnout as a result of sport organisations, which, again, appears to have been a contributing factor to Laura's situation. Laura also identifies with an element described in Schmidt and Stein's (1991) commitment-based model, which adds the dimension of the athlete feeling like they have to be involved as opposed to wanting to be involved in the sport. This was a key contributing factor to Laura's circumstance due to the array of challenges and sacrifices both she and her support network had made.

> The feeling of burnout does not arrive overnight, it creeps up on you over a period of time so that you hardly notice the disaffection settling in … I was training because that was just what I did, but I had lost the joy of the sport. For a while I wasn't even sure I wanted to recapture it and the belief that my parents and everybody in my team had all invested so much in me meant that I simply could not quit, even if I wanted to. This only engendered an element of resentment towards my sport.

Such a statement aligns itself with the investment model of burnout as proposed by Raedeke (1997). The model suggests that there is a cost/benefit relationship whereby if the costs outweigh the benefits there is an imbalance and the athlete becomes entrapped within the sport. For Laura the rewards of competing were low but the costs were now appraised as high.

Together, Laura and her sport psychologist identified the sources of stress and the key contributors were placed in order of importance so as to prioritise the intervention strategy. Money, attitudes from within the sporting world and college entry were identified and strategies for dealing with each one were developed through a structured and systematic action plan. Laura also wrote about her basic motivations in order to examine her levels of competence and autonomy. This was important because, as discussed by Rynne and McLean (2011), environments that are conducive to autonomy are said to have effects both long term on performance as well as on personal development and relatedness. As a result of the work done, Laura was able to rediscover her motivation and commitment to her sport, making her next competition a more pleasurable and rewarding experience.

Lessons learnt and future

With challenges and sacrifices also came growth. The amount of training Laura had adopted every day led to what she explained as 'accelerated performance', as was reflected in her progression from number one Cadet and Junior to Senior team member, and in her proudest sporting moments:

> Defeating two Olympic team members in competition, one of whom had won gold in 2008.

For Laura's parents the experience had been of a different kind. They have had to learn to live apart for more than half of the year and maintain a common goal despite not being able to share the entire load equally between them. Laura's father reflects:

> Given our time again, we would do some things differently. Probably, we should have saved up some money first before launching into the "Portland Plan".

As the family Team moves forward, they look towards the future and see 'many bright things on the horizon'. Laura continues to develop as an athlete, and continues to work towards her one unfulfilled goal: the Olympics. She also looks towards college, having been admitted to an Ivy League university from September 2012. She knows that the family Team is right behind her. It is clear that to promote and maintain a successful career athletes must have clear and effective interventions in place (Thiel et al., 2011). This involves enlisting the help of people beyond the family but with purpose and control. Overall, a key lesson learnt is do your research to ensure you have trust in those around you, as this can be highly beneficial to the successful functioning of a team.

Conclusion

All those working and dealing with athletes must understand the unique demands of each performer. Awareness, acknowledgement and understanding of athletes' individual stressors are essential to maintain healthy athletes. Coaches, parents, practitioners and athletes need to develop positive working relationships in order to ensure that organisational stressors are eliminated and productive support systems encouraged.

Burnout is a risk factor that needs to be monitored. Perhaps upon reflection Laura experienced burnout because of a lack of communication between the core team due to the divide of 'the pond' and thus key indicators were missed. Immediate team members must therefore be trained to identify early signs and symptoms so prevention rather than cures can occur.

The family team have dealt with many different challenges and sacrifices whether it is in the form of hours spent travelling, time apart, or pounds spent. However they have arrived at a singular conclusion:

> That no matter what, every challenge can be overcome, and that it is all, unequivocally and undeniably, worth it.

Acknowledgements

The authors would like to thank the participants of this study and all those who have contributed to the journey of the athlete and her family.

Notes on contributors

Amanda J. Wilding is in the School of Tourism at Bournemouth University where she works as Framework Leader for the undergraduate sport programmes. She is currently completing her PhD in the area of the diffusion and adoption of sport psychology.

Laura Hunter-Thomas is a student, writer and online magazine editor.

Roger Thomas is a member of the Bar of England and Wales practising from St Ives Chambers, Birmingham.

References

Abernethy, B. (2008). Introduction: Developing expertise in sport – how research can inform practice. In D. Farrow, J. Baker, & C. MacMahon (Eds.), *Developing sport expertise* (pp. 1–14). Abingdon: Routledge.

Adie, J.W., Duda, J.L., & Ntoumanis, N. (2008). Achievement goals, competition appraisals, and the psychological and emotional welfare of sports participants. *Journal of Sport & Exercise Psychology, 30*(3), 302–322.

Barth, B., & Beck, E. (2007). *The complete guide to fencing.* Oxford: Meyer & Meyer Sport.

Carlson, D.S., & Perrewe, P.L. (1999). The role of social support in the stressor-strain relationship: an examination of work-family conflict. *Journal of Management, 25*(4), 513–540.

Coakley, J. (1992). Burnout among adolescent athletes: a personal failure or social problem? *Sociology of Sport Journey, 9*, 271–285.

Fletcher, D., & Hanton, S. (2003). Sources of organizational stress in elite sports performers. *The Sport Psychologist, 17*, 175–195.

Fletcher, D., Hanton, S., & Mellalieu, S.D. (2006). An organizational stress review: conceptual and theoretical issues in competitive sport. In S. Hanton & S.D. Mellelieu (Eds.), *Literature reviews in sport psychology* (pp. 321–373). New York: Nova Science.

Fletcher, D., Hanton, S., & Wagstaff, C.R.D. (2012). Performers' responses to stressors encountered in sport organisations. *Journal of Sports Sciences, 30*(4), 349–358.

Frone, M.R., Russell, M., & Cooper, M.L. (1992). Antecedents and outcomes of work-family conflict: Testing a model of the work-family interface. *Journal of Applied Psychology, 11*, 65–75.

Goodger, K., Gorely, T., Lavallee, D., & Harwood, C. (2007). Burnout in sport: A systematic review. *The Sport Psychologist, 21*, 127–151.

Gould, D., & Maynard, I. (2009). Psychological preparation for the Olympic Games. *Journal of Sports Sciences, 27*(13), 1393–1408.

Gould, D., Jackson, S., & Finch, L. (1993a). Sources of stress in national champion figure skaters. *Journal of Sport & Exercise Psychology, 15*, 134–159.

Gould, D., Jackson, S., & Finch, L. (1993b). Life at the top: The experience of U.S. national champion figure skaters. *The Sport Psychologist, 7*, 354–374.

Gustafsson, G., Kenttä, G., Hassmén, P., & Lundqvist, C. (2007). Prevalence of burnout in competitive adolescent athletes. *The Sport Psychologist, 21*, 21–37.

Hadjistavropoulos, T., & Smythe, W. (2001). Elements of risk in qualitative research. *Ethics and Behavior, 11*(2), 163–174.

Hanton, S., Fletcher, D., & Coughlan, G. (2005). Stress in elite sport performers: A comparative study of competitive and organizational stressors. *Journal of Sports Sciences, 23* (10), 1129–1141.

Hanton, S., Wadey, R., & Mellalieu, S.D. (2008). Advanced psychological strategies and anxiety responses in sport. *The Sport Psychologist, 22*, 472–490.

Jeffreys, I. (2006). Lifestyle profiling in high school athletes. *Strength and Conditioning Journal, 28*(3), 77–79.

Kristiansen, E.G., & Roberts, C. (2009). Young elite athletes and social support: coping with competitive and organizational stress in 'Olympic' competition. *Scandinavian Journal of Medicine and Science in Sports, 20*, 686–695.

Long, T., Pantaleon, N., & Bruant, G. (2008). Institutionalization versus self-regulation: a contextual analysis of responsibility among adolescent sportsmen. *Journal of Moral Education, 37*(4), 519–538.

Lonsdale, C., Hodge, K., & Rose, E. (2009). Athlete burnout in elite sport: A self-determination perspective. *Journal of Sports Sciences, 27*(8), 785–795.

Mageau, G.A., & Vallerand, R.J. (2003). The coach-athlete relationship: A motivational model. *Journal of Sports Sciences, 21*, 883–904.

Mellalieu, S.D., Neil, R., Hanton, S., & Fletcher, D. (2009). Competition stress in sport performers: Stressors experienced in the competition environment. *Journal of Sports Sciences, 12*(7), 729–744.

McKay, J., Niven, A.G., Lavalle, D., & White, A. (2008). Sources of strain among elite UK track athletes. *The Sport Psychologist, 22*, 143–163.

Norris, F.H., & Kaniasty, K. (1996). Received and perceived social support in times of stress: A test of the social support deterioration deterrence model. *Journal of Personality and Social Psychology, 71*(3), 498–511.

Raedeke, T.D. (1997). Is athlete burnout more than just stress? A sport commitment perspective. *Journal of Sport and Exercise Psychology, 19*, 396–417.

Raedeke, T.D., Lunney, K., & Venanbles, K. (2002). Understanding athlete burnout: Coach perspectives. *Journal of Sport Behaviour, 25*, 181–206.

Rynne, S.B., & McLean, K.N. (2001). Enhancing coach-parent relationships in youth sports: Increasing harmony and minimizing hassle, a commentary. *International Journal of Sports Science & Coaching, 6*(1), 53–55.

Scanlan, T.K., Stein, G.L., & Ravizza, K. (1991). An in-depth study of former elite figure skaters: III. Sources of stress. *Journal of Sport and Exercise Psychology, 13*(2), 103–120.

Schaefer, C., Coyne, J.C., & Lazarus, R.S. (1982). The health related functions of social support. *Journal of Behavioral Medicine, 4*, 381–406.

Schmidt, G.W., & Stein, G.L. (1991). A commitment model of burnout. *Journal of Applied Sport Psychology, 8*, 323–345.

Sherman, D.K., & Kim, H.S. (2005). Is there an 'I' in 'team'? The role of the self in group-serving judgments. *Journal of Personality and Social Psychology, 88*(1), 108–120.

Shirom, A. (1982). What is organizational stress? A facet analytical conceptualisation. *Journal of Occupational Behaviour, 3*(1), 21–37.

Smith, B., & Sparkes, A.C. (2005). Analyzing talk in qualitative inquiry: exploring possibilities, problems, and tensions. *QUEST, 57*, 213–242.

Smoll, F.L., Cumming, S.P., & Smith, R.E. (2011). Enhancing coach-parent relationships in youth sports: Increasing harmony and minimizing hassle. *International Journal of Sports Science & Coaching, 6*(1), 13–26.

Stotlar, D.K., & Wonder, A. (2006). Developing elite athletes: A content analysis of US national governing body systems. *International Journal of Applied Sports Sciences, 18*(2), 121–144.

Sun, Y., & Wu, X. (2011). Self-regulation of elite athletes in China. *Social Behavior and Personality, 39*(8), 1035–1044.

Thiel, A., Diehl, K.E., Schnell, A., Schbring, A.M., Mayer, J., Ziptel, S., et al. (2011). The German young Olympics athletes' lifestyle and health management study (goal study): Design of a mixed-method study. *BMC Public Health, 11*(410), 1471–2458.

Williams, A.M., & Ford, P.R. (2009). Promoting a skills-based agenda in Olympic Sports: The role of skill acquisition specialists. *Journal of Sport Sciences, 27*(13), 1381–1392.

Woodman, T., & Hardy, L. (2001). A case study of organizational stress in elite sport. *Journal of Applied Sport Psychology, 13*(2), 207–238.

'Multi-directional management': exploring the challenges of performance in the World Class Programme environment

Dave Collins and Andrew Cruickshank

Institute for Coaching and Performance, University of Central Lancashire, Preston, UK

Driven by the ever-increasing intensity of Olympic competition and the 'no compromise – no stone unturned' requirements frequently addressed by HM Government and its main agency, UK Sport, a change in culture across Olympic team landscapes is a common occurrence. With a focus on process, this paper presents reflections from eight current or recently serving UK Olympic sport Performance Directors on their experiences of creating and disseminating their vision for their sport, a vital initial activity of the change initiative. To facilitate a broad overview of this construct, reflections are structured around the vision's characteristics and foundations, how it is delivered to key stakeholder groups, how it is influenced by these groups, the qualities required to ensure its longevity and its limitations. Emerging from these perceptions, the creation and maintenance of a shared team vision was portrayed as a highly dynamic task requiring the active management of a number of key internal and external stakeholders. Furthermore, the application of 'dark' traits and context-specific expertise were considered critical attributes for the activity's success. Finally, recent calls for research to elucidate the wider culture optimisation process are reinforced.

Introduction

As Olympic performance continues to push the boundaries of physical, technical, tactical and mental aptitude, it is crucial that athletes and their support staff operate within high performing cultures throughout the four-year competition cycle. Indeed, reflecting the energy, engagement and focus required to improve/refine all facets of performance, and ensure that these are robust to the intense pressure an Olympic Games, a minute-to-minute, second-to-second commitment to one's profession across this period is essential if peak success is to be achieved. As those responsible for managing and regulating individual, intra-group and inter-group features of the performance environment, the perception, decision making and action of the Performance Director (hereafter PD) is therefore central to the functioning, longevity and achievement of Olympic sports teams.

Certainly, while Olympic sport PDs typically deliver little if any 'hands on' coaching (or at least should if their role is not to become 'clouded'), their ability to influence pan-individual performance (positively, negatively or indifferently) is arguably the most significant of any in the performance department of a national sport organisation (i.e. that including team management, performance-specific administrative staff, support staff and performers) apart from the personal coach him/herself. Specifically, through holding ultimate responsibility for team policies, systems, structures and processes, at least in an optimum system, a PD's ambitions, principles and intentions will always, to at least some extent, be reflected in the perceptions, preferences and behaviours of all those 'lower down' the organisational chart (we place *lower down* in inverted commas as this principle applies to democratic as well as autocratic models). As such, due to growing awareness of this role's significance, attention has recently turned to consider these figures perceptions of best practice.

Specifically, from enquiry into the position's main facets and the qualities required for optimal performance, Fletcher and Arnold (2011, p. 223) revealed four areas of Olympic PD competency, namely: *operations*, *people*, *culture* and *vision*. Operations entailed "financial management, strategic competition and training planning, athlete selection for competition, and upholding rules and regulations"; people involved "staff management, lines of communication, and feedback mechanisms"; culture was represented by "establishing role awareness, and organizational and team atmosphere"; and, finally, vision, or "the team's ultimate aspiration" (p. 228) incorporated "vision development, influences on the vision, and sharing the vision". Providing much needed insight into the nuances of Olympic team management, this work offers a valuable overview of the required dimensions of proficiency, albeit that the competency construct may impose some limitations on our conceptual understanding of how exactly such 'competencies' are differentially blended and applied (cf. in coaching: Abraham & Collins, 2011; in support science: Martindale & Collins, 2007). Indeed, as alluded to by Fletcher and Arnold, it is reasonable to assert that the relative importance and operationalisation of each identified theme will vary substantially across contextually distinct phases and episodes of the real life PD challenge.

Expressly, while many of the sub-theme responsibilities identified by Fletcher and Arnold (2011) represent inherent and ongoing tests of the PD skill set, successful engagement in each area will undoubtedly be highly context-specific. For example, as in any complex and dynamic environment, factors such as history, tradition, systems, structures and interpersonal relationships will all interact to dictate/limit the options and directions available to the PD in their efforts to deliver sustained optimal performance (Bevir & Richards, 2009; Cilliers, 2000). Accordingly, the uncritical, pan-context application of generic 'advantageous' leadership behaviours, such as those espoused by transformational leadership theory (cf. Callow, Smith, Hardy, Arthur, & Hardy, 2009), across a variety of scenarios will presumably often generate sub-optimal impact or, in some instances, even be inappropriate.

Of further importance, some of the Olympic PD's broad activities also appear highly context-*dependent*. Specifically, the efficient and effective creation of a shared vision and culture will logically only occur if pertinent groups (i.e. team management, administrators, support staff, performers) and their members consider that: (a) the old vision/culture is no longer engaging and/or functional; or (b) the new vision/culture holds greater rewards and/or is more appealing. Normally generated (or demanded) by (usually) tacitly accepted watershed moments, the Olympic Games' four-year schedule provides one such 'natural' tipping point (Kim & Mauborgne, 2003) whereby a detailed review of performance provides a catalyst for determining the focus and approach in the next cycle. Beyond this structural feature, however, one exemplar 'unnatural' trigger is that of PD turnover. In this scenario a new, incoming director engages in a 'change management' programme aimed at fostering a high performing culture and, by association, consistent high performance (cf. Cruickshank & Collins, in pressa). Reflecting the sacking pandemic engulfing elite sport systems around the world (Bruinshoofd & ter Weel, 2003; League Managers Association., 2010; Zinser, 2008) and the lack of peer-reviewed knowledge on this performance-defining construct, our contribution is located within this latter context; in short, how may the benefits of such change be optimised, albeit from the perspective of the incoming director.

Returning to the competencies identified by Fletcher and Arnold (2011), but with a focus on the *process* of a new director's programme, we place the creation and dissemination of the team's vision as the chronological origins of a change imitative. Indeed, these authors' also conceptualised the Olympic PD's vision as a framework against which individual, team and organisational performance/process goals are harnessed, a point echoed by one of the PDs (individual sport) interviewed for the present contribution:

> Having a vision is first and the vision is within you ...The next stage only makes a difference if the other ones are in first ... People think attention to detail is compelling and necessary, which it probably is, but the environment and the attitude is way more compelling ... I can ... start introducing [performance] analysis and even physiological testing, but if we don't have a compelling performance environment that stuff's just a waste of time. In fact it's more than a waste of time, it's a distraction.

Recognising the programme- and outcome-shaping nature of the guiding vision, examining PDs' reflections on this construct is therefore both theoretically and practically intriguing. Beyond contributing to the developing literature and evidence-based practice of management-lead culture change elite sport performance teams (cf. Cruickshank & Collins, in pressa; Cruickshank & Collins, in pressb), we hope that such exposure will stimulate further reflection on the part of elite team managers, consultants who support their programmes and other pertinent members of elite sport organisations (e.g. CEOs; Board members).

Accordingly, to provide a descriptive account of the characteristics, components, interactions and limitations of the PD-facilitated team vision and examine these figures' role in optimising performance, reflections are structured around the following questions: What are the characteristics and foundations of Olympic PDs' visions? How are these best delivered to key stakeholder groups? How are such visions influenced by these groups? What qualities are required to ensure their longevity? Finally, what are their limitations? Mirroring the complexity of elite team environments (cf. Cruickshank & Collins, in pressa), we pay close attention to interactional elements, considering how PD decision making, action and reaction does not operate within an uncontested vacuum. The presented reflections come from interviews with eight PDs either currently or previously employed by British Olympic sport organisations within the past two Olympic cycles (2004–2012).

Characteristics and foundations of the Olympic PD's vision

As governed and reinforced by their continued operation within elite sport settings, all PDs articulated that their vision for their sport represented an enduring pursuit for/realisation of optimal performance, which in all cases was directly related to the attainment of desirable objective outcomes (i.e. medals/titles). Resonating with a number of acquired perceptions, the following quote conveys how one individual's vision (individual sport) was built upon a foundation of ambition, enticing possibility and positive engagement:

> Very simply … [the vision] was to produce or develop the best sports team in Britain and the best [sport] team in the World. And it's a very grand, broad statement obviously, backed up by the imagery it creates in people … They're dominant forces in whatever it is that they're contesting … it's a tidal wave, an unstoppable force … there will be a way in which they race or play … We wanted to race exciting, attacking races. We wanted to win races, not cross the line first by default having buried everyone into submission. We wanted to actually go win 'em.

Interestingly, while all interviewees held similar ideals regarding their long-term hopes and goals, it was also acknowledged, particularly by the PD quoted immediately above, that such aspiration was a mandatory but initially mysterious and elusive construct:

> Did I know the detail of what I was trying to achieve at the time? No. But you have this vision and I think perhaps that's actually worth stating: When you make that pledge [about] what…you [are] trying to achieve [to key stakeholders], you've got to have a compelling vision … And that pretty much bound [the strategic plan], we're gonna be the best sports team in the World … you want to get on board with that? Come on. What does it actually mean? Don't really know in all detail. But it's gonna be fun and it's gonna be dominant.

From this quote, ambition and optimism were vital components of this PD's initial efforts to immediately engage key stakeholders in their change programme. Importantly, although this and all other PD visions were largely ego-orientated (i.e. they involved winning events and/or comparison with others), it is also critical to note that all interviewees clearly clarified that objective rewards did not necessarily define the success of their programmes. Certainly, a key adjunct to the fundamental 'dream' was an acceptance that performance, and therefore the acquisition of medals/titles, is dictated by an innumerate range of athlete-related (e.g. physiological traits; technical expertise), programme-related (e.g. training facilities, sport science/ medicine support) and sport/competition-related (e.g. ability of competitors, rule changes) variables. In line with this recognition, one PD (individual and team sport) who described their intention to change a "culture of being a participant to trying to be a winner" reflected:

> [The Olympics are] the biggest meet of your life and if you can have the performance of your life, whether you come twelfth or first, you'll feel like you've won a medal 'cos you couldn't have done any better – you just had the performance of your life. And that's what I want to create … it doesn't matter where you finish, I just want *you* to come away and go "god, I couldn't have done any better" … there is nothing worse than ifs and buts.

Acknowledging the demands placed on Olympic PDs by their staff and performers, employers (i.e. national sports organisations), funders (i.e. UK Sport), external partners (e.g. service providers; sponsors) and the media/general public (particularly in the lead up to London 2012), understanding the personal context of why these individuals undertake such roles represents a further important point of reflection. Consistent across the present sample's perceptions, the personal challenge of realising their vision was a key motivator:

> I was driven, I was driven by winning, not being placed but by winning; [I] believed that we could find a way to get the right people to challenge the world's best ... I'm a proud person as well, I want to win medals ... as I did when I was an athlete so that was a massive driver for me. (Team sport PD)

As suggested by this quote, although Olympic PDs are required to facilitate the performance of a multitude of individuals (athletes, support staff, administrative staff), an important but perhaps often overlooked consideration, both academically and practically, is recognition that elite team managers are performers in their own right. Certainly, acknowledging the inherent competitiveness of elite sport environments and the likelihood that PDs will have previously performed, managed/coached or operated in high pressure sport environments, this oversight is surprising. Notwithstanding this point, however, while personal achievement emerged as central to the energy and commitment devoted to programme delivery, significantly none of the interviewees placed this as their sole or major pursuit. First and foremost, all PDs described a desire to introduce and/or optimise systems, structures and processes which would facilitate sustained peak performance in their athletes/staff and, consequently, provide a legacy for their sport:

> I saw this as an unbelievable challenge and I liked that ... Let's see if we can do it, let's give it a go, 'cos I liked that, let's see what happens ... [But] I want to build them a sporting system ... so that if I'm there 10 years and I leave does it just fall apart and crumble? If it does, that's a pretty poor job I did. If there's something there that helps keep producing medals for 50 years then I've done something right; so that's probably the biggest thing I'm trying to achieve. (Individual and team sport PD)

Reflecting the magnitude of these aspirations and the personal stake in programme success, all PDs also ardently reported that a robust and enduring personal belief was critical for optimal engagement with the vision and its effective and efficient proliferation within and across generations of the performance department:

> You've got to believe in it – if you don't you will not convince anybody else because it's going to be hard and you've got to compel people to come with you, and you've got to set a tone and it's got to be consistent ... Can someone like myself take that same change, that culture development from [sport] into [another sport]? I personally believe that you can to an extent, but in the end you are fundamentally limited because you actually don't care about it. There might be bits of it you care about it, you might care about being personally successful or something like that, but ultimately you don't understand the sport or fundamentally care about it. And I think that's limiting because you have to believe very strongly in what you're doing ... You're going to be up at 1 or 2 o'clock in the morning. (Individual sport PD)

The clear and stated existence of this longer-term goal, namely the generation and achievement of a legacy (cf. the basis under which the Singapore proposal which secured the games for London was based) stands in contrast to the explicit focus by management structures on this oft cited but insufficiently targeted outcome of the home games!

Making the vision work: ensuring credibility

While the foundations of the PDs' visions were purely performance-focused, there was widespread recognition that this aspiration's initial formation and dissemination was highly susceptible to a range of mediating factors. Primarily, whether the PD was from 'within' or 'outside' the sport emerged as central to how the vision was generated, delivered and established. For example, one PD (individual and team sport) with no history or previous association with their sport offered a particularly notable reflection on their 'status' at the time of their appointment:

> One of the benefits when you come from outside the sport ... is that you are not saddled by the history of the sport, ... relationships good or bad with people within the sport...[or] the politics of the sport ... As such, coming from outside the sport, the fact that you are unknown can be a double-edged sword: it can make people very defensive but it can also make people very, very open by the fact that you are not weighed down by history ... I think you have to be aware you're only in that unique position for a period of time.

While this PD valued the opportunity to work with a 'clean slate', as facilitated by their lack of connection, the hurdles facing those attempting to deliver sustainable change in unfamiliar settings was significantly reinforced by another PD (individual and team sport):

> At the most basic level, people want to follow a clear and 'face valid' lead; they want you to be clearly seen as a 'guru'...someone whose credibility is unquestioned. Personally, I think this is really dangerous, unless both they and you question what you say. Just because I am a successful coach in (sport), or even worse a successful performer, is almost totally irrelevant to whether I am making good strategic decisions. The media are the worst promoters of this bull**** truth! For example, consider the status of SCW (Sir Clive Woodward). One great success, several subsequent failures but still the man on almost every aspect of performance as far as the media are concerned. Surely, you need to carefully test what you think all the time, whether this is your sport or not.

Intriguingly, while the PD's stature may require careful handling if the desired vision is to be widely accepted, shared and driven by all performance team members (the principles of a high performing culture: cf. Cruickshank & Collins, in pressb), it was also considered invaluable in gaining support and minimising uncertainty and/or resistance from key stakeholder groups:

> I do think you need to have a level of credibility, whatever your background is. I think a precursor for being a PD is to have had, even if it's in a different sport, is to have had some success ... Credibility does count for an awful, awful lot ... you wouldn't be being questioned directly by the people who are going out to perform on your behalf. (Individual and team sport PD)

Importantly, while the PD's credibility at appointment emerged as a consistent reflection, it is also essential to note that the credibility of the vision itself also offered a mechanism by which the programme could be protected from derailment by powerful individuals:

What you're backing is your long-term vision to be the best team in the world: We're not the best team in the world at the minute so we have to move forward, we can't just do what we're doing now. And if I'm right it's going to require you guys getting better, and if I can have some demonstrable evidence that at least some of you, and significant ones of you [are] getting better then there's enough of a hook that when [a socially powerful, senior performer] walks you don't. (Individual sport PD)

In cases where such a vision lacked credibility, the role of other agencies (such as CEO, Board, UK Sport, etc.) was seen as crucial to keeping the plan on track.

Particularly in the early stages of selling the new vision, it's essential to get all the other stakeholders on board and publicly supporting the plan. Without this you are "a voice which crieth in the wilderness". (Individual and team sport PD)

This reflection notably emphasises the importance of multi-directional management if selling the vision is to be successful, a point which we now consider in greater depth.

Creating and disseminating the vision: multi-stakeholder influence

As identified above, although the PD's vision for their sport may be firmly grounded within a philosophy of facilitating enduring optimal performance, the preceding reflections support our earlier assertion that elite sport is a highly dynamic and contested environment which is both rooted to and shaped by fluctuating environmental contexts. Indeed, across the present dataset, powerful actors from a variety of stakeholder groups emerged as pivotal in constraining the PD's vision and associated activities. As such, multi-source information gathering and multi-stakeholder negotiation, focused on both internal and external parties, emerged as a critical success factor of vision formulation and dissemination.

Influences from within the performance environment

Highlighting the challenge of delivering a constantly coherent programme, one PD (individual and team sport) reported the importance of gaining the support of existing senior managers before fully engaging with the changes which would support the attainment of their vision:

They were very, very cautious ... and that somewhat dictated my approach ... I knew that I had to develop a relationship with those two [senior managers] in particular. Without a relationship with those two people ... then I would have been doomed to fail.

Beyond ensuring that the whole management team exuded a unified and consistent approach, another PD (individual and team sport) also reflected upon similar issues within their support staff, which often provided a distraction to immediately addressing the dissemination of their vision and pertinent performance-related issues:

Each and every provider is an individual, with all the baggage and agendae that includes. Unfortunately, but perhaps inevitably, they are each driven by what they want and need...and they will often fight tooth and nail to maintain their own status, irrespective of the logic or benefit of change.

Similarly, all PDs also revealed that sensitivity to performers' perceptions was critical in ensuring that the programme's new systems and processes were positively received:

> You're asking people to commit way above and beyond what it is ordinarily committed if you're going to be the best in the world, and it's an undefined quantity and it's a scary quantity for most people … If we're going to chop people on programmes every six months, they ain't going to [optimally] commit … They…will do it out of fear. Well now you're not free you're not liberated and in order to truly give you've got to be liberated. The brakes have got to come off, and fear is a break. (Individual sport PD)

Influences from outside the performance environment

As well as the constraining perceptions, expectations and actions of performers, support staff and team management, the PDs also reflected upon the influence which external groups have on the establishment and diffusion of their team's visions. Predominantly, such assessment related to interactions with UK Sport (the British Government's Olympic sport funding body and largest provider of finance to participating teams), the sport's wider membership and the media.

Influences from above

As suggested, managing interactions with UK Sport was portrayed as a particular challenge to the PD's efforts in establishing and sharing their vision. Primarily, this body's insatiable pursuit of medals provided significant issues for many and their desire to remain sensitive to the internal uncertainty in the performance environment triggered by the PD's impending new programme:

> The first role I [had] …was to write the four-year plan to UK Sport … The timing of it worked, personally, particularly poorly … I was keen to keep everybody happy and probably should have just looked at my own needs a little bit more … but we had to very quickly put together a concise summary performance plan as to the changes we were going to make during this cycle …, the significant events we were going to be attending and what our medal targets were for those events. (Individual and team sport PD)

In contrast, another PD (individual and team sport) felt the need to use the planning process as a line in the sand:

> My first plan was an important one; an exercise in managing upwards aimed more at creating the space necessary to operate against the performance models required than a pure box ticking exercise. I had to do it to keep them off my back! (Individual and team sport PD)

Indeed, rather than ensuring that PDs were liberated to create and deliver their own vision, one interviewee revealed that UK Sport's growing preference for involvement in performance matters caused a further significant distraction:

> I don't need to copy a blueprint from British Cycling … Although UK Sport tried to simplify everything, [and] there's definitely good practice that can go across all sports,

[they] aren't going to tell me about the nuances of [sport] and what I need to put in place. (Team sport PD)

Indeed, although not responsible for preparing athletes for Olympic competition, another PD (individual sport) provided detailed and insightful reflection on UK Sport's often authoritarian involvement and preoccupation with medals as *the* marker of successful investment:

> If UK Sport don't believe in [your] model then we have a problem ... I could have gone, yeah, I can see [the merits of UK Sport's ideas] ... but fundamentally we're on different pages ... Underpinning all this conversation ... compelling visions, real belief in what you want to do, absolute immersion and determination to see it through ..., if you're putting a lot into it on somebody else's agenda that's really dissatisfying... You have to absolutely believe, personally believe in what you're doing and [problems arise] if it has to be framed by somebody else.

Interestingly, while all PDs aimed to deliver long-term performance optimisation, another interviewee (individual and team sport PD) reflected on how the pressure for medals had ultimately shaped their initial focus and approach at the expense of changes which would facilitate such sustained achievement:

> I am answerable to UK Sport at the same time as being answerable to the sport itself so it does become a balance ...One of the things I've tried not to do ... is try not to get overly involved in changing the governing body per se ... that can become a massive distraction ... If my tenure was to last for an extended period of time maybe those are some conversations I would have further down the line. At this point in time, I'm certainly extremely focused on ... performance outcome.

Against this pragmatic focus a number of other influences were apparent. Some of these are considered in the next section.

Influences from the side

Of final note, interviewees also identified challenges to their vision from influential stakeholders outside of the performance and organisational environment, such as the sport's wider membership:

> The membership of the sport runs into the hundreds of thousands and of course the people involved in high performance are just a small fraction of that so of course there will probably be a raft of people who won't know me, won't understand my role ... There is always the dilemma in Olympic Sport that high performance tends to be hugely resource-intensive so you spend a lot of cash on a very ... small group ... it's either public money or membership money. (Individual and team sport PD)

Although not direct targets or recipients of the PD's change programme, the above reflection conveys that lower-level competitive and recreational athletes are nonetheless 'active players' in shaping and sustaining the vision and culture of the performance environment. Indeed, inherent within this quote is recognition that individuals will *always* have an opinion on the activities of their sport, regardless of their personal impact. As such, while not necessarily shaped by this group's views, the PD's vision must nonetheless be delivered in a manner which facilitates their acceptance or, perhaps more likely, minimises potential discontent.

Beyond the sport's wider membership, a number of PDs also highlighted the media as an important change agent. Indeed, one interviewee (individual sport) reflected on how this group's power could be harnessed to facilitate the realisation of their vision:

> We're a small programme, we're genuinely a small sport and I don't want to be a small sport – I want to be a big sport, I want to be a profile sport. So if we can get that out there then people think [sport] is significant and that's helpful ... If we can get a profile piece on [athlete] in national press ... media will pick up with [other individual athletes'] agents because [sport] is gaining momentum.

However, as with many of the vision-shaping factors described above, the same PD also reflected on the 'flipside' of media exposure:

> On one hand everyone's really grateful because everyone's benefiting. There's more money coming in, more individual sponsorships, everyone likes to see their name in the paper ... [But] then you've got to manage the egos ... It's a double-edged sword.

In 'higher profile' sports, these two competing pressures often coalesced as ex-athletes fulfilling powerful media roles took on an excessive influence, with funders if not with the general public!

> You get some guys on the TV with strong opinions and the ego to express them. The fact that these are often ill-informed and completely self-serving is often missed by the image conscious guys at UK Sport and in government. (Individual and team sport PD)

Delivering the vision: exemplar qualities required by the PD

Having offered reflection on the origins, drivers and mediators of the Olympic PD's vision, to maintain our focus on process we now examine the management qualities which these individuals have employed to successfully disseminate and protect this goal.

The 'dark side' of elite team management

As reported by Fletcher and Arnold (2011, p. 237), characterising Olympic PDs as holders of an array of socially desirable qualities (e.g. conscientiousness, openness, charisma) presents a "somewhat simplistic picture" of effective management in this domain. Indeed, strongly aligning with this point, the PDs interviewed for the present contribution also conveyed the need for 'darker' attributes in the facilitation and propagation of their vision. For example, take one (individual sport) PD's reflection on the need for soft traits:

> When you look at a lot of successful people they bulldoze ... because I think taking people with you is about a compelling vision not about a nice world ... The bulldozer analogy for me is: we're gonna go that way because it's right ...[and] if we're going that way then let's go that way. Does that make people go "that was a lovely discussion"; well not really. If we know the end point of this discussion lets go to ... that end point now. Whether I've said hello and have a nice day to you or not doesn't

really matter. Do people then reflect and go, "he's a very nice guy"? No, not necessarily. Really, it's a very outcome-generated thing.

As expressed by this quote, the possession and utilisation of an intense and no compromise attitude to performance issues emerged as crucial in ensuring that the PD's sport continually strived to address and solve performance-oriented issues. Indeed, such 'ruthlessness' (a word used by several PDs) was considered particularly valuable for vision dissemination and consequently generating and sustaining an entirely performance-focused culture; an arguably 'dark but positive' feature for these change agents. Further resonating with earlier reflections that placed the sport's enduring success ahead of personal achievement, another PD (team sport) also revealed how an unyielding stance was, at times, mandatory:

> Ultimately ... I made some decisions which made me quite unpopular but I never came into the sport to be popular anyway, I came in to drive things forward and win medals ... The bottom line for me is that [for] the support staff who didn't buy into that, [it] didn't make one bit of difference to me if [they] went or not.

Interestingly, and opposed to contemporary leadership theory assertions on the utility of individual consideration (cf. Callow et al., 2009), a similar direct approach was also often employed with performers:

> I was keeping as much as I could all the politics away from the other coaches and the players because they didn't need to know anything about that other than this is the four-year pathway ..., this is what it looks like on the playing side this is what you will be expected to do: are you wanting to be part of this or not because I'm not here to negotiate how little you can do, this is about Olympic [sport], you need to change your mindset. (Team sport PD)

Context-specific expertise

As noted in the introduction to this contribution, portioning responsibilities of the Olympic PD into generic competencies provides a valuable but ultimately unsophisticated picture of the skills required by such individuals. Indeed, as supported by the preceding reflections, the complexity inherent within elite sport environments demands the ability to make context-sensitive decisions which ensure that a short- and long-term focus on performance is sustained at all times. Reinforcing this key point, one PD (team sport) reflected:

> How much change do you make? When do you make that change? When is change like that too close to the major competition to then become disruptive? You're gonna get some backlash because ... the [athletes] will definitely have a downturn in performance and they're going to blame that on you ...

Similarly, the situation-specific challenge generated by a number of individuals interacting in ever-evolving environmental contexts was also manifest in efforts to engage key stakeholders in more macro-level decisions aimed at facilitating the vision's actualisation:

> The process was different for different pieces of work ...The selling of the idea ... of posts and people was a very different process to the consultancy approach when it

came to revising ... the policy of how we supported athletes; in the same way as [it was different to] ... the process of ... being a lot more prescriptive about the processes that were put in place for bringing people onto and taking people off of the WC programme. (Individual and team sport PD)

As such, the picture painted by the present sample was one whereby the dynamic, resource-demanding nature of managing an elite performance department relies on moment-to-moment expertise rather than the ability to deliver prescriptive, generic response patterns. Indeed, one PD (team sport) noted how such a top-down approach is rarely viable:

In the heat of the battle ... you're making decisions on the hoof ... the reality is you aren't that clear in the middle of it but you use instinct and ... gut feeling which defines you ... Certainly communication with the players was massive.

Limitations of the vision

Having considered the characteristics, components and interactional elements of Olympic PDs' visions, a final important consideration lies in perceptions of their restrictions; or more simply, what the vision is *not*. Indeed, although this ultimate aspiration provides a cornerstone against which long-term culture optimisation is consequently delivered, it is significant to note that a number of PDs reflected on the construct's frailties for generating *sustained* application and high performance throughout the four-year cycle:

The first hook's the compelling vision: do you want to be a part of this? [However] that can only last so long, that's rather like the motivational speaker that actually gives you nothing tangible ... There's probably enough in your background and track record that says "maybe this guy can do that" and that lasts a little while, but not long. (Individual sport PD)

Accordingly, this reflection suggests that any 'honeymoon' period of heightened optimism, motivation and harmony, as driven by a new and fresh impetus, is relatively short-lived. In essence, if any initial wave of excitement is not followed up with continued dissemination and the introduction, optimisation and monitoring of vision-consistent systems, structures and processes, then it runs significant risk of becoming an historical artefact as opposed to a guiding ideology. Significantly, however, context yet again appears to dictate the PD's possibilities for action, as evaluated by the PD (individual and team sport) who earlier reflected on the 'lip service exercise' requirements of UK Sport:

Whilst the personal timing of my appointment was poor as I came in, the timing of it in relation to giving me the [full four-year] cycle to develop the programme, I can see that as a positive now. So I suppose if I was ever looking in future, I'd probably be quite mindful of when those key milestones were: how much time you have to make change. I think anybody that comes into the role of PD now (June, 2010) in relation to London has a pretty thankless task, certainly for significant under-performers.

Once again, context-specific expertise is clearly necessary if the PD's change management programme is to be successful. Certainly, the practical prudency of applying *general* competencies to *specific, socially-complex* events is, at best, sub-optimal.

Lessons learned: reflections on the key messages

Having presented a broad overview of the range of factors which may shape the characteristics, components and agency of the Olympic PD's vision, we now conclude with some reflections of our own regarding the principle messages to emerge from this contribution. Recognising that reflective practice facilitates experiential learning, enhances practice-based knowledge and optimises practice itself (Ghaye & Lillyman, 2000), such a synopsis, we hope, will encourage similar reflection by other support consultants, their PD clients and other relevant members of national sport organisations (e.g. CEOs).

Primarily, as reflected by the coverage above, creating and sustaining a shared vision in Olympic sports teams (at least British Olympic teams) appears to be a highly dynamic and multifaceted task. While we have focused on one initial component of a pan-individual change programme, the complexity inherent within this process alone suggests that top-down approaches to performance optimisation in Olympic sport settings are neither appropriate nor likely to be successful. Indeed, due to the multitude of groups and individuals which have a 'stake' in performance or performance-related matters, it appears that the Olympic PD would be wise to *actively* manage the perceptions, expectations and agency of such parties to ensure that their programmes run as effectively and smoothly as possible.

Accordingly, rather than a unidirectional model of action whereby stakeholder feedback is neither embraced nor encouraged, the PD challenge seems best represented by a multi-directional framework (see Figure 1). Indeed, a failure to engage with this style of management may be a fundamental error when recognising such groups' power to derail a PD's programme through: (a) direct, overt resistance (cf. solid arrows in Figure 1); or (b) indirect, covert proliferation/reinforcement of contradictory/rogue perceptions and behaviours with fellow stakeholders (cf. broken arrows in Figure 1). Of course, if managed well then such interactional relationships may be harnessed to subtly facilitate and strengthen the PD's intended vision and culture.

A second key note is the emergence of 'dark' practices and context-specific expertise stimulates significant re-evaluation of traditional approaches to sports team leadership. Regarding the former, even though Fletcher and Arnold (2011) highlighted the prevalence of dark qualities in Olympic PDs (e.g. Machiavellianism; dominance), little insight was provided as to their behavioural manifestation. As detailed above, the present PD sample reflected upon the utility of an unwavering and forceful approach to vision-related decision making, often at the expense of socially desirable action. Indeed, this appeared a conscious approach with many, which is perhaps unsurprising when considering these figures drive for success and the pressure they are under to deliver medals for outcome-focused funders.

In addition, and in direct contrast to competency-based models of performance leadership, the emergence of context-specific expertise as a critical marker of successfully creating and disseminating the team's vision is significant. Arguably driven by the post-positivist facilitation of global leadership models (e.g. transformational leadership: cf. Callow et al., 2009), knowledge on how team managers select, deploy and monitor their behaviour in precise situations is largely

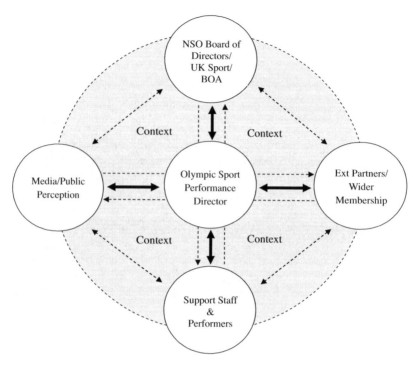

Figure 1. Multi-directional management model of the Olympic sport Performance Director.

unknown. Although this paper has focused on just one feature of Olympic team direction, the reflections offered here suggest that the ability to efficiently compare and contrast the utility of disparate courses of action against the demands of the specific scenario and long-term cultural ideals is critical.

Finally, as evidenced by the PDs' perceptions of their vision's limitations, the call for research on the culture optimisation process is significantly reinforced (cf. Fletcher & Arnold, 2011; Cruickshank & Collins, in pressa; Cruickshank & Collins, in pressb). Indeed, recognising that the PD's vision may be an initially necessary but consequently transient feature of a long-term programme, the need for a framework which supports the effective and efficient delivery of a high performing culture is crucial for both the consistency of the Olympic sports team's performance and the long-term career prospects of the PD!

Notes on contributors

Dave Collins is professor of Coaching and Performance and Director of the Institute for Coaching and Performance at the University of Central Lancashire. As a long term research-practitioner in the promotion of performance, Dave's work has increasingly focused on the crucial role played by management systems and organisational environments. As Performance director of UK Athletics, Dave 'enjoyed' the practical challenges and pressures inherent in the change management process.

Andrew Cruickshank is a PhD student within the University of Central Lancashire's Institute for Coaching and Performance, examining management-led culture change in elite sport performance teams. Formerly a professional footballer, Andrew is also completing his final stages of training in becoming a British Psychological Society-chartered sport and exercise psychologist.

References

Abraham, A., & Collins, D. (2011). Taking the next step: New directions for coaching science. *Quest, 6*, 366–384.

Bevir, M., & Richards, D. (2009). Decentring policy networks: A theoretical agenda. *Public Administration, 87*, 3–14.

Bruinshoofd, A., & ter Weel, B. (2003). Manager to go? Performance dips reconsidered with evidence from Dutch football *European Journal of Operational Research, 148*, 233–246.

Callow, N., Smith, M.J., Hardy, L., Arthur, C.A., & Hardy, J. (2009). Measurement of transformational leadership and its relationship with team cohesion and performance level. *Journal of Applied Sport Psychology, 21*, 395–412.

Cilliers, P. (2000). What can we learn from a theory of complexity? *Emergence, 2*(1), 23–33.

Cruickshank, A., & Collins, D. (in pressa). Change management: The case of the elite sport performance team. *Journal of Change Management.*

Cruickshank, A., & Collins, D. (in pressb). Culture change in elite sport performance teams: Examining and advancing effectiveness in the new era. *Journal of Applied Sport Psychology.*

Fletcher, D., & Arnold, R. (2011). A qualitative study of performance leadership and management in elite sport. *Journal of Applied Sport Psychology, 23*, 223–242.

Ghaye, T., & Lillyman, S. (2000). *Reflection: Principles and practice for healthcare professionals.* Wiltshire, UK: Quay Books.

Kim, W. Chan, & Mauborgne, R. (2003). Tipping point leadership. *Harvard Business Review, 81*(4), 60–69.

League Managers Association. (2010). *LMA end of season statistics 2010.* Retrieved from http://www.leaguemanagers.com/news/news-6585.html

Martindale, A., & Collins, D. (2007). Enhancing the evaluation of effectiveness with professional judgment and decision making. *The Sport Psychologist, 21*, 458–474.

Zinser, L. (2008, December 17). One loss away from unemployment. *The New York Times.* Retrieved from http://www.nytimes.com/2008/12/18/sports/18coaches.html

Politics, power & the podium: coaching for Paralympic performance

Anthony J. Bush and Michael L. Silk

Department of Education, Faculty of Humanities and Social Sciences, University of Bath BA2 7AY, UK

This paper considers the cultural politics of working with elite athletes with a disability. The focus of the paper is a coach who has dedicated his career to performance athletes with a disability – Robert Ellchuk – and draws on the coach's personal experiences and ethnographic work with four different coach-Paralympic athlete dyads. These data are (re)presented in the form of a reflexive conversation supplemented with post-conversation reflections. Important questions are raised about the structure of 'coach education', the role of a coach, hierarchies within disabled sport, the impact of commodification on the disabled body and the (perceived) barriers to physical activity for disabled participants. The article concludes with an invitation to readers to make their own meaning of this polysemic narrative, especially at a time when specific representations of 'acceptable' disabled bodies will be circulated in, and through, the London 2012 Olympic and Paralympic Games.

As the Paralympic Games have made the transition from pastime to global spectacle, the profile of Paralympic athletes has been increased (Howe, 2008). Drawing upon our recent work that has attempted to reconceptualise the field of sports coaching – through reorienting knowledge within this field towards a social justice agenda – this paper seeks to make sense of the cultural politics surrounding coaching elite athletes with disabilities. Our specific focus derives from the experiences of a rare commodity: a coach who has dedicated his career to performance athletes with disabilities. While his record is impressive – three World Championship gold medals, a Commonwealth Games champion, a number of other podium finishes in World Championships and Paralympic Games – we aim to explore the challenges that are faced by coaches working with elite athletes with a disability. By drawing on the coach's personal experiences and ethnographic work with four different coach-Paralympic athlete dyads, we present a reflexive conversation. Supplementing the conversation will be our post-conversation reflections (following the work of Lee, Shaw, Chesterfield, & Woodward, 2009), which will be represented in boxes throughout the transcript. Through so doing, we aim to draw out key issues relating to the power relations inherent in, and the cultural politics of, coaching athletes with disabilities: understanding the impaired body, representations of disabled athletes, accommodation of Paralympic bodies, the status of, and challenges for, coaching elite Paralympians, and, the politics of Paralympic exclusion and discrimination. Through our representations of this reflexive conversation, it is envisaged that we will shed light on cultural politics of working with elite athletes with a disability, the power relations that permeate this practice, and the ways in which realising the Paralympic dream is not just about the drive for sporting excellence, but importantly, the infusion and discovery of a much broader philosophy of life – a conversation which is especially pertinent as we consider the legacies (both forecasted and actualised) of the London 2012 Olympic and Paralympic games.

After some introductions …

RE – Robert Ellchuk
AB – Anthony Bush
MS – Michael Silk

AB: There is no question that successful coaches need to be knowledgeable. How coaches acquire that knowledge – through education systems and personal learning – is open to debate. How would you describe your education as a coach?

RE: I have always had a problem with the educational system, but not with education. I am inquisitive, I want to know things. I want to go out and find things out. If I can't find it out and understand it, then that make me an ignorant person, this is how I view that. When I use the word ignorant, it is because I have not taken the opportunity to learn something. I don't always understand it; no one can always understand everything, but get in there, get involved and get familiar. You know I was injured a lot as an athlete, not because I was coached wrong, but my body was wrong. I just couldn't keep up with the demands of the sport.

Part of the reason that I don't like the education system is that it comes back to the fact that it has to be done their way. You are not really allowed informal education at any level, to be as idiosyncratic as you can be, to learn your way. I was extremely lucky, in that when I went 'off-piste' in my learning experiences, I was supported in the most part. If you try to do that these days, no matter where you are in the world – where you take control of your own education basically – the yoke could be reined in or thrown out.

The constraints that are put on people's learning these days are ridiculous. Now as a coach, it is the same thing. I need to know, otherwise how can I have an impact in a positive manner on anything. Now I've got people in front of me that I am working with, and in order to get the best out of them, I have got to know everything. I am never going to know everything, but I have got to try. And I have to work as hard as I can to make sure that for each individual in front of me, that I know as much about them as I possibly can and I also need to know everything about everything to do with training. There can be no blind spots.

AB: It's noticeable that you omit to mention vocational, National Governing Body coaching awards in your educational profile; what about the place for these in your learning to be an elite coach?

RE: I never did any coaching levels in Canada, because I was an athlete and I was in the system and people just came to me for advice. Once I started learning stuff, I didn't walk around telling people what to do, but if people had questions then I wanted to be able to answer the question, I didn't want to look like an idiot and say no, I don't know. And if I don't know, I want to make sure that I can point myself or you in the right direction to find out. So, when I was in Canada I never did a formal coaching anything.

AB: What about during your time in the UK (United Kingdom)?

RE: Well, these have been the biggest waste of time that I have ever experienced in my entire life. When I did the very first course that I had to do in the UK – to get my level one – I had to commit to a weekend; there's a waste of a weekend. Did I learn anything? No, I didn't learn anything. In the UK we have got the system set up now where we have UK Sport and Sports Coach UK dictating levels of coaching awards, but they are not tied in any way to – and this would make sense to me – coach education courses or even the sports science courses that you do at university. This is where the actual academic stuff is. So the coach education courses that are put on by the National Governing Bodies give you nothing with no back up or no background.

Your level one course tells you how to treat kids; if you don't know how to treat kids what the hell are you doing coaching? Then your level two course basically let's you be a head coach; which means that now you can do these sessions on your own. What a waste of time. I'd just keep my mouth shut and keep my head down and not engage at all. My philosophy tends to be in direct conflict with what they are trying to tell us to do. The reason for that is that I am following experience and the academic stuff that I have gone through, and all they are giving me is some kind of sanitised health and safety version of what it is that you can do, which is wrong. It doesn't fit. It is not what coaching is about. It is not what sport is about. It is not what being a human being is about.

I keep getting asked to get involved and go along to seminars and workshops that are put on by the National Governing Body; and I keep saying no. And I keep saying no, I have already done it. You are not giving me more information, you are giving me the same information and potentially some little tick box somewhere that says I have done something … As far as I am concerned, personal satisfaction is what it is about. And once you get that, you don't need anything else. I don't need a certificate to tell me that I can coach international athletes.

I sat down and I looked at what was required to do for a level four UK Athletics coach – which is effectively the top level – and I looked at it and said, 'well I have done all of that'. I don't qualify as a level four coach, but I have mentored several of them and helped them through, but I don't qualify as one. I have got university degrees in coaching and university degrees in sports science, university degrees in sports psychology; university degrees in all the things that they are trying to teach me on these courses in a dumbed down level. Do I need it? No, it doesn't help my coaching.

Reflection 1: Learning to be an expert coach

In the profession of sports coaching there is an inexorable link between knowledge and competence. Coaching knowledge is a complex entity, comprising of both sports specific (for example, subject matter content knowledge, curriculum content knowledge) and non-sports specific (for example, pedagogical knowledge, sub-discipline sports science knowledge, inter / intra personal knowledge) domains. How coaches gain this knowledge is therefore important to understand. Typically, coaches acquire knowledge through formal (certified qualifications), non-formal (workshops and conferences) and informal (for example; playing experience, reflection on coaching, communities of practice) processes.

Question: In the culture that pervades coaching where certification infers competence, how can we ensure that the formal coaching qualifications are fit-for-purpose and not just discarded by expert practitioners?

AB: What's interesting is that you haven't mentioned the fact that your coaching practice has become synonymous with working with athletes with a disability. Do you think that perhaps your thirst for knowledge and your experience positions you uniquely in track and field to work with elite athletes with a disability?

RE: Yes, because basically the thing is that if you make everybody welcome, everybody feels good. You know, who doesn't like to be made to feel welcome. So, what do I care if you have got cerebral palsy or you have got an amputation or you're visually impaired? I don't care about that, not in the slightest. What I care about is trying to find a way to do what you want. Through discussion with you, at some point, this has got to be about getting you faster and stronger. That's where my education and natural inquisitiveness comes in, because I don't need to go on some 'stupid waste of time little course' that somebody gives on disability or children or whatever. I know what you need to do to engage. I was an athlete, I know what it took and I know what it takes, therefore we can work together on this and I can help give that to you.

And if I can't do it, then I have to find somewhere where I can get it for you. You know, the first thing you have to do as a psychologist is to know your referral list. If I can't deal with this, who am I referring you to? Now that doesn't mean that I don't spend a lot of time trying to work on it, but it does mean that if I have got a wall in front of me of whatever kind, I need to know who I can refer you to so that we can get around this wall. Because it is not about me, I have been there and I have done it and I don't care about it any more. It is about *you* and that *you* are different on an individual basis with everybody.

Now, a few years ago a kid came down and was training with us a little bit. That day I had between 12 and 18 people training. I had one Paralympic athlete at that point – a very good one, but only one – out of a group of 12 people; and I am subsequently labelled a Paralympic coach! Everybody, as far as I can tell, has improved when I have been coaching them. Now, that can be for a lot of different reasons and might have absolutely nothing to do with me and it might have absolutely nothing to do with the training programme; it could just be from being away from home, who knows? There are loads of things that it could be. But, every one of them has got better. Out of all the hundreds of people that I have worked with, right now I have got five Paralympic athletes; yet I am a Paralympic coach. I am pigeon-holed into a mentality that states 'you can only do Paralympic stuff'. I don't accept that limitation. I know personally, from all the medallists at BUSA [British Universities Sports Association; now BUCS, British Universities and Colleges Sport] that I have worked with in sprints, the medallists at 'three

As' [Amateur Athletics Association] and other national and international events (in a variety of sports) that I have worked with, that I am quite good in a lot of different things.

AB: So you are good at making people faster?

RE: I make people faster, I make people stronger. It doesn't matter what you show up with; what matters is what you leave with. And my job is to make sure that you are leaving faster and stronger than you showed up. Because that is what you are there for.

AB: You really believe that it doesn't matter what your participants show up with and that it is all about what they leave with. Can this mean anything from an Olympic gold medal to just feeling better about themselves?

RE: So, yes you have a continuum of good things carrying over for everybody, but the most noticeable is with the Paralympic athletes. And the most noticeable within that tend to be with CP [Cerebral Palsy] athletes. One of the things is that if you have been suffering with discrimination and ableism all your entire life and then you find out that you can do things; that self-confidence is massive. The change in the way that you carry yourself is massive and you won't be as accepting of all the things that are thrown at you in society. It does change the way that you deal with your life.

With all of the disability people that I have ever worked with, the first thing I get just after say a week, is a message from the parent saying that they have noticed the change in their child in a positive way. Well, isn't that what sport ultimately should be doing for everybody? You can have a really big impact with sport by including them in a general sense. Not in a special sense, you know where you run disability specific things because that is still segregation. Segregation doesn't work. But you do the hard thing and you include people properly ... You don't have to do anything special. You can just include them as an individual.

Reflection 2: Dualisms in sports coaching literature

Extant within coaching literature are dualisms that frame the practice of sports coaching. Examples of the dualisms presented in the literature are; elite / participation, able bodied / disabled, male / female, child / adult, and competition / fun. Thus, to work with particular groups (such as Paralympic athletes) then it is assumed that you need to have specialist knowledge and skills to be able to do this effectively. Coaches get pigeon-holed or labelled as participation coaches or coaches of children, athletes with a disability or elite athletes. The result of these dualisms is a compartmentalised approach to coach preparation programmes.

Questions: What do these dualisms mean for the profession of sports coaching? Should we challenge these taken-for-granted assumptions that frame coaching literature and coach preparation programmes?

MS: We're interested in your role as a coach and your philosophy related to working with people who, as you say, have been discriminated against for much of their lives.

RE: When I was in grade three my best friend in that class had cystic fibrosis. Mainstream school, no big deal. The kind of society [Canada] that I grew up in, there was racism and sexism and all the kinds of 'isms' and everything, but for the most part, 'you have a kid with cystic fibrosis in the class ...yes, so?' He was treated like the rest of us; dealt with as the rest of us. You know when I was an athlete we didn't have people with amputations come down. I really don't remember anyone coming down when I was an athlete who had an amputation of any kind. But, I do remember when a friend of mine showed up on his very first day as a 9-year-old in a wheelchair that was far too big for him. He is a multi-Paralympian now.

What happened was, at the training centre, time was booked when everybody trained – not just one club – and he just showed up and wanted to train, and just got on with it. We shared the track with a bunch of special Olympians; they were down there training every day as we were. We were aware of, engaging with, and familiar with a load of kids that were special Olympians. We had a guy in our training group who was a Paralympian. He was a Canadian record holder; but we didn't know it until he went to Seoul for the Paralympics. We had no idea; nor did we care. We were all really good friends that hung out together, all training hard. Respect to everybody was given. You have come down, you train, and you work hard, fantastic. Any elitism was just the result of your competition. Did that mean anything to us, well yes, fantastic, you are a really good athlete; so what else have you done? Some of these guys were in university, some of these guys were working. Some were Olympians, multi-Canadian record holders, all alongside people there for fitness and all working within the same group. The coaches were friends to you. You know, they were there for you, there for anything. Actually, the second coach was the person that taught me to drive a manual car; my mum wouldn't as she wouldn't let me in her car. But, this coach did. I was at that coaches wedding ... I still see both coaches. These are people that there is a connection with. Now that connection didn't matter if you were elite or not; neither one of them had special coaching qualifications; both of them were teachers.

Reflection 3: 'Coach as bricoleur'

Throughout the literature, the intimation is made that sports coaching is fundamentally about improving the sporting performance of others. This narrow understanding pervades coach preparation programmes and in many cases the expectations of the participants. This reductionist view simplifies the practice of coaching to be about motivating and organising participants and then systematically applying methods to make them better at a sport. In reality, coaching is a complex, contextual, dynamic, relational and pedagogical activity and to understand the everyday lives of coaches we need to challenge traditional definitions of what it means to be a coach. A coach might act as a friend, pseudo-parent, taxi driver, fundraiser, social worker, administrator, innovator, pedagogue, biomechanist, nutritionist and much, much more (Bush & Silk, 2010). Claude Levi-Strauss (1966) used the French word *bricoleur* to describe a handyman or handywoman who makes use of the tools available to complete a task. The concept of 'coach as bricoleur' is one that could be useful in helping frame the reality of what it means to be a coach.

Questions: How can we ensure that the practice of coaching, and therefore what it means to be an effective practitioner, doesn't get reduced to simply making a person better at reproducing a skill? To what extent can we embrace the concept of 'coach as bricoleur' in helping the way that we think about a coach's practice?

MS: It is really interesting that you talk about the Paralympic and Olympic stream extreme divisions and the hierarchy that is evident. What about within the Paralympic movement? Do you see that there is a hierarchy that is evident there?

RE: There is a massive hierarchy. I mean, it's highly media driven and based on who they can sell. Well, the only things they can sell you are – forget about all the disabilities – the people that will resonate with the public. This relates to the problem we have with the medical model of disability and the social model of disability and the inadequate bio-psychosocial model. The medical model says that disability is all about loss and about, 'oh you poor little disability person, you have lost this and we can fix you and we can make you better and we can bring you on to nirvana. We can do these things for you, you used to be one of us … you could be one of us'. To be frank, I couldn't disagree more with this, but that is effectively the main discourse that people get out of the Paralympics. It just goes hand in hand with all returning soldiers who have become amputees and who are now in wheelchairs or using prosthetic limbs. They have been made athletes, but given that they are the same as us, we are able to connect with them. Oh, but for the grace of God goes I. Of course, I am not saying that they are bad individuals. What I am saying though if that is the only way that you can sell stuff, society still has got a problem. This becomes part of the social model of disability. It is not about the fact that you have had a limb removed – whether you are born with it or it has got blown off somewhere in one of the wars that is being fought – for whatever reason you have had an amputation, you become somebody everyone can identify with.

The media can build on that because you are easily identifiable, so those are the people that sit right at the top of the Paralympic media coverage. This past summer, for example, there was an event in London put on by UK Athletics; it was not actually covered in the press. It was a major event with major athletes there and there was no television. I was following it on the Channel 4 Paralympic twitter feed, getting some updates. One of the problems with this competition though was that they were collapsing categories; that is they were having people with cerebral palsy competing against amputations having people compete against different levels of visual impairment, yet the only information coming from the media was who had won, which is just ridiculous.

A kid I coached was running in a race that was just like that. He has got CP and was racing against other guys with CP from other categories that are at least 10 seconds faster than he is, as well as visually impaired athletes and amputees. Now my athlete is one of the best in the world but these guys in these other categories are so much faster because of the differential impairment is different are much faster. So I know that he is not going to win, but I know that he is ready to run a good time. There was no media coverage, so what do I do? I know that somebody from our training group is actually in the stadium, so I ask them to give me feedback. He is running 800m and I need to know his first 400m split. I get that. Fine no problem. Now this person in the stadium takes it on their initiative to time the whole race and feeds me back the time. I said, please can you confirm that time, because if you are correct on that time – and I didn't say this part in the first message – then it was a new world-record. The time was confirmed but UK Athletics didn't pick up on it; he'd finished fifth or sixth in the race. But it was a world record, and not just by a hundredth of a second, he took nearly a second off the 800m world record which has stood for years. UK Athletics didn't pick up on it, no media picked up on it, and the athlete didn't even pick up on it.

A Paralympic athlete drops his personal best by two seconds and breaks the world record by almost a second; he doesn't even get a mention. Is that fair? Channel 4 do an update a week later on the event – highlights of what happened that day – nothing, not a mention even though they now knew about the record. Who was featured in that update? An amputee who has got social recognition as he is identifiable. A wheelchair athlete, again social recognition. They also featured two VI [visually impaired] athletes; yet in the entire highlights there was not a minute devoted to any athlete with CP. So, if you are a CP athlete, don't expect to get any inclusion within Paralympic media coverage.

Reflection 4: Commodification of the disabled body

Grue (2011, p. 534) suggested that 'while disability has a material component that is inextricably linked to individual bodies – for instance, a lack of vision, hearing or the ability to walk – the consequences that the biophysical has for the individual in question is to a huge extent a matter of socio-political dynamics'. Serious questions can be raised when the Paralympic movement becomes bound with the logics of spectacle, when, very loosely paraphrasing Debord (1967), all that there is to see is the commercial direction of social practices and subjectivities. The ability to 'sell' socially identifiable – or acceptable / palatable – discourses of disability privilege certain forms of disabled bodies over others; in this sense, those most heroic (the returning wounded soldier who once again serves 'his' country through being funnelled into a Paralympic podium possibility) and the most accepted (those, like us, but with just a bit missing) become the most celebrated and visible Paralympic bodies.

Question: In corporatised representations of disabled athletes – such as those desirable bodies promulgated through London 2012 Olympic and Paralympic Games coverage – who becomes valorised, celebrated and championed? Conversely, who disappears, who is absent from such discourses; which disabled bodies are silenced, marginalised or pathologised and thus subject to further stigmatisation, oppression and discrimination?

MS: Following on from this point, there has been so much press coverage surrounding the bi-lateral below the knee amputee Oscar Pistorius – the blade runner – who is seeking out new challenges beyond the shelter of the Paralympic umbrella. How do you as a 'Paralympic' coach feel about that and do you see it as turning his back on what the Paralympics is seeking to do? Equally as important as that, what do your athletes, especially the ones with cerebral palsy that are seen as 'the others' view this?

RE: Oscar has to milk it; and I have got no problem with Oscar milking it. Oscar is special case because he is a T43 and there are not very many of those on blades or upright. Anybody that is born like that generally has the lower limb amputated and then ends up in a wheelchair so they become wheelchair athletes. Oscar for the longest time was the only T43 out there. Now because he is bi-lateral he has got an advantage – over the other amputees – because both sides of his body are working in conjunction with each other in the same way. So, the difference between Oscar Pistorius and an Olympic stream athlete is only the blades because the movement is going to be equal. It's not like he has got cerebral palsy where there are issues with the nervous system, or it's not like he is a single leg amputee where there are issues with co-ordinating the leg with the blade on it with the leg that doesn't; which leads to big issues with co-ordinating what are essentially different types of movement. Oscar has got a stable movement just like the rest of us do that don't have an amputation. This is why he is so far ahead of the rest of the people over 400m. And, he is fast enough and can qualify for the Olympics; where is the harm in that?

Natalie Du Toit does it in swimming and Marla Runyan did it as an American VI [Visually Impaired] in the 1500m and 800m and I think the 5K. If you are that good and you need the challenge, then yes, you do need to move on because the rest of the people are just too slow. It has got nothing to do with whether you are a 'lovely little Paralympian' as this is still elite sport. Oscar barely wins if he wins his 100m because you have others like Jerome Singleton – Jerome is in the T44 classification, so he is a single leg amputation – and he beat Oscar in the 100m at the world championships. So, Oscar doesn't have it all his own way in the 100m. The 200m Oscar tends to win by a decent margin, but there are others who are beginning to challenge. It is the 400m in which Oscar is so far ahead of everybody else. So, why shouldn't he go and race against the able bodied guys?

MS: I wonder then what impact this has on your athletes who are not amputees, in wheelchairs or who do not have an 'acceptable' disability, what you called 'social recognition?'

RE: Absolutely it has an impact. I had a discussion with one of those athletes last week. The athlete had, in a separate interview with somebody, stated that 'If I didn't have cerebral palsy then I wouldn't be good'. They were focusing on their times. So, yes, in an absolute sense, they are more than two seconds behind Usain Bolt. But Usain Bolt doesn't have cerebral palsy. Cerebral palsy does have some effect on genetic expression, but not a lot. If you are an incredible athlete and you have got CP, you're an incredible athlete. Yes you are good, take the CP away; you are still going to be good. I find myself explaining this a lot and reassuring these athletes that they are Paralympians. Many don't actually understand how good they really are. They don't understand that having cerebral palsy, however bad it is, affects initiating every movement, affects every reflex, and affects everything to do with movement. It is mind boggling when you think that it affects absolutely everything. But they don't understand exactly that because they are constantly dealing with it. So they don't get the fact that OK I reach for my coffee cup, I do it, I don't think about it. They do it now as adults, they don't think about it. But there are issues if you have CP with reaching for that cup. And, you just don't think about this as you just accept these things. And then, someone at some point asks to push themselves past what they think they can do. 'Look kid, you have got CP, you are an incredible athlete – forget the CP – you are an incredible athlete and get what you deserve from it'.

But, and here is the problem, in the Paralympic movements the CP athletes sit at the bottom of the ladder. They are at the bottom of the totem pole as far as public awareness is concerned. Why? They haven't got the social recognition because of the constant twitching, the constant issues that those people are having. The rest of us have issues identifying with them, there is no social recognition, and they are not covered in the media. This is so wrong, but I really think this is how they are treated and viewed. Further, there is extra pressure on my CP athletes. Those on 'podium' funding are on around £30K a year tax free; they also get 'in kind' support that could equate to another £55K. Even those athletes on B level funding are pulling in £20K a year and those C level athletes just under £15K. Where are these kids going to earn that sort of money away from the sports arena? I suppose this puts more pressures on the athletes to keep going and on me to keep them in their funding stream. For some, retiring is not an option; I just worry about what will happen to some of them after London 2012.

Reflection 5: Les Autres

David Howe (2011) has argued that those Paralympic bodies that use the latest technology (e.g. carbon fibre blades, those that he would term, following Berger 2008, the cyborgified 'supercrip') become closer to the 'norm' of acceptability in sport. 'Supercrips' are those successful (in terms of 'winning') disabled athletes who are able to live a relatively 'normal' life and who gain a high-profile media exposure. They are, simply, those with 'social recognition'. However, we might question what will happen to even these disabled bodies once the media circus moves on to the next town after London 2012. Further, with Howe (2011), we would suggest that the more marginal the physicality of the body (e.g. cerebral palsy), the further away it is from the potential of cyborgification and the more likely the athlete will be painted with a tragic rather than a heroic allegory during the London 2012 Paralympic Games: while cyborgification may well enhance the social pedestal / podium potential for certain categories of athletes, this may act to further increase the liminality of those categories of athletes who do not use (or cannot afford to use) such technologies (both in their sport and in society generally).

Question: Will the representations of the London 2012 Paralympic coverage focus mostly on heroic allegories of the cyborgified supercrips? If so, and in advancing a technocentric ideology (Howe, 2011) of disability, will such representations serve to empower disabled (athletic) bodies?

AB: Interestingly you mention financial implications of disability sport. Do you think that for your athletes to discover and achieve their potential, access to resources is crucial or is it more a question of the mind?

RE: It is not their mind, it is their money. I currently am dealing with a teenage girl that is a single leg amputee, T44. Prior to – and she's a young women who as it happens is a very good athlete – she had been competing on what was effectively a wooden stump and was not getting good results; surprise, surprise. You know what happens is that the National Health Service will only provide one leg so there are financial implications there. So, what leg are you going to get? A sporting leg—and they will get you the cheapest model that they can get you – or are you going to get a day leg that you can walk around with, be with your friends, use all day long every day? Well obviously you are going to get a day leg; anything else is just stupid. But, a day leg can't do sport. So, now you have got an individual in a fairly well to do area of a fairly well to do country whose access to sport is limited because an appropriate leg will not be provided; and isn't easily provided.

There is another teenager who has just been introduced to using a sport wheelchair. There is a big problem there. I was talking to his father one evening and he was trying to wait to find out if his son is really interested in continuing on with doing sport, which is stupid! As I said to this guy's father, look, I want to go for a run, for whatever reason, I want to do a 5K run or a half marathon and I go down to the shops and pick up a pair of trainers and away I go. If you are in a wheelchair, you are provided with your day chair, but you cannot actually do any sport in one of those things. Those pair of trainers that I picked up is the equivalent of a specialist made sporting wheelchair. Now in my wildest dreams I would never think of getting a pair of trainers that cost £4000. That is basically the price of a base model of a specialist wheelchair. And the father, relatively well to do, in a relatively well to do area, is hesitating. Now his son is not accessing sport, not because he doesn't want to, but because he can't.

Now there was a third year university student and she had never been exposed to sport before. She saw a friend of hers in the library and they were chatting and he said, 'Well, why don't you go down and see Rob at the track?' She wasn't about being an elite athlete, just like every one of the university students that does the Bath half [marathon] at some point during their time here. You can't do it in a day chair. You see her friends are doing the Bath half, so she says that she knows that all these not fit people go on to do the half marathon, so why can't I? She comes down to the track and we start doing some stuff together. I did what I could as we were working with her day chair; there was no way she could do the half marathon but she was now engaged in physical activity. There is no real thought about the need for healthy lifestyles for these disabled young people. She recently did the Great North run. I suppose the point is, how many people would do something in sport, such as the Great North run, if that to go and do it you have to do your fund-raising to get four grand to buy yourself a pair of shoes? Equal opportunity? Equal thought given to what is going on? It's not happening.

Reflection 6: Barriers to sport for disabled: weighing up the legacy of London 2012

The Active People Survey (2008–2009) shows that 57.1% of the overall population do not participate in sport. Importantly, the survey shows that this rises considerably to 79.2% when considering disabled people, and perhaps even more alarmingly, only 6.5% of disabled people regularly participate in sport. The London 2012 Olympic and Paralympic Games legacy is being driven by a rich variety of organisations. A central tenet of the government's 2012 legacy is to encourage the whole population to be more physically active. Indeed, the British Paralympic Association (BPA) see as one of the biggest obstacles to future success in Paralympic sport being the strength of grassroots involvement and the number of people playing sport at community level. There are multiple reasons why disabled people face barriers to participating in sport, for example, equipment costs, accessibility, transportation, and perceptions on coaching expertise. In addition, disabled people who wish to coach face barriers such as lack of accessible training resources, opportunities to practice or appropriate coach mentors.

Questions: With approximately 8 million disabled people in the UK, should we dismiss these barriers and participation rates as unimportant? What can we do to ensure that as many barriers to participation are removed for disabled participants? What can the organisations tasked with driving the London 2012 Games' legacy do to help remove these barriers to participation? Where, we might ask, are all the coaches with a disability?

A transpositional opening

Our reading of the experiences of this 'disability' coach raises a number of important questions about the structure of 'coach education', the role of the coach, the hierarchies within disabled sport, the impact of commodification on the disabled body and the (perceived) barriers to physical activity for disabled participants – questions we feel are timely, yet have received very little attention, and are worthy of being opened to reflective critique. We recognise that there may well be polysemic readings of this narrative, as such we invite further musings on the cultural politics, governance and policing of disabled bodies, especially at a time when specific representations of 'acceptable' disabled bodies will be circulated in, and through, the London 2012 Olympic and Paralympic Games.

Notes on contributors

Dr Anthony Bush is a lecturer in the Faculty of Humanities and Social Science at the University of Bath. His research interests include the development of interpretive-critical research methodologies and engaging a cultural studies sensibility with sports coaching research; an on-going project that democratises sports coaching research, opening it to critical conversations about social justice, cultural politics, violence, and progressive futures.

Dr Michael Silk is a reader in the Faculty of Humanities and Social Science at the University of Bath. His research and scholarship focuses on the production and consumption of space, the governance of bodies, and, the performative politics of identity within the context of neoliberalism.

References

Berger, R.J. (2008). Disability and the dedicated wheelchair athlete: Beyond the 'supercrip' critique. *Journal of Contemporary Ethnography, 37*(6), 647–678.
Bush, A.J., & Silk, M.L. (2010). Towards and evolving critical consciousness in coaching research: The physical pedagogic bricolage. *International Journal of Sports Science and Coaching, 5*(4), 551–565.
Debord, G. (1967). *La société du spectacle*. Paris: Buchet-Chastel.
Grue, J. (2011). Discourse analysis and disability: Some topics and issues. *Discourse and Society, 22*(5), 532–546.
Howe, P.D. (2008). *The cultural politics of the Paralympic movement: Through an anthropological lens*. London: Routledge.
Howe, P.D. (2011). Cyborg and supercrip: The Paralympics technology and the (dis)empowerment of disabled athletes. *Sociology, 45*(5), 868–882.
Lee, S., Shaw, D.J., Chesterfield, G., & Woodward, C. (2009). Reflections from a world champion: An interview with Sir Clive Woodward, Director of Olympic Performance, the British Olympic Association. *Reflective Practice, 10*(3), 295–310.
Levi-Strauss, C. (1966). *The savage mind*. University of Chicago Press.

THOUGHT PIECE

The political process of constructing a sustainable London Olympics sport legacy: three years on

Vassil Girginov

Brunel University, School of Sport & Education, Heinz Wolff Building, School of Sport & Education, Brunel University, Middlesex, UB8 3PH, UK

The paper follows on from an earlier study and addresses our understanding of the construction of Olympic legacy. It poses the question what counts as knowledge and who is responsible for producing it and questions the value of rational, objectively-produced knowledge which continues to dominate the sport legacy policy agenda at the expense of other forms of knowledge.

In a paper in the *International Journal of Sport Policy*, three years ago, Girginov and Hills (2009) interrogated the political process of constructing a sustainable London Olympic sport legacy. The aim of the study was 'to better understand the processes involved in conceptualizing and researching sustainable Olympic sports development legacy construction and its implementation' (p. 163). The study was worth pursuing because it concerned the global Olympic Movement's explicit aim to use sport for the betterment of society. Moreover, for the first time in history a host country's government has made a commitment to use the Olympic Games to deliver a range of legacies not just for London but for the whole of the UK (DCMS, 2007, 2008, 2009).

The current Olympic Special Issue of *Reflective Practice* is dedicated to understanding coaching for performance and therefore provides a perfect outlet for revisiting the main thrust of the paper. After all, the modern Olympism of Pierre de Coubertin was premised on a new form of athletic education and the physical education teacher-coach was to be its chief proselytiser. The Olympic hype would not be possible without the visionary figure of the teacher-coach who has been instrumental in developing the athletes who represent the foundation of the Olympic edifice and the main participants in the Games' spectacle. Equally, the same teacher-coach figure has been responsible for some of the damage done to Olympic ideals in the form of cheating, doping and violence. Modern day coaches and the sport organisations that employ them are at the forefront of knowledge production and dissemination and should rightfully be considered as legacy makers.

The 2009 study identified six key elements of the process of social construction of the sport legacy of the Games and a number of pertinent research questions. The paper argued for the importance of studying the process of knowledge creation and its use to inform policy making in sport. A call was made that 'researchers, therefore, should question prevailing social and political discourses representing naïve, commonsense understandings of sport as well as the validity of some sport forms, and their capacity to deliver particular outcomes based on the notion of sport as "self evidently a good thing"' (p. 174). Epistemologically, the study was located within the constructivist perspective with its insistence on understanding what counts as knowledge and who is responsible for producing it. What the study did not address, however, was the relationship between knowledge and power, and how the knowledge about sport legacy creation has been used to inform current and future policies and practices.

The aim of this Thought Piece is to submit an important issue concerning our understanding of the construction of Olympic legacy. In particular, it asks the question 'what counts as knowledge and who is responsible for producing it?' This question was raised in the 2009 paper as a central element of the notion of 'collective intentionality' which is concerned with the deliberate policies and actions of the state and other agencies in promoting sport. A main assumption of collective intentionality is the creation of subjective meanings and a mandate for action, both of which help determine what Olympic sport legacy should look like. Traditionally, legacy has been framed as a retrospective project and studied using an after event mode of reflection (Girginov, 2011). However, Boud (2001) suggested that this is just one form of reflective practice. He proposed two other forms, including reflection in anticipation and in the midst of events. These two modes of reflection are particularly suitable for a constructivist enquiry as they allow for engaging with the event both before it happens and during its unfolding. Reflection, according to Moon (1999), is:

> a form of mental processing – a form of thinking – that we use to fulfil a purpose or to achieve some anticipated outcome. It is applied to relatively complicated or unstructured ideas for which there is no obvious solution. (p. 10)

The sport development legacy of the London Games presents one such complicated and unstructured set of ideas which offer no clear cut solutions to the politically diverse issues of sport. This has been vividly exemplified by the rift between the UK government's visions of Olympic legacy and the five host Olympic boroughs of East London (HBSU, 2009) strategic plan for achieving it. However, the legacy framing, or its intersubjective meanings, has been created by favouring an after event mode of reflection and rationally conceived and objective knowledge in the form of evidence. Following from the UK government's six promises (DCMS, 2007, 2009) the DCMS (Department for Culture Media and Sport) have commissioned a large-scale longitudinal meta-evaluation of the legacy of London Olympics. This has never been attempted before and naturally presented a number of conceptual and methodological challenges. An apparent contradiction has been between the nature of sustainable sports development as a moving target, and the DCMS's evidence-based approach to understanding it. Most of the sport programmes subject to the meta-evaluation have been evaluated in terms of their input and output. Very little attention has been given to the actual processes responsible for those outcomes. This is because the evaluation of those processes requires different methods of enquiry that favour critical and transformative forms of knowledge. Silk, Bush, and Andrews (2010) made a convincing argument against the methodological fundamentalism on which evidence based research is based and its detrimental effect on the sociology of sport.

The London Olympic Games has generated substantial interest within the host and international academic community. A main feature of the constructivist methods of enquiry has been the study of reality with the people concerned not to use them as a subject of investigation. Inevitably, some research on the London Games will capture the experiences and voices of sport participants. However, it has been notoriously difficult to conduct research with the main legacy developers. These include a range of organisations (e.g. DCMS, London Organising Committee of the Olympic Games (LOCOG), Olympic Delivery Authority (ODA)), key officials and the interactions in the legacy field. This is partly because of the highly politically sensitive nature of the organisational processes of the Games and of the aura of confidentiality surrounding the knowledge needed for that, which is an intellectual property of the International Olympic Committee (IOC). While the commercial value of know-how for the IOC has to be acknowledged, it should not be forgotten that the London Games have only become possible because of the substantial amount of public money (£9.3 billion) that have been invested in them (DCMS, 2011).

Therefore, our understanding of what counts as knowledge about sport development legacy of the Games is going to be constrained by the point of view of the DCMS as a commissioning agency responsible for its production. The limitations of the meta-evaluation framework have been acknowledged by the consultancy company undertaking it (Grant Thornton, Ecorys and Loughborough University, 2011). Two reasons for that put forward are worth mentioning – the limited funding available and the need to prioritise evaluation by focusing on flagship programmes with more structured forms of evaluation. Small bottom-up initiatives are not likely to be considered and the knowledge generated through them will be largely lost. Kuhn (1970) has long observed that specific regimes of power are underpinned by specific regimes of truth and vice versa. The link between political regimes and knowledge in the UK has been clearly demonstrated by the current Coalition government's shift from the previous Labour government's obsession with targets, performance and evidence-based policy, to an emphasis on more opportunities for sport. Yet, rational objectively-produced knowledge continues to dominate the sport legacy policy agenda at the expense of 'lay knowledge'.

Note on contributor

Vassil Girginov is Reader in Sport Management/Development at Brunel University. Recently he has been researching the sports development legacy of the 2012 London Olympic Games and the relationship between the culture of national sports governing bodies and participation in sport. Vassil is editing the official two volume collection on the London 2012 Games to be published by Routledge, and is an Executive Editor of Routledge Online Studies on the Olympic & Paralympic Games (http://www.routledgeonlinestudies.com/). He is also an Executive Editor of the 2012 Routledge Special Olympic Journals Issue that involves some 45 journals from a range of academic disciplines. Vassil is currently working on two research projects: 'Creation and transfer of knowledge within LOCOG', and 'UK National Governing Bodies of sport use of the London Olympics for capacity building'. His research interests, publications and industry experience are in the field of Olympic movement, sport development and comparative management and policy analysis. His most recent books include Sport Management Cultures (Routledge, 2011), The Olympics: A Critical Reader (Routledge, 2010), Management of Sports Development, (Elsevier, 2008) and The Olympic Games Explained (Routledge, 2005, the book has been translated in 6 languages).

References

Boud, D. (2001). Using journal writing to enhance reflective practice. *New Directions for Adult and Continuing Education, 90*(Summer), 9–17.

DCMS. (2007). *Our Promise for 2012: How the UK will benefit from the Olympic and Paralympic Games*. London: Department for Culture Media and Sport.

DCMS. (2008). *Before, during and after: Making the most of the London 2012 Games*. London: Department for Culture Media and Sport.

DCMS. (2009). London 2012: *A legacy for disabled people: Setting new standards, changing perceptions*. London: Department for Culture Media and Sport.

DCMS. (2011). Government Olympic Executive London 2012 Olympic and Paralympic Games. Annual Report. February. DCMS: London.

Girginov, V., 2011. Governance of London 2012 Olympic Sport Legacy, *International Review for the Sociology of Sport*, 1–16.

Girginov, V., & Hills, L. (2009). The political process of constructing a sustainable London Olympics sports development legacy. *International Journal of Sport Policy, 1*(2), 161–181.

Grant Thornton, Ecorys and Loughborough University. (2011). Report 2: *Methods meta-evaluation of the impacts and legacy of the London 2012 Olympic Games and Paralympic Games*. Final Report, April, London: DCMS.

HBSU. (2009). *Olympic and Paralympic legacy: Strategic regeneration framework*. London: Host Boroughs Strategic Unit.

Kuhn, T. (1970). *The structure of scientific revolution*University of Chicago Press.

Moon, J.A. (1999). *Reflection in learning and professional development*. London: Kogan Page.

Silk, M., Bush, A., & Andrews, D., (2010). Contingent intellectual amateurism, or, the problem with evidence-based research. *Journal of Sport and Social Issues, 34*(1), 105–128.

Index

Note: Page numbers in **bold** type refer to figures
Page numbers in *italic* type refer to tables